Queering Italian Media

Queering Italian Media

Edited by
Sole Anatrone and Julia Heim

LEXINGTON BOOKS
Lanham • Boulder • New York • London

Published by Lexington Books
An imprint of The Rowman & Littlefield Publishing Group, Inc.
4501 Forbes Boulevard, Suite 200, Lanham, Maryland 20706
www.rowman.com

6 Tinworth Street, London SE11 5AL, United Kingdom

Copyright © 2020 The Rowman & Littlefield Publishing Group, Inc.

All rights reserved. No part of this book may be reproduced in any form or by any electronic or mechanical means, including information storage and retrieval systems, without written permission from the publisher, except by a reviewer who may quote passages in a review.

British Library Cataloguing in Publication Information Available

Library of Congress Cataloging-in-Publication Data

Names: Anatrone, Sole, 1981- editor. | Heim, Julia, editor.
Title: Queering Italian media / edited by Sole Anatrone and Julia Heim.
Description: Lanham : Lexington Books, [2020] | Includes bibliographical references and index. | Summary: "Queering Italian Media offers queer readings of LGBTQIA+ representation in Italian media. The contributors discuss the relationship between the political and social lives of queer populations in Italy and investigate their representations in film, news media, television, social media, and viewer-generated media sites"—Provided by publisher.
Identifiers: LCCN 2019055086 (print) | LCCN 2019055087 (ebook) | ISBN 9781793616104 (cloth) | ISBN 9781793616111 (epub)
ISBN 9781793616128 (pbk)
Subjects: LCSH: Sexual minorities in mass media. | Mass media—Italy.
Classification: LCC P96.S58 Q48 2020 (print) | LCC P96.S58 (ebook) | DDC 306.76/6—dc23
LC record available at https://lccn.loc.gov/2019055086
LC ebook record available at https://lccn.loc.gov/2019055087

Contents

Preface　　　　　　　　　　　　　　　　　　　　　　　　　　vii
Julia Heim and Sole Anatrone

Acknowledgments　　　　　　　　　　　　　　　　　　　　　　ix

Introduction　　　　　　　　　　　　　　　　　　　　　　　　　1
Julia Heim and Sole Anatrone

1　The Lavorini Case: The Mediatic Confection of the
　　Homosexual Ogres and the Homosexual Counterattack　　　　13
　　Alessio Ponzio

2　We Want Lesbians Too: A Lesbian Feminist
　　Counter-History Inspired by *We Want Roses Too*　　　　　　31
　　Alessia Palanti

3　A Queerer Road: Crossing Borders On and Off the
　　Screen in *Corazones de Mujer*　　　　　　　　　　　　　　57
　　Sole Anatrone

4　The Queer Potential of Mainstream Film　　　　　　　　　　75
　　Dom Holdaway

5　An All Italian *Game of Thrones*: A Social Media
　　Investigation of Maria de Filippi's Gay Male Version
　　of the Trash, Dating Show *Uomini e Donne*　　　　　　　　97
　　Luca Malici

6	Queer Italian Communities and Alternative Televisual Re/Mediations *Julia Heim*	133

Index	155
About the Editors	161
About the Contributors	163

Preface

In September 2017, the Queer Italia Network (QuIR) held a workshop in New York for scholars, artists, and activists to discuss their approaches to and research on queer Italian media.[1] This two-day event, held both at the CUNY Graduate Center and New York University's Casa Italiana, was part of a series of five workshops, which took place across Italy, in the United Kingdom, and in the United States, each with a different focus under the intersectional umbrella of queer studies, queer politics, and Italy (e.g., migration, translation, art, activism, and media). The scope of the research presented in New York and the extensive discussions led to productive interdisciplinary collaborations; this collection is born from those encounters. We present it as a useful resource for those with an active interest in the topic or a burgeoning curiosity about queerness and/in Italian media.

—*Julia e Sole*

NOTE

1. The QuIR was established by Charlotte Ross, S. A. Smythe, and Julia Heim in 2016. The network was founded with grant support from the British Arts and Humanities Research Council, in order to create a transnational community of academics, activists, and artists, working in various ways at the intersections of queerness and Italianness.

Acknowledgments

This book would not have been possible without the Queer Italia Network (QuIR) and our fellow organizers SA Smythe and Charlotte Ross who helped organize the Queer Italian Media Workshop in New York in September of 2017. We give thanks also to the CUNY Graduate Center and the Casa Italiana who sponsored the event and the Arts and Humanities Research Council which funded QuIR.

We would also like to acknowledge the people who gave their time and minds to work with us through the various iterations of all of the works within this book, contributing their ideas, comments, and suggestions so that our chapters might optimally negotiate the balance between scholarly rigor and approachability.

Finally we give our queerest thanks to those within and without our universities who have supported us emotionally, financially, and physically so that we could produce this work and attend the community-building and academically (dis)mantling events that made this scholarship possible. We hope that the words within these pages help uplift anyone whose embodiment, thoughts, scholarship, and/or positionality exists, even temporarily, within the margins and liminal spaces of our societies.

May we find power in our collective otherness.

Introduction
Julia Heim and Sole Anatrone

HISTORY / NATIONS / MARGINS

Attending to the complex trajectory of the (historical and transnational) relationship between Italianness, media, and queerness requires a constant redefinition of terms as they are adapted in various contexts and temporalities. By way of introduction, we offer some words on the interwoven nature of these categories and on the discursive and sociopolitical consequences of this relationship.

The idea of Italian national identity and nationhood has always been very dependent upon mediatic cultural representation. In the era of national unification—from the mid-1800s to the early 1900s—print media and literature were the primary vehicles for engendering public support and establishing a narrative of shared history and cultural identification. Italian media historian Peppino Ortoleva reminds us that "[t]he move toward cultural unification prevailed, however, and it was radio, television and cinema which brought it about."[1] The notion of Italianness—as understood and defined initially by the formation of its national geopolitical borders—has maintained a symbiotic relationship with media through this contemporary age of convergence culture wherein media content is created and consumed across multiple platforms. When cinema and radio replaced newspapers and print as the dominant media forms, they further reinforced the role media played in creating and reiterating specific ideas of national identity. As Áine O'Healy notes: "Clearly implicated in the construction of identity and difference, cinema has played a significant role in nation building, particularly in Italy."[2] This interrelation between cultural representation and national identity becomes multimediatic as new technologies are created, reaffirming media's role in shaping how Italian national identity is defined. For example, with the advent of television in 1954, and primarily through the broadcasting of *sceneggiati* (serialized scripted novels with literary and historical content that dominated narrative television through the 1970s), Italian television worked not only toward legitimizing itself but also toward creating a unifying common "national" history and culture.[3]

Though we may speak of the "parallel and interconnected development of the notion of Italian national identity alongside the Italian media system," it is important to also reflect on the assumptions and limitations imbedded in the very notion of "Italian national identity" itself.[4] Scholar Michela Ardizzoni emphasizes that Italian television continues to portray "conceptions of Italianness that were at the heart of the country's unification in the 19th century," creating bio-essentialist notions of identity that necessarily marginalize those people who don't easily fit into "Italian" racial, religious, sex, and gender categories (to name a few).[5] The Italian media industry produced and continues to reproduce very specific ideas about sociocultural norms that privilege and even concretize ideas of a homogenous, white, heterosexual Italianness. In fact, Alessio Ponzio's chapter highlights the relationship between identity and print media in the 1970s, pointing specifically to the ways that heteromasculinities and marginalizations are created through the linguistic interpellation of "new" minority voices, and to the ways that minority communities are formed through discriminatory utterances. Cultural theorist David Morley speaks of the social, cultural, and political consequences of cinematic representational marginalization and othering. However, his ideas should be considered beyond the limits of the cinematic medium, extending to all cultural discursive forms, in particular, to media:

> Definitions of national cinema always involve the construction of an imaginary homogeneity of identity and culture, apparently shared by all national subjects; this involves mechanisms of inclusion and exclusion whereby one definition of "the nation" is centralised and others are marginalised—what Higson refers to as a process of "internal cultural colonialism."[6]

These marginalized spaces created by and through Italian media discourse are characterized by the contradictory condition of being loci of both oppression and potentiality. As Sole Anatrone discusses in this book, queer subjects forced to live at the social, political, and geographical borders can find new modes of being and community formation in those sites of excess.

The reification of "Italian national identity" has always been facilitated by the media's (re)production of invented models of normativity that are limiting in the ways they are racialized, gendered, religiously and linguistically coded, heterocentric, and geographically specific. The social, cultural, and political construct—that is, national identity—is as imaginary as it is pervasive, and renders liminal any display of difference. The result is that minorities are relegated—both in media and in society more generally—to the *space-off*. As Teresa de Lauretis explains, the space-off is "the space not visible in the frame but inferable from what the frame makes visible."[7] What becomes clear here is that not only is minority positionality socio-physically enforced by these framings of national identity, but their own identity categories are in turn defined by what they are not.

QUEER / NOW

Today[8] we can point to LGBTQIA+ visibility across all forms of Italian media. At the same time, however, Italy is home to an alarming uptick in instances of verbal, physical, and legislative aggression against queer bodies. The contemporary climate surrounding LGBT rights in Italy is fraught at best. On the one hand, we saw the legalization of civil unions for same-sex couples pass in 2016, followed by numerous public demonstrations of support and successful collective actions. For instance, the boycott against Barilla pasta after homophobic remarks from the company's chairman resulted in a complete reversal of policy by the company, which now receives a perfect score on the Human Rights Campaign's Equality Index. In the media, more specifically, significant symbolic measures have been taken, like the development of Diversity Lab's Diversity Media Awards, which began in 2016 as a way of recognizing valuable and affirming representations of LGBT people in the media. On the other hand, right wing and church groups continue to lead movements that reaffirm the compulsory heterosexuality of the nuclear family, and that perpetuate fear about the dangers of gender variance. One such effort that has garnered significant media coverage and received public opposition as well as an alarming amount of public support is the World Congress of Families (WCF). In March 2019, Verona hosted the WCF, which focused a great deal of attention on developing strategies to combat things like gender theory education and nonheterosexual family formations. The event was organized with financial support from the religious and political right and drew international media coverage, featuring current political leaders like Deputy Prime Minister Matteo Salvini. The event spread dehumanizing rhetoric and mobilized dangerous language about hunting gay people and preventing the infectious spread of homosexuality, which was likened to an illness. The WCF conference came on the heels of a series of campaigns over the course of the past few years organized in concerted opposition to the Italian LGBT movement.[9] These campaigns have taken specific aim at preventing gender and sex education in schools, and seek to reaffirm heteroprimacy by employing a "new" pseudoscientific language. This opposition occurs in all aspects of Italian life, for example, it is a stance reinforced by Pope Francis who, in 2018, urged parents with young gay children to consider psychiatry as a way of curing the sickness of homosexuality. Furthermore, the negativity surrounding LGBTQIA+ people in Italy can be quantitatively evidenced by the ILGA's (International Lesbian Gay Bisexual Trans and Intersex Association) annual report, published in May of 2019, which ranked the country as number thirty-five out of forty-nine countries in terms of the country's LGBTQIA+ inclusivity, with a total grade of 22 percent out of 100 percent, receiving its lowest score (0) in the category that measured anti-homophobia laws.[10]

QUEER / ING

Within this text there is an emphasis on LGBTQ[11] identities and bodies, and an analysis of their positionality within Italian society as reflected in and produced by Italian media. Exploring these subject positions allows us to reflect on current and historic patterns of exclusion, to begin expanding notions of social and academic legibility and legitimacy, and to reflect on and celebrate the potential within sociocultural precarity. By considering these questions in the context of media representation we point to the importance of media's discursive contributions to identity formation, especially for marginalized minorities.

One of the aims of this book is to highlight the ways that LGBTQIA+ people are being interpellated into society through mediatic discourse. In turn, as media theorist Jason Mittell notes, it allows us to stress that "[d]iscursive formations often appear to be 'natural' or internal properties of beings, such as humans or texts, but they are actually culturally constituted and mutable."[12] Thus, the sociocultural position of the people represented by this acronym is a constructed one, and not dependent on essentialist notions of identity, no matter how *naturalized* they have become through the continual repetition of negative mediatic representation.

When we use "queer" as an identity category, we use it with an intentionality and awareness of the specificity of its origin in the Anglophone (and, more specifically, North American) world, because in the Italian context this word is not often used and is frequently misunderstood. For example, prominent trans activist Porpora Marcasciano finds that the meaning of the term "queer" has shifted as it is put in continued conversation with feminism, but she feels still more represented by *frocia* than by "queer."[13] *Frocia*, she explains, best represents her lived experience in 1970s Italy: "*Frocia* was a word that traversed the boundaries of identity categories [. . .] so gays, lesbians, and trans—which were the three main categories that one *could* and,

I should include myself, *should* use to identify—could all define themselves as *frocia*."[14] Marcasciano's comment speaks to the contradictory position queer bodies inhabit in contemporary Italy; a contradictory position further complicated by a distinction between what Massimo Prearo calls a "theoretical queer"—which (was and) continues to be brought to Italy through the translated texts of canonical theorists such as Michel Foucault, Giles Deleuze, Eve Sedgwick, Judith Butler—and an "experiential queer," of which militant thinkers such as Mario Mieli were a part.[15] Within this introduction and throughout the anthology, we attempt to bridge the divide between these two lineages, to muddle their definitions and practice the potential of bleeding theory into identity and vice versa. This in no way devalues the precarity, and marginality of the term "queer" as an identity category in Italy, which is indeed mirrored by the social, cultural, and economic positions of those represented by any culturally specific form of "queerness." Rather, it seeks to highlight the politics inherent in the positionality of the queer Italian subject.

The authors in this book use queerness also as a theoretical framework that reorients ways of thinking about "media," "Italy," and "Italian media" in addition to exploring it as an identity category. As Sara Ahmed notes in *Queer Phenomenology*, "Queer happens precisely when such legislation fails, when bodies meet that would be kept apart if we followed the lines given to us."[16] In other words, to use the geopolitical and industrial frameworks that define "media" and "Italy" in mainstream society would be a failure to acknowledge other ways of being, other ways of looking, and other ways of engaging with these concepts: ways that are queer. By queering Italian media we underscore that national understandings of media production do not account for contemporary modes of media creation and consumption, and we resist prioritizing mainstream and industrial media products. While the media discussed in these pages were all created within the geopolitical boundaries of the Italian nation-state, the "Italian space" we refer to exceeds the confines of the peninsula, both in its diaspora and because of the convergence of media cultures across nations.

ACADEMICS / POLITICS / ACTIVISM

In the landscape of Italian cultural studies, the term "queer" is often used as a stand-in for gay or lesbian identities, signaling a difference in sexual identity—which is often quite homonormative—without reflecting on either gender variance or nonnormative identities and practices.[17] By substituting queer for gay and lesbian in these instances, this kind of work ends up stripping the queer signifier of its already marginalized signified. Studies on lesbian and gay subjects in the Italian context are fundamental for creating political, social, historic, and academic legitimacy, and are necessarily intertwined with both feminist and queer activism, bodies, and theories.[18] But, as Alessia Palanti discusses in her chapter, these processes are often complicated by changing understandings of what it means to be feminist, queer, lesbian or otherwise occupy positions within these histories. The scholarship itself, Palanti argues, perpetuates certain notions of belonging and practices of othering even as it works in the service of enacting change in the Italian sociopolitical landscape.

Similarly, English-language queer scholarship engages rigorously with theory at the cost of prioritizing Anglophone-centric cultures and narratives. While some cultures may not necessarily embrace the term "queer" as an identity marker, rejecting the term outright risks limiting understandings of queer bodies, cultures, theories, and modes of being to not just Western, but Anglo-centric investigations and thus universalizes these very specific subject positions and shuts down the possibility for transnational queer discourse. Broadening queerness to encompass lives, theories, and politics beyond Anglophone cultures in a way that does not force those objects of study to identify with the term creates an open queer transnational and transcultural conversation that will surely increase the potential for queer visibility and queer theory. Some of this work is being done today by groups that exceed the academic sphere and put theoretical examination in conjunction with arts, community-building, and political practice. These include Archivio Queer, a virtual platform bringing together queer art, theory, and politics specific to Italian culture in Italy and abroad; and GendErotica, a festival with performances, roundtables, and exhibitions about gender and sexuality. Movimento Identità Trans (Trans Identity Movement) and MigraBO are both Bologna-based organizations dedicated to offering legal, social, and emotional support, as well as arts and community space for trans people (MIT) and LGBTI migrants (MigraBO). Within the sphere of higher education we find networks and research centers like Centro Interuniversitario di Ricerca Queer (Interuniversity Centero for Queer Research), PoliTeSse, and GIFTS: Genere Intersex Femministi Trans Sessualità (Gender Intersex Feminist Trans Sexuality) for queer scholars and those interested in queering their work.

QUEER / ITALIAN / MEDIA

As a whole, the chapters in this book investigate queer positionality, and work to queer notions of Italianness as it relates to and is reflected in media, while also queering understandings of viewer engagement and participation in media consumption and production. We maintain, however, the disciplinary frameworks of "media" as they are socially and academically understood because the mercurial nature of all that is embodied by this term undergoes a constant social and technological queering by definition. As such we engage with both the technological and social facets of which media is constituted. As cultural theorist Henry Jenkins states, building on historian Lisa Gitelman's definition: "On the first, a medium is a technology that enables communication; on the second, a medium is a set of 'protocols' or social and cultural practices that have grown up around that technology."[19] The people watching and participating in media creation and consumption are necessarily subject to (and complicit with) its sociopolitical messages and structures. The chapters that make up this book discuss media—specifically print media, film, television, user generated content sites, and social media platforms—primarily through an analysis of its content, consumer production, and response. Each chapter acknowledges the significance of each medium in the historical moment under investigation, while also participating in a collective reflection on the expansive influence of the entirety of our mediatic universe.

The varied lenses and discourses shared and explored in this book showcase the large reach of Italian media, and highlight the diverse ways that queerness, Italianness, and media can and should be put in conversation. The methodological variance of queerness mirrors the diversity of LGBTQIA+ lives and communities that are, in part, represented by the depictions discussed here, as well as by those consuming and/or investigating them.

Opening the anthology, Alessio Ponzio finds the intersection of these terms in the media coverage of a 1969 murder of a teenage boy in Tuscany; in his chapter we see the way a media-induced moral panic surrounding gay culture propelled the formation of gay cultural codes and community in Italy. Through an investigative analysis on representations of gays in the press, and the rise of contemporaneous discourses criminalizing homosexuality, on the one hand, and promoting gay rights awareness, on the other, Ponzio demonstrates that the dominant deviancy narrative fed into stereotypes of gays as child predators and as corrupting, unwelcome presences in "proper" Italian society. At the same time, however, this increased media focus on homosexuality had an unintended effect as this coverage helped educate the general public about certain aspects of gay life in Italy by shedding light on a community that had previously been relegated to the shadows, and sparked a response from gay Italians who began writing to these publications to defend themselves. Ponzio locates some of the early rumblings of the Italian gay rights movement within the public voices that spoke out during the years following the murder. The tensions that can be seen in the public discourse surrounding this murder are indicative of the dramatic sociocultural transformations Italy underwent in the late 1960s and early 1970s, making this case a critical milestone in Italian gay history.

Attention to this critical period in LGBT history is also at the heart of Alessia Palanti's chapter, which focuses on the interplay between documentary film and Italian lesbian feminism. Palanti takes a critical look at Marazzi's award-winning documentary film *We Want Roses Too*, as a way of reopening an important conversation about lesbian marginality in Italian second-wave feminism and its legacies. Second-wave feminism occupies a privileged position within Italian radical and activist history, and critical analyses of that moment are often denounced as attempts to discredit the movement and its achievements (which are many and include securing the right to divorce and abortion). Palanti enters this fraught territory by bringing a North American style of feminist film theory to bear on this deeply national topic. Her historical analysis brings to light a gap between feminist and lesbian activism, which is echoed by the film. Providing an in-depth description of the film and a consideration of the politics of documentary filmmaking, Palanti argues that while the formal structures of *We Want Roses Too* could very well be used to support a feminist reading of the film, the actual stories themselves weaken its radicalism, and essentially render invisible nonnormative sexualities.

The question of visibility is also central to Sole Anatrone's discussion of immigration and gender roles in the 2008 film *Corazones de Mujer*. Here the author invites us to reflect on the question of migration in Italy through an interrogation of assumptions of national identity and cultural coherence. While the film is often considered a "road trip movie," and part of the "migrant cinema" genre, Anatrone pushes past the limitations of this categorization by examining the ways this film rehearses iconic moments from Italian and US cinema in order to challenge assumptions of national identity that have been disseminated through the cinematic medium. Using Jose Muñoz's theory of queer utopianism, this chapter explores how the nomadic nature of both the film's narrative and its form, trouble both actual and filmic political and cultural borders. Elaborating on Rosi Braidotti's theory of nomadism, Anatrone makes the case that "nomadism becomes, in this way, a radical political practice that seeks to reconfigure the ways in which we understand ourselves in relation to geo-political borders; it is an intentional divorcing of the subject from the fixity imposed by state structures."[20] This theory of strategic nomadism is uncovered through an analysis of the film's intertextual, formal, and production elements, which, when taken together, work to disrupt a heteronormative narrative that is deeply tied up in preserving national boundaries.

The following chapter continues the discussion of cinema in a study of the changing representation of LGBT characters in contemporary Italian comedies. Dom Holdaway's chapter makes a convincing case about the generative queer substratum of recent comedies and its potential for unlocking radical experiences and epistemologies. Through a discussion of popular films from 2009 to 2016 including *Cado dalle nubi*, *Maschi contro femmine*, *Nessuno mi può giudicare*, *Una piccola impresa meridionale*, and *Perfetti sconosciuti*, Holdaway refutes the widely held idea that mainstream Italian cinema features few, and always stereotyped, LGBT characters; instead, he argues that these films differ in significant ways from the homophobic representations that characterized Italian films in the last century. As Holdaway demonstrates, it is precisely through the use of humor that the characters in this contemporary brand of cinema are able to leverage pointed critiques of homophobia in Italian society. Though both the critiques and the types of LGBT characters are limited, Holdaway locates queer potential within the oppositional spaces of these films.

Holdaway explains the strategic and multipronged way in which queer is deployed, "to foreground the same presence that queer people have always had around popular culture, especially as interpreters of it, and to maintain the term as a space of resistance, even to restrictive representational codes."[21] This simultaneous attention to the specificity and precarity of the individual, and to the revolutionary potential of queer life and art is operative throughout this book.

The discussion Holdaway begins regarding the tensions and potentials in normative representations of LGBTQIA+ lives is also central to Luca Malici's chapter, "An All Italian *Game of Thrones*: A Social Media Investigation of Maria de Filippi's Gay Male Version of the Trash, Dating Show *Uomini e Donne*." Malici's case study analyzes the gay version of the reality television show *Uomini e donne* (*Men and Women*), in which participants sit on a throne and are courted by suitors. After a rigorous quantitative analysis of Italian Twitter users' responses to LBGTQIA+ representation on "trash" television, Malici offers a productive queer reading both of the social commentary and the televisual text itself, arguing that "trash" TV has the potential to be a generative space for LGBTQIA+ representation and fandom. His investigation reveals LGBTQ mainstream televisual representations to be sites of discursive struggle. While addressing LGBTQ issues on daytime television helps to challenge stereotypes and behaviors often perceived as dissident, shows like *Uomini e donne* push the boundaries of prescriptive morality, as many of the tweets under investigation prove. However, what Malici shows is that the potentiality of trash television as a locus for queerness is being overshadowed by the television program's choice to privilege conventional members of sexual minorities, a move which ultimately stigmatizes many within the categories it purports to celebrate.

The concluding chapter by Julia Heim examines both industrial television and alternative prosumer media content and practices such as webseries, remediations, and slash fiction. Heim offers a queer lens through which to consider the complicated and unstable relationship between Italian consumers, producers, and televisual content. This chapter looks at representations of LGBTQ lives within mainstream Italian television, independently produced webseries, and fan remediations. Heim makes the case that contemporary developments in digital media have helped create a virtual space for the formation of queer communities. Engaging with J. Halberstam's theorization of the "technotopic," Heim identifies four discrete bodies as a productive tool for understanding the relationship between queerness and contemporary television: "The individual consumer/producer as body; the community as body; the consumed televisual text as body; and the produced televisual text as body."[22] Picking up on Malici's and Holdaway's discussions about potentiality in the spaces of contradiction and omission, Heim argues that, by taking these extended networks of production, consumption, and interaction into consideration, true queerness lies not in the products themselves, but in contemporary modes of mediatic engagement.

Throughout this book, queer theory, depictions of LGBTQ populations, and various mainstream and nonmainstream media are all put into conversation in an effort to speak across and through as many media platforms and content and approaches to them; each chapter works, in different ways and across different media, to queer normative texts, investigate queer lives in Italy, and bring to the fore queer media texts, and Italian queer mediatic communities. This kind of queer (re)reflecting is particularly important because it gives visibility to marginalized peoples and stories. It creates other ways of understanding media and our relationship to it. We present the work collected here as a beginning in the hopes that others will build on and continue to expand and transform understandings of Italianness and queerness, as critical theory, embodiment, and radical political practice.

NOTES

1. Peppino Ortoleva "A Geography of the Media since 1945" in *Italian Cultural Studies: An Introduction*, ed. David Forgacs and Robert Lumley (Oxford: Oxford University Press, 1996), 194.

2. Áine O'Healy, "Mediterranean Passages: Abjection and Belonging in Contemporary Italian Cinema" in *California Italian Studies* 1, no. 1 (2010): 4.

3. Milly Buonanno, *Italian TV Drama and Beyond* (United Kingdom: Intellect Books, 2012), 15–16.

4. Michela Ardizzoni, *North/South, East/West: Mapping Italianness on Television* (Lanham, MD: Lexington Books, 2007), 8.

5. Ibid., 110.

6. David Morley and Kevin Robins, *Spaces of Identity: Global Media, Electronic Landscapes, and Cultural Boundaries* (New York: Routledge, 1995), 90–91.

Introduction 11

7. Teresa de Lauretis, *Technologies of Gender* (Bloomington: Indiana University Press, 1987), 26.

8. The subheading "Now" addresses the contemporary condition of queer subjects in Italy while also referencing Eve Kolofksy Sedgwick's *Tendencies* and her and other's discussions of queer identity in conjunction with queer theory, which comprise a queer lineage that informs our work.

9. Two such examples are as follows: the Fertility Day campaign organized in 2016 by the Minister of Health as a way of promoting the heterosexual family and reinforcing gender stereotyped roles; and the Anti-Gender campaign organized by Citizen Go and Generazione Famiglia which used the #StopGender nelle scuole (in the schools) to promote discriminatory forms of digital activism.

10. According to the association, Italy's ranking has dropped by three places from May 2018 to May 2019. ILGA—Europe, "Rainbow Europe Index," May 2019, https://rainbow-europe.org/#8640/0/0.

11. LGBTQ is part of a larger group of subject positions linked together in response to a marginalization based on sexuality and gender: lesbian, gay, bisexual, trans, queer, intersex, asexual, plus (LGBTQIA+). While our sociopolitical and theoretical discussions and investments speak to every part of the LGBTQIA+ acronym, we have intentionally abbreviated it here so as to reflect the subject positions under investigation in this book.

12. Jason Mittell, "A Cultural Approach to Television Genre Theory," *Cinema Journal* 40, no. 3 (Spring, 2001): 8.

13. "Frocia" comes from the Italian word "frocio," meaning "faggot"; by adding the "a" at the end, the gender implications of the label are subverted, making space for a reclaiming and proposing of new expressions of identity, similar to the way the term "queer" was reclaimed and redefined by English-speaking gays, trans, and lesbians.

14. "Frocia era un termine che travalicava quei confini identitari [. . .] per cui potevano definirsi frocia invariabilmente gay, lesbiche, e trans, le tre principali categorie in cui ci si poteva e, aggiungerei io, doveva identificare." Marco Pustianaz, "Qualche domanda (sul) queer in Italia," *Italian Studies* 65, no. 2 (2010): 265. *Translation is our own.*

15. Massimo Prearo, "Le radici rimosse della queer theory. Una genealogia da ricostruire," *Genesis* IX, nos. 1–2 (2012): 96–97. For an elaboration of queer theory and activism in contemporary Italy, see Cesare di Feliciantonio's "Exploring the Complex Geographies of Italian Queer Activism," *Lambda nordica* 2 (2014).

16. Sara Ahmed, *Queer Phenomenology* (Durham: Duke University Press, 2006), 149.

17. Works like Giordano Bassetti and Andrea Jelardi's (2006) *Queer TV: omossessualità e transgressione* and *Mondo queer: cinema e militanza gay* by Pier Maria Bocchi (2005) are some of the only titles available to Italian-speaking audiences, though here too, as the subtitles suggest, "queer" is largely used as a stand-in for "gay."

18. There are works such as Luisa Passerini's (2007) *Fuori dalla norma: storie lesbiche*, Derek Duncan's (2005) *Reading and Writing Italian Homosexuality: A Case*

of Possible Difference, and Andrea Pini's (2011) *Quando eravamo froci: Gli omosessuali nell'Italia di una volta* that engage directly with these subject positions and their place within Italy's sociopolitical context.

19. Henry Jenkins, *Convergence Culture* (New York: New York University Press, 2008), 13–14.
20. Sole Anatrone, Infra., 58.
21. Dom Holdaway, Infra., 76.
22. Julia Heim, Infra., 135.

BIBLIOGRAPHY

Ahmed, Sara. *Queer Phenomenology*. Durham: Duke University Press, 2006.

Ardizzoni, Michela. *North/South, East/West: Mapping Italianness on Television*. Lanham, MD: Lexington Books, 2007.

Buonanno, Milly. *Italian TV Drama and Beyond*. Bristol: Intellect Books, 2012.

De Lauretis, Teresa. *Technologies of Gender*. Bloomington: Indiana University Press, 1987.

ILGA—Europe. "Rainbow Europe Index." May 2019. https://rainbow-europe.org/#8640/0/0.

Jenkins, Henry. *Convergence Culture*. New York: New York University Press, 2008.

Mittell, Jason. "A Cultural Approach to Television Genre Theory." *Cinema Journal* 40, no. 3 (Spring, 2001): 3–24. https://pdfs.semanticscholar.org/b61f/4d25fc18a49df8daaa2523af8f46530eac19.pdf.

Morley, David and Kevin Robins. *Spaces of Identity: Global Media, Electronic Landscapes, and Cultural Boundaries*. New York: Routledge, 1995.

O'Healy, Áine. "Mediterranean Passages: Abjection and Belonging in Contemporary Italian Cinema." *California Italian Studies* 1, no. 1 (2010). https://escholarship.org/uc/item/2qh5d59c.

Ortoleva, Peppino. "A Geography of the Media since 1945." In *Italian Cultural Studies: An Introduction*. Edited by David Forgacs and Robert Lumley, 185–198. Oxford: Oxford University Press, 1996.

Prearo, Massimo. "Le radici rimosse della queer theory. Una genealogia da ricostruire." *Genesis* IX, nos. 1–2 (2012): 95–114. http://massimoprearo.com/wp-content/uploads/2014/01/Le_radici_rimosse_della_queer_theory.pdf.

Pustianaz, Marco. "Qualche domanda (sul) queer in Italia." *Italian Studies* 65, no. 2 (2010): 263–277. https://doi.org/10.1179/016146210X12593180182856.

Chapter 1

The Lavorini Case

The Mediatic Confection of the Homosexual Ogres and the Homosexual Counterattack

Alessio Ponzio

On January 31, 1969, the thirteen-year-old Ermanno Lavorini disappeared in Viareggio, a Tuscan seaside resort. On the same day Lavorini's family received a call. The telephone rang in Lavorini's father's shop, a well-known fabric store, and Lavorini's sister answered. A male voice coldly asked to collect 15,000,000 lire, and ordered she refrain from calling the local authorities.[1] Despite the kidnappers' request, the family contacted the police immediately, and the search began soon thereafter. For thirty-seven days everyone hoped that Lavorini would come back home alive. However, on March 9, 1969 Lavorini's corpse was accidentally found buried on the beach of Marina di Vecchiano (about 4 miles away from Viareggio). The autopsy revealed that he had died the same day of his disappearance, and the corpse did not show evident signs of sexual abuse.[2]

The literature produced over the years about Ermanno Lavorini has offered more or less detailed chronicles of the homicide. It has described the dynamics of the assassination, the investigation, and the trials. But it has not adequately analyzed the ways in which media, demonizing Italian homosexuals, made them more visible. In this chapter I will show how the murder of this adolescent from Viareggio caused the wide circulation of pictures, magazines, and newspapers that gave visibility to "nonnormative" sexuality. Such visibility inflamed bigots, but it also catalyzed the emergence of homosexual self-awareness, and incited the politicization of inchoate homosexual communities. If many Italian homosexuals reacted, resisted, and organized themselves at the beginning of the 1970s it was also because of the exceptionally hostile atmosphere surrounding them after Lavorini's death. In this chapter, after having briefly talked about the investigation and resolution of the case,

I will focus my attention on the anti-homosexual media campaign, and I will then conclude by looking at the homosexual counterreaction.

From the very beginning police and media decided that to solve Lavorini's case it was necessary to seek answers in what they considered to be the "homosexual underworld." On the day of his disappearance Lavorini had been seen around the *pineta* (pine forest). In the summer this forested area was replete with tourists, but in the winter it was a totally different place. Here *travestiti* (transvestites), homosexuals, and young hustlers hung out. According to the investigators this population needed to be grilled to understand what actually happened to Lavorini. The police interviewed many *ragazzi di pineta* (pine forest boys)—as the young hustlers of Viareggio were rebaptized by the press. One of them was Marco Baldisseri, aged sixteen, unemployed, and recently accused of having been part of a gang rape of a twelve-year-old girl. After days and days of investigation and questioning, on April 19, 1969 Baldisseri confessed: he had killed Lavorini. In the following days two other youth confessed to be present when the kid was killed: Rodolfo della Latta (twenty years old) and Andrea Benedetti (twelve). Thus began a blur of continuously changing versions of how Lavorini was killed. These young hustlers defamed several prominent adults. Among them were Adolfo Meciani, owner of a beach resort, and Giuseppe Zacconi, rich son of a famous actor. According to one of the versions offered by Baldisseri and his friends, Lavorini was killed during a homosexual orgy gone bad. Meciani and Zacconi professed themselves innocent. However, Meciani could not handle the shame of being outed and committed suicide after a long and cruel media lynching, whereas Zacconi died of a heart attack in 1970.[3]

The investigating judge Pierluigi Mazzocchi was not convinced by the ragazzi di pineta's story and started thinking that homosexuals might have nothing to do with the case.[4] Marco, Rodolfo, and Andrea had something else in common—besides hustling: they were far-right activists. Rodolfo was a member of the neo-Fascist *Movimento Sociale Italiano*. Marco and Andrea instead were active supporters of the Monarchist Front led by Pietro Vangioni. Mazzotti began putting pressure on them, until Marco changed his version for the umpteenth time: Lavorini was kidnapped to extort money and organize far-right terrorism in Tuscany. Andrea Benedetti corroborated this new version in a letter sent to the investigators. He retracted his confessions and asserted that Della Latta and Vangioni convinced him to talk about homosexual exploiters and male-male prostitution in the pineta so that authorities could lose sight of the neo-Fascist trail. One year after Lavorini's disappearance Vangioni was arrested.

In 1977, after three trials, the Italian justice system finally condemned Della Latta (eleven years), Vangioni (nine years), and Baldisseri (eight years) for kidnapping and unpremeditated murder. According to the judges

Lavorini was kidnapped for ransom, and killed by Della Latta and Baldisseri. Vangioni was the mastermind of the criminal act. Andrea Benedetti was not tried because he was too young at the time of the murder. Meciani and Zacconi were completely innocent. Lavorini's death had nothing to do with homosexuality. He had been kidnapped to finance neo-Fascist terrorism. But Lavorini's case caused a discursive explosion in the Italian media against homosexuality and still today many in Italy think that he was a victim of sadistic homosexual pedophiles.[5]

THE ANTI-HOMOSEXUAL CAMPAIGN

Almost a decade after the *Balletti Verdi* (green ballets) scandal, when—in 1960—hundreds of homosexuals were accused of organizing sex parties with under-aged lads in Brescia, homosexuality hit the headlines of Italian newspapers and magazines again stirring panic and revulsion.[6] A presumed case of murderous pedophilia, thanks to the insatiable attention of the media, showed not only how at the end of the 1960s homosexuals were still perceived as dangerous child predators, but it also highlighted the very confusing ideas Italians had about what homosexuality was. In 1969, beside Lavorini's case, two other cases ignited the press: Giovanni Borri, a homosexual man, was killed in Florence by a young hustler, Andrea Vozza,[7] and in Reggio Emilia a very active male-male prostitution circle, involving mature clients and young hustlers, was discovered.[8] Because of these three cases, Italian homosexuals were branded as corruptors and killers.

Browsing the most popular newspapers and magazines it is very clear that the Italian press had decided from the very beginning who had killed Lavorini. Finding voices vaguely sympathetic to homosexuals is all but easy. The press labeled them—the group that suddenly became a collective culprit—as *pederasti* (pederasts) and *sodomiti* (sodomites), but also as *invertiti* (inverts), *pervertiti* (perverts), *contronatura* (against nature), and *capovolti* (upturned).[9] The *Corriere della Sera*, one of the most important Italian newspapers, described the homosexual milieu as a filthy "world of vice" and talked about its inhabitants as squalid, shameful, lewd, and depraved *anormali* (abnormal individuals).[10] The Viareggio local newspaper *Il Telegrafo* used very similar language and did not make any distinction between homosexuals and perverted sex maniacs. These terms were used as interchangeable synonyms.[11] *La Nazione Sera*, a Florentine newspaper particularly fond of the word "anormale" to describe homosexuals, argued that they lived in a world of "secrecy and insanity," in "a limbo of eternal damnation" where "the most unbelievable, the most grotesque, the most infamous maliciousness happens." Homosexuals, according to this newspaper, were ontologically different and had nothing in common with "the other men."[12] The right-wing magazine *Lo Specchio*, talking about the "*sordido ambiente*" (sordid milieu) and the "*sporca matassa*" (dirty skein) of Viareggio, the new Italian Sodom where kids were corrupted and even killed,[13] brought up again the old-fashioned expression "*terzo sesso*" (third sex) to talk about homosexuals,[14] an expression used also by the newspaper *La Nazione Sera*[15] and by the more progressive magazine *L'Espresso*.[16] The magazine *Epoca* seemed to be less aggressive against homosexuality. In an article published in June 1969 entitled *Siamo diventati più viziosi?* (Have We Become More Depraved?) the author underscored that Italy had not been punishing homosexuality for decades and that this had to be considered as proof of Italian tolerance. In his view, homosexuality between adults and without scandals did not need to be criminalized. However, and here the open-mindedness of the journalist showed its cracks, "when this vice, instead of remaining secret and recognizing in this way its own abnormal nature and its own moral condemnation, becomes public, and is displayed and almost praised on the streets, in movies and in some magazines, then it is necessary that the law intervenes to protect young people."[17] While claiming to be more tolerant than others, the journalist underscored: "We are not talking about prosecuting homosexuals, but about avoiding that their vice, which is tolerated when circumscribed, become an object of imitation and almost admiration, a reason for corruption, an incentive to crime, prostitution, and blackmailing."[18]

Protecting the youth against the vice became the press' favorite refrain. Before Baldiserri's confession, homosexuals were considered the culprits in Lavorini's disappearance and death, but even after Baldisseri's admission of guilt the Italian press continued to blame them. Even if they did not seem to be directly involved in the case, they were responsible anyway. They were at fault because they *infected* Marco and guys like him. According to *Il Corriere* the homosexual corruptors—the "mafia of vice"—pushed innocent kids to depravity. Those who corrupted—the homosexuals—rather than those who were corrupted—the ragazzi di pineta—were to be condemned.[19] *Il Telegrafo* talked about homosexuals as exploiters who turned kids into instruments of degradation.[20] According to *L'Espresso* homosexuals were imagined as being "obsessed with making proselytes on the road to vice."[21] And the mothers of Lavorini and of his young killers, interviewed by the popular magazine *Gente*, agreed that vicious homosexuals had to be blamed because they infected poor children's minds.[22]

La Nazione accused not only homosexuals who seduced and lured the ragazzi di pineta but also these kids' fathers. Their argument was that these youth were easily corrupted because their fathers were absent and, as a consequence, they had lacked positive male models.[23] The communist press tended to blame the entire Italian society that turned money into the supreme goal, a goal the youth wanted to achieve by any means, even hustling.[24] The right-wing *Il Borghese* instead proudly maintained that the Italians should not feel guilty for what had happened. Only the *"pederasti maledetti"* (damned pederasts), the *"gran clan degli invertiti"* (grand clan of the inverts) had to be condemned.[25] However, reading the interviews granted by the ragazzi di pineta, we see that they did not consider themselves as victims led astray by the anormali. Andrea Benedetti in his interview to *Gente* underscored that no one forced him to hustle. Ragazzi like him accepted proposals and invitations, he explained, because "they wanted to." To his opinion such choices were not reprehensible, because "[e]veryone can do what they want."[26] Another ragazzo di pineta interviewed by *Oggi* confirmed that the kids were not corrupted because no one really forced them to hustle. They decided to do it for money. Furthermore, he explained that he was not disgusted by this life—defined "depraved" by the journalist—because he knew that it was just a phase that would not affect his future as a man.[27] But these youth were different from Lavorini. He was presented as an innocent victim. The picture taken during his first communion, published by some Italian magazines, aimed at distinguishing him from the young hustlers of Viareggio, and criminalizing even more the cruel "abnormal men" who allegedly caused more or less directly his death.[28]

The idea of homosexuals as child predators coexisted with the idea of homosexuals as "sexual inverts." *Il Borghese* powerfully visualized the feminization of the homosexual men and the ambiguity of their gender identity on its cover of May 22, 1969 (see figure 1.1). The diagonal band at the top of the front page—*"Da Viareggio con amore"* (From Viareggio with Love)—aimed at associating this picture with Lavorini, Viareggio, and the *habitués* of the pineta. The picture was a collage of a dark-haired and hirsute man hiding his face, and of a female figure disguised by a blonde wig, bright red lipstick, and black mascara. Looking at the picture the subject seemed to be the same person, but the ambiguity and the uncertainty communicated by the cover aimed at increasing societal anxiety about sexual and gender nonconformity: What is a man? What is a woman? What is a homosexual? How can we be sure about the "real" nature of the people we meet every day? Looking at this image we see how homosexuality was represented as a schizophrenic identity, and how the homosexual appeared as an assemblage of masculinity and femininity. The "male" half is covered, symbolizing not only shame but also deceit. The female "half" is larger, expressing a fear of "feminization," epitomized also by the shaved hand contrasted against the hairy forearm. In the image femininity is represented as creeping dangerously and inexorably into this male body destined to be sooner or later completely devoured. In this image the distinction between homosexuality, cross-dressing, and gender nonconformity was blurred.

Figure 1.1 Cover of *Il Borghese*, May 22, 1969.

Il Borghese was not alone in trying to *explain* what homosexuality was, and presenting homosexuality as gender inversion. *Oggi*, a popular tabloid with a very large readership, did the same in an investigative report published in the summer of 1969. The tone was all but indulgent. The title and the subheading of the first installment say it all: "When sex becomes vice or sickness" "Why is the scourge of the abnormal men spreading?"[29] *Oggi* explained that their articles were the final result of long conversations with policemen, doctors, priests, sociologists, psychologists, and lawyers about the seedy underworld of homosexuals. The goal of the magazine not only was to understand "the actual spread of this 'social disease'" but also wanted to figure out "how the abnormal have to be judged." The journalist asked in the first installment: "Are we transforming into a country where the third sex reigns, we, always proud of our reputation of virility and of our reputation as Latin lovers (to the point of turning them into tourist attractions)?"[30] And he explained he was particularly worried about violent crimes perpetrated by homosexuals. The investigative report wanted to understand how big the homosexual problem was, what caused homosexuality, till what point homosexuality had to be considered a disease, what therapies could cure it, what tools the society had to protect itself from criminal degenerations of homosexuality, till what point the image of Italy emerging from homosexual scandals corresponded to reality, and if the perception of homosexuality as a spreading phenomenon was distorted by scaremongering.

The second installment of the report tried to understand, thanks to a priest, a psychologist, and a neurologist, if the anormali deserved scorn or pity, and if they could recover. The article concluded asserting that the homosexual was an unhappy human being because he was "the first to consider his condition as opposite to normalcy."[31] This was the reason why he tried "to keep his true nature desperately secret, controlling his behavior, and showing off virile tastes and habits."[32] However, the double life he was forced to live was exhausting and turned him into a neurasthenic. Doctors considered homosexuality a biological or a psychological disease. Therapies were so difficult and results so uncertain that many men suspended their treatment.[33] The last installment of *Oggi*, entitled *I sessi sono due o tre?* (Are Sexes Two or Three?), turned into a criticism of the existing (and nonexisting) laws. The Italian open-mindedness and the inadequacy of the Italian penal system, according to the journalist, was dangerously favoring the growing number of male hustlers on the streets. A law to keep homosexuality under control was due.[34]

In this atmosphere of media lynching against homosexuals the communist press emerged—I would say astonishingly—as an exception. *Vie Nuove*, underscoring that the Lavorini case had brought the phenomenon of homosexuality to the attention of the public opinion, made an argument very different from the rest of the Italian press. The magazine underlined that being homosexual did not mean being a criminal. This does not mean that the magazine was devoid of judgmental overtones. We read in fact: "It is obvious that homosexuals, like sexually normal people, can commit crimes, but as homosexual they are not intrinsically guilty, they are what they are."[35] The magazine, trying to answer the question *Cosa sono gli omosessuali*? (What Are Homosexuals?), argued that some of them were sick, whereas others were physically and mentally healthy. They were normal. *Vie Nuove* explained that saying this could spark scandal, but it also added that because of the "Kinsey report" it became more and more difficult to classify homosexual tendencies as "abnormal."[36] However, in spite of this unexpected tolerance, the magazine fell into the *disease paradigm* again underlining that despising a homosexual is as absurd as despising a diabetic. Furthermore, trying to keep a salutary distance from homosexuals, *Vie Nuove* underscored that what they wrote did not have to be understood as an apologia of homosexuality, but only as a clarification of this scarcely known phenomenon.[37] *Il Borghese* did not wait long to respond. The right-wing magazine argued that the Italian communists were protecting homosexuals because the capovolti had leading positions in their party, and because homosexuals were fulfilling an important communist task: the destruction of the traditional Italian family.[38]

Lavorini's case pushed people to express their own opinions about homosexuality. Newspapers and magazines published many readers' letters. Most of them were rather, we would say today, homophobic. They expressed fear about the alleged increasing number of abnormal men. Some talked about the "third sex" as a plague that needed to be eradicated, as a "sick and morally disgusting milieu threatening children's innocence."[39] One reader of *Il Telegrafo*, the lawyer G. P., wrote in his letter: "You will find in me the most severe of the censurers. 48 hours after Ermanno Lavorini's disappearance, I thought immediately that the kidnapper had to be searched for in the third sex's world." And he concluded, "From an emotional point of view I am with the sheik of Amman, who finishes off the pederasts shooting them in the back of the head. From a legal point of view, I believe the kidnappers should be killed on the electric chair as they do in the United States of America."[40] Other readers invoked the introduction of a law to penalize homosexuality. In his letter to *Oggi* a lawyer from Milan wondered why the law to prosecute "pederasty" in Italy had been covered up and never discussed. Given that the presence of "pederasts" in "normal" society was a danger, according to this lawyer, it was necessary to get rid of this "national shame." And he concluded: "If the pederast is sick, he has to be institutionalized, if he is depraved, he has to be incarcerated."[41] A reader of *La Nazione Sera* was instead more worried about the loud noise around homosexuality and about the presence of homosexuals in delicate positions. He thought that it was necessary to talk less about homosexuality because the more people discussed it the more it produced dangerous effects in the Italian society. And, using a typical 1950s lavender scare argument he concluded, "We need to focus our attention on identifying homosexuals so that they will not be able to become educators or fill positions that can allow them to be aware of military and industrial secrets."[42]

HOMOSEXUAL COUNTERREACTION

Homosexuals too appeared in mainstream media to talk about themselves. Some homosexual readers of the magazine *Oggi* used the words abnormal and normal to make distinctions between them and the others. They underscored that there were sick people on both sides, but they also asked the *normal* to understand that there were some *abnormal* who had jobs, did not cause any scandal, and just wanted to be left in peace. Others pathologized their sexual orientation asking for compassion: "Why are we homosexuals abhorred? Do people despise blind, mentally ill, or paralytic people because they lack something the others have? Before judging, normal people should think about what they would have done if such a big disgrace had happened to them."[43] The magazine *ABC* also published several homosexuals' testimonies in an article entitled *Questi ragazzi di vita si possono recuperare?* (Can We Recover These Hustlers?). Given the preamble of the article though, a preamble about homosexuality as an evil infection, we are not surprised that most testimonies talk about it as a damned vice, as a secret to hide, as a disease, as a torment, and as a curse. Homosexuals in these letters described their disgust for having sex in dirty toilets, confessed to having become homosexuals when lured by older men, and talked about their desire for a "normal" family. One man, obsessed with hiding his identity, explained: "I am a representative of the most revolting category in the world, the category of the inverts."[44] He was happy to be very masculine and discrete but he ended up his testimony saying, "If my abnormal tendency got out, I would have to run away or kill myself."[45]

Looking at these documents, many homosexuals seemed to have internalized hatred, blame, and pathologization, but, as the magazine *Cronaca* underlined, there were many who resisted and counterattacked rejecting the degrading adjectives used to describe their world, and excluding that their relationships had to entail crimes. Particularly significant, according to *Cronaca*, were the letters sent to *La Nazione*.[46] The director of this newspaper admitted that the Lavorini case caused a flood of letters written by homosexuals who were appalled by the ways in which his correspondent from Viareggio was talking about homosexuality.[47] *La Nazione* published a small amount of fascinating letters written by homosexuals. On March 16, F. G. sent a letter to the director of the Florentine newspaper criticizing the use of the word *squallido* (sordid) made by the magazine in order to describe the homosexual milieu. F. G. explained that he was homosexual, but he did not think about himself as squallido. Moreover, the homosexual milieu was so large that one adjective was not enough to describe its complexity. F. G. argued that it would be easier to be "normal" for practical reasons but, at the same time, he did consider himself "normal." He had a job, a life, friends, lovers, and he did not cause problems or scandals. In the end, he reminded, "brute and insane people exist also among the so-called 'normal,' but despite this 'we' don't think that these people represent 'the other side' in its entirety, therefore I do not think it is right to generalize when we talk about homosexuals."[48] Another homosexual L. A., in his letter published on March 23, maintained:

> I am a citizen who, as others, works, pays taxes, did the compulsory military service, and has not done any wrong to anyone, so shouldn't I have the right to be what I am without being tormented and humiliated? Many of us live in the terror of being discovered, of losing our jobs and the love of our families; we are blackmailed by criminals who remain unpunished and we are damned to loneliness. Dear director, believe me, I do not want anyone's pity, I just want the justice I deserve.[49]

F. G. sent another letter on March 29 proclaiming: "Like it or not, homosexuals exist, they exist, you bet . . . and they are determined to stay; and this is something people will have to accept, sooner or later, and then they will have to take off those blinders they are used to wearing—like donkeys—and learn to treat us as human beings, because this is what we are."[50] And another reader of the newspaper wrote on April 26, after Baldisseri had confessed to the murder, "I think it is time to stop considering homosexuals as causes of every human evil; it is time to stop considering this minority, who does not harm anyone, as an ill-fated and repulsive sect."[51] But homosexuals did not just write letters, they also began organizing and taking action.

On May 26, 1969 *La Nazione Sera* published an article entitled "*Incredibile manifesto diffuso da giovani del 'terzo sesso'*" ("Incredible Manifesto Published by Young Members of the 'Third Sex'") (see figure 1.2). This

Incredibile manifesto diffuso da giovani del «terzo sesso»

Ieri in vari punti del centro cittadino - Protestano contro le operazioni di polizia nei luoghi frequentati da personaggi ambigui iniziate da qualche tempo dalla questura - Ridicole pretese

Figure 1.2 Article from *La Nazione Sera*, May 26, 1969.

manifesto was posted around the city center to protest against the actions carried out by the police in cruising and hustling areas of Florence.[52] In this statement homosexuals demanded the end of their marginalization, and asked for their full recognition as Italian citizens. This public declaration was one of the very first concrete actions carried out by an organized homosexual group asking to be recognized as legitimate full members of the Italian society. The flyer declared:

> Patience is limited and the patience OF HOMOSEXUALS HAS EXCEEDED EVERY LIMIT.
> ITALIAN HOMOSEXUALS are free citizens of a free and democratic state and, as such, they ask for FREEDOM and for official acknowledgement.
> HOMOSEXUALS work, are active members of society, pay taxes and the Italian government has to deal with their problems, preventing them from being victims of capricious and unfair persecutions by the Police that mortify and destroy the most sacred rights of these human beings.
> On the basis of what laws do the Italian Police drag off HOMOSEXUALS to the police central station and keep them there for hours?
> HOMOSEXUALS ARE NOT CRIMINALS! THEY ARE NOT CORRUPTORS!!
> Parents have to raise their children.
> Stop these NAZIFASCIST persecutions!
> Prisons are full of normal criminals.
> Stop racist media speculations!
> Citizens, each one of you can have a HOMOSEXUAL son, a HOMOSEXUAL brother.
> ITALIAN HOMOSEXUALS are tired of enduring unfair 'ENDLESS WARS.'
> They will fight united against those who want to exacerbate their problems.
> Stop police persecutions!
> Stop the abuse of power!
> Stop cease and desist orders![53]

The war on homosexuals, *La Nazione Sera* underscored, was a consequence of new tensions emerging after Lavorini's murder, but it also caused "the counter-battery fire" of "the third sex 'front.'" Insolent groups of youth, the journalist argued, "who under their male garments hide deviant feelings and habits, handed out in the underground passages of the train station and in other zones of the center . . . anonymous flyers asserting those things said again and again . . . in many letters sent to our newspaper in the last weeks."[54]

Media denigrated Italian homosexuals, but they also allowed many men to come to terms with their own sexuality. Many youth realized their own homosexuality thanks to the media lynching. Thus, I would argue, if many Italian homosexuals reacted, resisted, and organized themselves at the beginning of the 1970s it was also because of the exceptionally hostile atmosphere surrounding them after Lavorini's death. The people who wrote combative letters, the young homosexuals handing out flyers in Santa Maria Novella in the spring of 1969 were probably among those who flocked into the Italian gay movement a few years later. Homosexuality was in the press before 1969—for example, *Cronaca* devoted a report to sexual deviations, and male and female homosexuality in sixteen installments in 1967—and in 1969 there were cultish magazines—such *LSD*[55] and *Men*[56]—that were trying to *normalize* same-sex sex. But the Lavorini case turned homosexuality into a mainstream topic and favored a more severe repression against homosexuals,[57] as a result these alleged *homosexual ogres* became aware they needed to fight back. Obviously I am not arguing for a monocausal explanation of this very complex phenomenon, that was deeply transnational, however Lavorini's case—as constructed by the media—gave an essential boost to the 1970s Italian homosexual counterattack. The unprecedented tide of hate roused by the murder of a thirteen-year-old kid was one of the elements that between the end of the 1960s and the beginning of the 1970s fed that rage Italian homosexuals needed to understand who they were, express themselves, get organized, and intensify their battle.

NOTES

1. According to the website of *Il Sole 24 Ore* (http://www.infodata.ilsole24ore.com/2016/05/17/calcola-potere-dacquisto-lire-ed-euro-dal-1860-2015/?refresh_ce=1) 15,000,000 lire of 1969 would be 143,000 Euro in current money ($165,000).

2. For a history and chronology of the Lavorini case, see Adolfo Lippi-Fernando Galli, *Ermanno il Primo?* (Massarosa: Edizioni attualità, 1969); Benzio Bernabò, *L'infanzia delle stragi. Il caso Lavorini* (Trento: Reverdito, 1989); Marco Nozza, *Il pistarolo: da piazza Fontana, trent'anni di storia raccontati da un grande cronista* (Milano: Il Saggiatore, 2006); Sabina Marchesi, *I processi del secolo: enigmi, retroscena, orrori e verità in trenta casi giudiziari italiani da Gino Girolimoni a Marta Russo* (Sesto Fiorentino: Olimpia, 2008); Luca Steffenoni, *Nera: come la cronaca cambia i delitti* (Cinisello Balsamo: San Paolo, 2011), 187–202.

3. See, for example, Fabio Galiani, "I ragazzi mentono perché temono il vero colpevole," *Oggi*, November 26, 1969, 140–142; "Parlano le vittime della calunnia," *Oggi*, November 26, 1969, 142; Franco Pierini, "Hanno sconvolto la mia vita ci dice il figlio di Ermete Zacconi," *L'Europeo*, November 27, 1969, 36–39. See also Nozza, *Il pistarolo*, 32; Marchesi, *I processi del secolo*, 268, 272.

4. For Mazzocchi, see, for example, Franco Pierini, "Il dramma del giudice che deve svelare il mistero della morte di Ermanno Lavorini," *L'Europeo*, October 30,

1969, 34–38; Lorenzo Iacona, *Gli anni 70: Il caso Lavorini. Una narrazione tra storia e cronaca giudiziaria*, Chair Prof. Giovanni De Luna, academic year 2003–2004, Università di Torino. Facoltà di Lettere e Filosofia, 50–51; Nozza, *Il pistarolo*, 32; Steffenoni, *Nera*, 198–199.

5. Marchesi, *I processi del secolo*, 274.

6. See Stefano Bolognini, *Balletti verdi: uno scandalo omosessuale* (Brescia: Libere edizioni, 2000).

7. See, for example, Piero Magi, "Ha confessato a Roma il delitto un giovane di diciannove anni," *La Nazione*, April 6, 1969, 1–2.

8. See, for example, T. B., "Reclutavano i ragazzi anche con la violenza," *La Nazione*, June 12, 1969, 7.

9. The word "capovolto" was used as a synonym of homosexual after the publication of Giò Stajano's queer-themed book *Roma Capovolta* in 1959.

10. See, for example, Sergio Cabassi, "Indagini nel mondo del vizio," *Il Corriere della Sera*, February 12, 1969, 5; Arrigo Benedetti, "Emozioni e pensieri," *Il Corriere della Sera*, March 7, 1969, 3; Sergio Cabassi, "Interrogatori sospesi a Viareggio," *Il Corriere della Sera*, March 13, 1969, 5.

11. See, for example, Renzo Pellegrini, "È un bruto il rapitore," *Il Telegrafo*, February 12, 1969, 1 and 12.

12. Mauro Mancini, "Perché non si trova l'assassino," *La Nazione Sera*, March 17, 1969, 3.

13. F. A., "Il giallo che fa arrossire," *Lo Specchio*, May 4, 1969, 46.

14. F. A., "Orrore in Versilia. Come il terzo sesso ha ucciso Ermanno Lavorini," *Lo Specchio*, May 11, 1969, 46.

15. Ugo Dotti, "Ermanno: sul 'carnet' della polizia lucchesi pisani fiorentini e massesi," *La Nazione Sera*, March 25, 1969, 3.

16. Giuseppe Catalano, "Pollicino fa la vita," *L'Espresso*, May 11, 1969, 11.

17. "[. . .] quando questo vizio, invece di essere segreto e di riconoscere così il proprio carattere anormale e la propria condanna morale, diventa pubblico, e viene ostentato e quasi magnificato nelle strade, nei film e in certi giornali, allora bisogna che la legge agisca a garanzia soprattutto dei giovani," Domenico Bartoli, "Siamo diventati più viziosi," *Epoca*, June 22, 1969, 29.

18. "Non si tratta, dunque, di perseguitare gli omosessuali, ma di impedire che il loro vizio, tollerato quando è circoscritto, diventi di imitazione e quasi di ammirazione, un motivo di corruttela, uno stimolo al crimine, alla prostituzione, al ricatto," Ibid.

19. Enzo Passanisi, "Gli angeli dalla faccia sporca," *Il Corriere della Sera*, May 4, 1969, 11.

20. C. A. Di Grazia, "La responsabilità degli adulti," *Il Telegrafo*, May 4, 1969, 3.

21. "Malati di proselitismo sulla strada de vizio," Camilla Cederna, "La caramella di Erode," *L'Espresso*, March 30, 1969, 13.

22. Ornella Ripa, "I ragazzi non sono colpevoli," *Gente*, May 28, 1969, 12–16.

23. Giancarlo Zanfroghini, "Ragazzi corrotti," *La Nazione*, May 21, 1969, 3.

24. See, for example, "Scandalo vero e falso a Viareggio," *Vie Nuove*, May 15, 1969, 6–7; Maria Rosa Calderoni, "Attentato alla città," *Vie Nuove*, May 22, 1969, 17–19; "Il giovane anormale," *Vie Nuove*, September 25, 1969, 19–22.

25. Luciano Cirri, "Il paradiso dei capovolti. Ipocrisia per il delitto di Viareggio," *Il Borghese*, March 20, 1969, 630–631.

26. "Ognuno è libero di fare ciò che vuole," Ornella Ripa and Renzo Allegri, "Così hanno corrotto i nostri poveri figli," *Gente*, May 14, 1969, 13.

27. "Come siete diventati 'ragazzi di vita,'" *Oggi*, May 21, 1969, 113.

28. See, for example, the pictures published in *Gente*, May 7, 1969, 7.

29. Silvio Bertoldi, "Perché si sta diffondendo la piaga degli anormali," *Oggi*, July 16, 1969, 54–57.

30. "Ci stiamo trasformando in un paese dove impera il terzo sesso, proprio noi, sempre orgogliosi (fino a farne un'attrattiva turistica) della nostra fama di virilità, di latin lover?" Ibid., 54–55.

31. "L'omosessuale è spesso un infelice: egli stesso per primo considera il suo stato contrario alla normalità."

32. "Per questo di solito cerca disperatamente di mantenere segreta la sua vera natura, controllandosi nel comportamento, mostrando gusti e abitudini virili."

33. Silvio Bertoldi, "Gli anormali possono guarire,'" *Oggi*, July 23, 1969, 38–42.

34. Silvio Bertoldi, "I sessi sono due o tre?" *Oggi*, July 30, 1969, 52–56.

35. "È ovvio che gli omosessuali, come qualsiasi altro individuo a sessualità normale, possono commettere dei delitti; ma in quanto omosessuali essi non sono colpevoli di nulla, sono semplicemente quello che sono."

36. The sexologist Alfred Kinsey, after many years of research, published in the United States two volumes for which he became very famous: *Sexual Behavior in the Human Male* (1948) and *Sexual Behavior in the Human Female* (1953). The Italian translations of the reports were produced by Bompiani: *Il comportamento sessuale dell'uomo* (1950) and *Il comportamento sessuale della donna* (1955). When they appeared they found full voice in the Italian press. The responses to the publications were all but positive, and the reports were rejected as morally dangerous. In the 1950s many magazines and newspapers in Italy talked about the reports as examples of the sexual "otherness" of Kinsey's America trying, in this way, to close down further public discussion of Italian sexuality. However, the every appearance of the reports, of their reviews, and of articles about the reports in newspapers and magazines inevitably produced effects among the Italian readers in subsequent decades. See Penelope Morris, "'Let's Not Talk About Italian Sex': The Reception of the Kinsey Reports in Italy," *Journal of Modern Italian Studies* 18, no. 1 (2013): 17–32.

37. Flavio Casale, "Che cos'è l'omosessualità? La norma e l'antinorma," *Vie Nuove*, May 15, 1969, 8–9.

38. Carlo Cusani, "Da Viareggio con amore," *Il Borghese*, May 22, 1969, 170–172.

39. "[Un] ambiente malsano e moralmente repellente che insidia da vicino l'innocenza dei bambini," *Il Telegrafo*, March 15, 1969, 10.

40. "Troverà in me il più drastico dei censori. Quarantotto ore dopo la sparizione di Ermanno Lavorini, ho subito pensato che il rapitore dovesse essere ricercato nel mondo del terzo sesso . . . . Sul piano sentimentale la penso come lo sceicco di Amman, che finisce i pederasti con un colpo alla nuca. Sul piano giuridico ritengo che dovrebbe essere comminata ai rapitori la pena che è prevista negli Stati Uniti d'America, vale a dire la sedia elettrica." Ibid.

41. "... se il pederasta è un malato, in manicomio; se è un vizioso alla galera," "Lettere a Oggi," *Oggi*, August 13, 1969, 3.

42. "Piuttosto cerchiamo di riconoscerli e identificarli per impedire di ritrovarceli educatori dei nostri figli o in posti dove possano conoscere segreti industriali o militari," "Lettere al direttore," *La Nazione Sera*, May 19, 1969, 2.

43. "Perché noi omosessuali siamo così spesso disprezzati? Si disprezza forse un cieco, un deficiente, un paralitico perché sono privi di qualcosa che altri hanno ed essi no? Prima di giudicare, gli uomini normali dovrebbero pensare che cosa avrebbero fatto se fosse capitata loro una così grande disgrazia," "Lettere a Oggi," *Oggi*, August 13, 1969, 3.

44. "Sono un rappresentante della più schifosa categoria che ci sia al mondo, quella degli invertiti." See "Questi ragazzi di vita si possono recuperare?" *ABC*, May 23, 1969, 15.

45. "... se qualcosa delle mie tendenze anormali trapelasse non mi resterebbe che la fuga o il suicidio." Ibid.

46. "Viareggio sì e no," *Cronaca*, April 19, 1969, 10.

47. "Lettere al direttore," *La Nazione*, April 2, 1969, 3.

48. "... i bruti e i pazzi esistono in larga misura anche tra i cosiddetti 'normali,' ma non per questo 'noi' ci riteniamo autorizzati a pensare che essi rappresentino tutta l''altra parte' per cui credo non sia molto giusto generalizzare parlando di certi omosessuali," "Lettere al direttore," *La Nazione*, March 16, 1969, 9.

49. "Io sono un cittadino che come gli altri lavora, paga le tasse, ha fatto il servizio militare e non ha mai fatto male a nessuno e allora devo o non devo avere il diritto di essere come la natura mi ha creato, senza dovermi tormentare e umiliare? Molti di noi vivono nel terrore di essere scoperti, di perdere il lavoro, gli affetti familiari; siamo sottoposti ai ricatti di criminali che restano impuniti, siamo condannati alla solitudine. Mi creda, signor direttore, io non voglio la pietà di nessuno, io voglio solo la giustizia che mi è dovuta." "Lettere al direttore," *La Nazione*, March 23, 1969, 9.

50. "Che piaccia o no a questi signori, gli omosessuali esistono, esistono eccome! ... essi ci sono e ben decisi a restare: e questo è un fatto che prima o poi dovranno accettare, e allora dovranno togliersi quei paraocchi da somari che sono avvezzi a portare e imparare a trattarci come esseri umani poiché tali siamo." "Lettere al direttore," *La Nazione*, March 29, 1969, 12.

51. "Credo che è l'ora di finirla di considerare gli omosessuali come capri-espiatori di tutti i mali dell'umanità; è l'ora di finirla di considerare questa minoranza, che non fa del male a nessuno, come una setta nefasta e ripugnante." "Lettere al direttore," *La Nazione*, April 26, 1969, 2.

52. "Una radicale pulizia nel mondo dei 'travestiti,'" *La Nazione*, May 13, 1969, 4; "Giovanotto di nome Massimo la 'vistosa ragazza bionda,'" *La Nazione*, May 22, 1969, 5.

53. The text of the flyers was reported in Gianna Preda, "Domande e risposte-Uno che si vergogna," *Il Borghese*, July 24, 1969, 714.

54. "Incredibile manifesto diffuso da giovani del 'terzo sesso,'" *La Nazione Sera*, May 26, 1969, 14.

55. See, for example, Giò Stajano, "Lungo viaggio nell'Italia omosessuale," *LSD*, April 9, 1969, 10–12.

56. See, for example, Andrea Silveri and Giovanni della Valle, "Gli omosex in Italia," *Men*, July 14, 1969, 8–17.

57. See files about repression of homosexuality in 1969 in Archivio Centrale dello Stato, Ministero Interni, Gabinetto 1967–1970, busta 56.

BIBLIOGRAPHY

"Come siete diventati 'ragazzi di vita'." *Oggi*, May 21, 1969.
"Giovanotto di nome Massimo la 'vistosa ragazza bionda'." *La Nazione*, May 22, 1969.
"Il giallo che fa arrossire." *Lo Specchio*, May 4, 1969.
"Il giovane anormale." *Vie Nuove*, September 25, 1969.
"Incredibile manifesto diffuso da giovani del 'terzo sesso'." *La Nazione Sera*, May 26, 1969.
"Orrore in Versilia. Come il terzo sesso ha ucciso Ermanno Lavorini." *Lo Specchio*, May 11, 1969.
"Parlano le vittime della calunnia." *Oggi*, November 26, 1969.
"Questi ragazzi di vita si possono recuperare?" *ABC*, May 23, 1969.
"Scandalo vero e falso a Viareggio." *Vie Nuove*, May 15, 1969.
"Una radicale pulizia nel mondo dei 'travestiti'." *La Nazione*, May 13, 1969.
"Viareggio sì e no." *Cronaca*, April 19, 1969.
"Reclutavano i ragazzi anche con la violenza." *La Nazione*, June 12, 1969.
Bartoli, Domenico. "Siamo diventati più viziosi." *Epoca*, June 22, 1969.
Benedetti, Arrigo. "Emozioni e pensieri." *Il Corriere della Sera*, March 7, 1969.
Bernabò, Benzio. *L'infanzia delle stragi. Il caso Lavorini*. Trento: Reverdito, 1989.
Bertoldi, Silvio. "Perché si sta diffondendo la piaga degli anormali." *Oggi*, July 16, 1969.
———. "Gli anormali possono guarire'." *Oggi*, July 23, 1969.
———. "I sessi sono due o tre?" *Oggi*, July 30, 1969.
Bolognini, Stefano. *Balletti verdi: uno scandalo omosessuale*. Brescia: Libere edizioni, 2000.
Cabassi, Sergio. "Indagini nel mondo del vizio." *Il Corriere della Sera*, February 12, 1969.
———. "Interrogatori sospesi a Viareggio." *Il Corriere della Sera*, March 13, 1969.
Calderoni, Maria Rosa. "Attentato alla città." *Vie Nuove*, May 22, 1969.
Casale, Flavio. "Che cos'è l'omosessualità? La norma e l'antinorma." *Vie Nuove*, May 15, 1969.
Catalano, Giuseppe. "Pollicino fa la vita." *L'Espresso*, May 11, 1969.
Cederna, Camilla. "La caramella di Erode." *L'Espresso*, March 30, 1969.
Cirri, Luciano. "Il paradiso dei capovolti. Ipocrisia per il delitto di Viareggio." *Il Borghese*, March 20, 1969.
Cusani, Carlo. "Da Viareggio con amore." *Il Borghese*, May 22, 1969.
Di Grazia, C.A. "La responsabilità degli adulti." *Il Telegrafo*, May 4, 1969.
Dotti, Ugo. "Ermanno: sul 'carnet' della polizia lucchesi pisani fiorentini e massesi." *La Nazione Sera*, March 25, 1969.

Galiani, Fabio. "I ragazzi mentono perché temono il vero colpevole." *Oggi*, November 26, 1969.

Iacona, Lorenzo. "Gli anni 70: Il caso Lavorini. Una narrazione tra storia e cronaca giudiziaria." Diss., Università di Torino, 2004.

Lippi, Adolfo and Fernando Galli. *Ermanno il Primo*. Massarosa: Edizioni attualità, 1969.

Magi, Piero. "Ha confessato a Roma il delitto un giovane di diciannove anni." *La Nazione*, April 6, 1969.

Mancini, Mauro. "Perché non si trova l'assassino." *La Nazione Sera*, March 17, 1969.

Marchesi, Sabina. *I processi del secolo: enigmi, retroscena, orrori e verità in trenta casi giudiziari italiani da Gino Girolimoni a Marta Russo*. Sesto Fiorentino: Olimpia, 2008.

Morris, Penelope. "'Let's Not Talk About Italian Sex': The Reception of the Kinsey Reports in Italy." *Journal of Modern Italian Studies* 18, no. 1 (2013): 17–32.

Nozza, Marco. *Il pistarolo: da piazza Fontana, trent'anni di storia raccontati da un grande cronista*. Milano: Il Saggiatore, 2006.

Passanisi, Enzo. "Gli angeli dalla faccia sporca." *Il Corriere della Sera*, May 4, 1969.

Pellegrini, Renzo. "È un bruto il rapitore." *Il Telegrafo*, February 12, 1969.

Pierini, Franco. "Il dramma del giudice che deve svelare il mistero della morte di Ermanno Lavorini." *L'Europeo*, October 30, 1969.

———. "Hanno sconvolto la mia vita ci dice il figlio di Ermete Zacconi." *L'Europeo*, November 27, 1969.

Preda, Gianna. "Domande e risposte-Uno che si vergogna." *Il Borghese*, July 24, 1969, 714.

Ripa, Ornella. "I ragazzi non sono colpevoli." *Gente*, May 28, 1969.

Ripa, Ornella and Renzo Allegri. "Così hanno corrotto i nostri poveri figli." *Gente*, May 14, 1969.

Silveri, Andrea and Giovanni della Valle. "Gli omosex in Italia." *Men*, July 14, 1969.

Stajano, Giò. "Lungo viaggio nell'Italia omosessuale." *LSD*, April 9, 1969.

Steffenoni, Luca. *Nera: come la cronaca cambia i delitti*. Cinisello Balsamo: San Paolo, 2011.

Zanfroghini, Giancarlo. "Ragazzi corrotti." *La Nazione*, May 21, 1969.

Chapter 2

We Want Lesbians Too

A Lesbian Feminist Counter-History Inspired by We Want Roses Too

Alessia Palanti

Lesbians are a rare species in Italian cinema. The very term "lesbian" is itself barely uttered lest it should become a more viable reality in modern-day Italy. So, I was pleasantly surprised when I read a scraggy, white, skinny block-letter graffiti spelling "Woman is beautiful, witch is better, lesbian is excellent," in Alina Marazzi's film, *We Want Roses Too,* (hereon, *Roses*).[1] Yet, what started as a welcome surprise was swiftly replaced by perplexity. The word scrawled on the Roman Women's Center's paint-chipped wall acquired no depth in the rest of the film: *Roses* never quite elaborates on lesbianism. And I wanted to learn because, indeed, Marazzi's film announces itself as a feminist cinematic pedagogical project intent on unpacking the complexity of women's sexuality.

Roses takes its viewers on a journey into public spaces like the Women's Center, and also into the private, interior lives of Italian women during the 1960s and 1970s. Three anonymous women's diaries dating 1967, 1975, and 1979 organize the film and provide first-person accounts, covering the period of the Italian women's Second Wave movements. The entries are voiced-over by modern-day actors, visually supported by kaleidoscopic video-art, Monty Python-like stop-animation, and punctuated by interviews, archival and home video footage, television clips, and magazine commercials. From sexual liberation, to abortion, to divorce, the film traces a number of political and legal changes taking place in Italy concerning women at the time, where sexuality is at the epicenter of its investigation (see figure 2.1).

Undoubtedly, *Roses* is a feminist treasure chest. Both its narrative and its formal anatomy—the sound/image disjunctions, the juxtaposition of disparate temporalities, the concatenation of different media—constitute the very

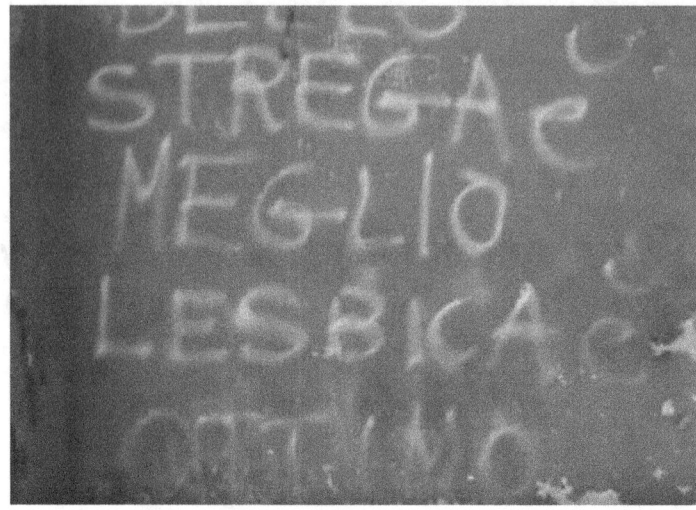

Figure 2.1　Graffiti at the Casa della donna in *Vogliamo anche le rose*. *Source*: Screenshot.

fibers of a feminist project. For one, the film grants private, ordinary women a public platform; it gives women the space to share what being a woman was like in a tense sociopolitical climate; it shapes historical memory that elevates and dignifies women's movements often left on the margins of historical grand narratives. Second, the film challenges cinema's taxonomical borders that would, on the one hand, place it squarely in the "documentary" category and, on the other hand, consider it an experimental film. Third, by integrating different media—like placing footage in conversation with animated sequences and having cut-outs of *fotoromanzi* (romances in comic-strip form) enact the passages being read from the diaries—the film reminds us that history is a fragile multimedia discourse. *Roses* contributes to the annals of feminist history not (only) because it's *about* women during the Second Wave, but because it experiments with cinema's potentials to tell history differently. The film's mesmerizing aesthetics—its fast-paced, chromatic visual virtuosity—are a *nouvelle politique*.

Marazzi's innovative and exciting feminist project is committed to interrogating systems of power like the patriarchy via the very media that was instrumental in constructing a heteronormatively desirable female subject. Therein lies the film's paradox: in the same moment it critiques media's role in producing heteronormative[2] women, it reflects back a heterosexual female experience of feminist history. To be clear, my intention is not to condemn the film's exclusion of lesbian activism in the historiography of Italian feminisms, for it isn't fair to expect any one film to represent all facets of such diverse communities. But I believe the film grants me permission for further investigation when it chooses to mention (if so subtly) same-sex desire. I argue that, unwittingly, the fleeting nature of the graffiti etches the dynamics of exclusion between lesbian and non-lesbian feminists during Italy's Second Wave. The feminist history that Italy already struggles to memorialize is—even in this avant-garde cinematic project—commemorated as a heterosexual woman's struggle. I, therefore, use this shot as a launching pad to give voice to lesbian activists whose efforts too frequently go unrecognized.

Yet, what is remarkable is that, in reality, *Roses* presents a transparently damning representation of heterosexuality. As my analysis will show, the film strings together a set of images that form a tacit critique of heterosexuality and heteronormativity more broadly. Using Marazzi's framework, I also move chronologically from diarist to diarist to set the challenges for women in Italy during each specific period (1967, 1975, 1979) against interventions, events, and experiences specific to lesbians. In this way, I take the baton from Marazzi and advance her project using similar means: by interjecting her history with a counter-history. In addition to amplifying lesbian narratives, I also name the very underlying ideological antagonist that subtends this film but that is only indirectly censured: heterosexuality.[3]

In the first section, I primarily unpack issues related to media and society's roles in shaping female subjects through the case of diarist, Anita. In the second section, I explore the dawning of sexual liberation from the perspective of heterosexual and lesbian women via diarist Teresa's abortion story. And in the third section, I discuss the dynamics within feminist collectives from the point of view of diarist, Valentina, just before the scission between feminists and lesbian feminists in 1978. I will refer to feminist activists who identified as lesbians prior to the separatist chasm as "lesbian feminists," and to the separatist activists subsequent to the rupture as *lesbofemministe*.[4]

ANITA'S DIARY 1967–1975: MEDIATED SEXUALITY

"There was a man whose back I caressed. The only thing I'd seen them do in films. In a dream, I thought: 'I should feel this and that. We should do this and that.' Why is nothing happening?"[5] *Roses*' first diarist, Anita (interpreted by actor Anita Caprioli), recounts a dream of her first sexual encounter with a man. A late-bloomer compared to her peers, Anita deals with an oppressive father, is sent to a psychoanalyst who diagnoses her as sexually frigid, and is caught between the incongruous messages of a masculinist social context that encourages sexual attractiveness and messages promoting chastity from religious conservatives. Given the ideological tug of war—not too unlike today's—Anita's anxieties seem absolutely justified.

Italian feminist theorist and film scholar Teresa De Lauretis avers that cinema has a pivotal role—pedagogical and affective—in shaping sexual experiences. She writes: "Cinematic representation can be understood as a kind of mapping of social vision into subjectivity . . . cinema's binding of fantasy to significant images affects the spectator as a subjective production, and so the movement of the film actually inscribes and orients desire."[6] Anita is a case in point. Cinema instructs, exemplifies, and indoctrinates in ways that textbooks, family or peer discussions, especially in a pre-May 1968 culture where sex did not enter private, let alone public, discourse with ease.[7] Anita's idea of sexuality reads like an instruction manual authored by cinema, setting the parameters of that which *should* or *should not* be performed, that which should or should not be felt. Her entry is accompanied by scenes of a man and a woman acting out what she describes, further underscoring the connection between her private, psychic space and the very public life of cinema.

Sequences preceding and following Anita's dream accentuate discourses on love and romance. We see: boyfriends and girlfriends holding hands walking down the street; men and women dancing together, kissing; colorfully drawn cut-outs of cis-hetero couples from the 1932 film *Grand Hotel*, accompanied by Nilla Pizzi's song "Le signorine da marito" (1969); parents pushing strollers; housewives' calling hotlines asking tarot card readers how to satisfy their husbands; interviews with couples who speak of the burgeoning of their relationship like they were following an instruction manual (our relationship "started like all young relationships do"). From a heterosexual perspective, what stands out in these sequences is misogyny, masculinist biases, conservative family values, and oppressive gender roles. From a lesbian perspective, in addition to all of the above, the sequences look like a bombardment of heterosexual propaganda.

It is not surprising, in a climate in which sexuality exists at the epicenter of a flurry of mixed messages, that Anita's first diary entry, at the age of eighteen, reveals an internal conflict she experiences upon encountering boys and discovering "emotional problems." Unlike her peers with burning desires to explore their sexualities, for Anita intimacy is an anxiety trigger. Anita's case frames the paradoxical situation of what it meant to be a woman in Italy in the late 1960s. Italian society's virgin/whore paradigm is practically unaltered today: on the one hand, young women are encouraged to guard their virginity until after marriage; on the other hand, their worth is evaluated according to sexual attractiveness. Either case leaves women with an indelible sense of *vergogna* (shame) and unattainable standards. Although this appears to be somewhat of a cultural platitude, the degree of damage this systemic misogyny once had, has only shape-shifted today.

Anita's male psychologist diagnoses her as frigid within the first five minutes of their meeting, and commits her to a women's group therapy that Anita describes as a mental asylum. Basing his conclusions on Rorschach tests, Anita's doctor diagnoses a refusal to be a woman, and claims that she has "a strong but repressed sexual instinct."[8] Simultaneously, Anita's conservative, oppressive father fortifies her terror of intimacy. Like many young women in Italy in the 1960s, her father expects her to get engaged, get married (in a church), and raise a family (preferably in that order), and while she may be disturbed by such conventions, she still asks: "But how can one live outside social conventions?"[9] While not exclusive to Italy, the misogynist social conventions Anita refers to are an effect of heteropatriarchal family structures that student movements and early feminist collectives in the late 1960s were challenging.[10]

Since I was expecting the film to make a statement about what is an obvious illustration of—to put it in Adrienne Rich's terms—"compulsory heterosexuality," its lack of address was surprising but also telling. On the one hand, *Roses* exposes the mechanisms by which various media indoctrinate women into a heteronormative lifestyle. On the other hand, *Roses* isn't making that connection more explicit for its viewers. Thus, it is unclear whether or not the film is denouncing heterosexuality specifically (as opposed to misogyny, patriarchy, etc.), leaving open the possibility that the film is, paradoxically, playing into the concealment that has methodically sustained the heteronormative project: it is so pervasive, so normalized that it is difficult to even see it as a dogma in its own right.

One of Italy's most prominent voices of the *movimento lesbofemminista*, Bianca Pomeranzi, expressly discusses what she calls society's "compulsion towards exclusively heterosexual sexuality," and the ways in which it "has resulted over time in the total, or almost total, cancellation of lesbian existence." She writes:

> Based exclusively on the needs of male sexuality, heterosexuality as the norm has been imposed, often brutally and violently, or else by making subtle generalizations about women, as the only possible choice for women's consciousness. In a universe constructed on heterosexual values and models, from the example of our parents to the models of happiness offered to us as women from our childhood (from fables, to love songs, from comics to bestsellers, from films to TV scripts), we have been inoculated with heterosexual behavior by a thousand daily pointers which sanction our complementarity to the male, and our completeness as women only in emotional and sexual synthesis with the "other sex."[11]

Pomeranzi denounces a culturally enforced heterosexual propagandism: a presentation of male-female sexual engagement saturating media content to the point of making other forms of sexual expression not only invisible, but also outright unimaginable. The heterosexual imagination she outlines reduces sexually nonconforming women to celibates or spinsters; in other words, asexual.[12] *Roses* exposes the heterosexist agenda that puts pressure on the meanings and expectations of sexual/romantic relationships but does not problematize the heterosexual credo underlying its own material. And so, *Roses* seems to quite adequately illustrate Pomeranzi's same accusations but, unlike her, does not name its nemesis.

The Case for Separatism

Anita's diary is but a glimpse into the realities of being a woman navigating a toxic patriarchal milieu.[13] Her diary seems to be the only space she has to explore her emotional landscape. And since many women at the time suffered silently, separatism—a practice that would have women create women-only spaces precisely to generate a sense of community and begin to define their own relationships with one another—began to take hold.

Although separatism was a practical reality for lesbians before it became a christened political stance, the more popular (and heterosexual) feminist thinker Carla Lonzi is usually credited as the its pioneer. Certainly, Italian feminisms are indebted to Lonzi for making sexuality a core part of mainstream feminist discourse, and for vouching for separatism as a means of cultivating a reality uncontaminated by masculinist social spheres. She openly denounced the 1970s glorification of "sexual liberation" as a mere etymological hallmark of sexual emancipation that reified the same privileges men already enjoyed.

Florentine-born Lonzi was the leader of Rivolta Femminile in 1970 which authored the "Manifesto di Rivolta Femminile" containing virtually all of Italian feminisms' primary principles, like the proud commitment to sexual difference instead of equality, a resistance to complementarity to men, and a critique of the institution of marriage.[14] Lonzi argues that by divorcing from the common social sphere—one that women never coauthored in the first place—women can begin "to achieve equality on the creative level historically defined by the male and arrive at the autonomous liberation of the woman who can claim a creativity of her own, fueled by the dominant sex's imposed repression" (My translation).[15] In other words, separatism would play a restorative and creative role for female subjectivity.

But Lonzi is perhaps best known for her most famous essay, "The Clitoral Woman and the Vaginal Woman." Here, Lonzi identifies two female social archetypes: "The vaginal woman is she who, in captivity, has been made to consent to the enjoyment of the patriarch, while the clitoral woman is one that does not comply with the emotional narrative of integration with the other, which the passive woman, for instance, accepts. Instead, she expresses herself in a sexuality that does not coincide with coitus" (My translation).[16]

Heterosexual Lonzi could not have crafted a more sapphic treatise on the exceptional potentials of female sexuality! She challenges the standardization of reproductive sexuality by bringing to light women's libidic experience and its independence from the supposed male counterpart, and begins to deflate the humiliation nourished and normalized by patriarchally monopolized medical institutions including, most notably, psychoanalysis. The same biological essentialist weapon wielded by heteropatriarchal institutions to construct a reality in its own interest becomes the very instrument Lonzi uses to invalidate it.

Although Lonzi's ideological impact is undeniable, according to Emma Baeri, it was lesbian feminists who "have made manifest both the violence of the patriarchal colonization of the body and of all women's sexuality through mandatory heterosexuality, and of the different political responses as evidenced by a complex and mature movement" (My translation).[17] Lesbians embodied their critique of patriarchy and publicly pushed for feminists to be politically coherent and not only condemn patriarchy as an ideology but to also challenge men—in flesh and blood—themselves. Politically speaking, then, lesbianism appears to be a more radically oppositional force against misogyny than the feminism to which we have easier access.

In 1970s Italy, lesbian feminists had to deal both with repudiation from within gay collectives (as I will discuss) and from within feminist groups for whom, intentionally or not, heterosexuality was still a natural default (a stance we can observe in *Roses*' footage). While numerous feminist groups voluntarily adopted separatist practices, for lesbian women, separatism was the outcome of segregation internal to feminist collectives. De Lauretis refers to feminist theories of sexual difference as "a conceptual paradox corresponding to what is in effect a real contradiction in women's lives: the term, at once, of a sexual difference (women are, or want, something different from men) and of a sexual indifference (women are, or want, the same as men)."[18] The intersectional complication of being a feminist and being a woman with same-sex desires was initially met with reticence. Unhinging the private from the political was a nearly impossible feat for lesbian feminists as the private inevitably circumscribed their political identities; claiming a sexual identity, in fact, strategically demystified women's complementarity to men.

In addition to managing feminist collectives' internal disputes, lesbians had to assert themselves as autonomous political subjects and foster more robust identity politics. Several lesbian activists joined FUORI!, the gay collective that formed in Torino in 1971, and participated in the first public protest on behalf of gay rights in Italy. On April 5, 1972, in Sanremo, Italy experienced its very own Stonewall; it was, in effect, the event that introduced homosexuality more fluidly into public discourse. A group of approximately forty gay and lesbian activists protested the Italian Center for Sexology (Centro Italiano Sessuologia, or, CIS) a Catholic-leaning group—ancestor to present-day "conversion therapy" associations—that was holding a convention titled "International Conference on Sexual Deviance" ("Congresso internazionale sulle devianze sessuali"). Although lesbian participation in the FUORI! collective was strong, it was numerically subordinate to men's, as most activist women generally took to the feminist cause. But numbers were not arbitrarily low. As lesbian feminist Maria Schiavo wrote:

> It is not merely a numeric minority. The fact that within our group we do not have a precise lesbian physiognomy and our own autonomy is partly our own fault. We are absorbed in the men's group. We would like not to say that this happens voluntarily on their behalf, but surely there is still much ground to cover before phallocracy is translated into concrete behaviors, into interpersonal relationships that are truly egalitarian. (My translation)[19]

To become absorbed in an androcentric, *homo*sexual collective would mean surrendering the feminist credo of sexual difference and yielding, once again, to structures that were not built with women in mind. The need to distinguish lesbianism from homosexuality became urgent.

The 1974 issue of FUORI!'s journal titled *Fuori! Donna* was entirely drafted and compiled by women. It focused on the ongoing deliberations in feminist groups, and specifically denounced patriarchy, capitalism, and the "homosexual brothers'" ("fratelli omosessuali") misogynist posture (omofonie.it). At that time, although lesbians still constituted a mere one-tenth of FUORI! adherents, they nevertheless summoned an international convention in Rome, where attendance was extremely low, leaving just over a dozen women debating over consciousness-raising methods. Lesbian activist and philosopher Nerina Milletti narrates the difficulty with which lesbians could find space in other collectives. She writes: "If it was difficult to find space in the homosexual movement, monopolized by men who often despised them, it was almost as tiring to be in a movement of women who considered lesbian relationships very private affairs of which it was better, perhaps, not to talk" (My translation).[20] Thus, lesbian feminists were caught between the proverbial rock and hard place: FUORI!'s misogyny and feminist collectives' lesbophobia.[21]

Via Anita's personal narrative, *Roses* makes visible the multitude of ways in which patriarchally monopolized sexual discourse had the power to create and destroy female subjectivity (heterosexual in particular). But it is only when we also consider what was happening off-screen—when sexuality becomes the linchpin of personal and social negotiations between members of different marginalized groups—that we can realize the reach of this monopoly.

TERESA'S DIARY 1975–1979: WHOSE SEXUAL LIBERATION?

Almost diametrically opposed to Anita's fear of sexuality, Teresa's first journal entry effusively retells of a lovemaking experience with her boyfriend. The healthy, loving sexual experience is refreshing after the darkness of Anita's anecdotes. But a drawing that morphs from being an outline of a passionate sexual embrace into a textbook-like anatomical illustration of the moment of conception reads like an oblique mockery of copulation. "We are mad about each other" ("Ci amiamo alla follia"), Teresa (interpreted by actor, Teresa Saponangelo) shares as the image outlines the consequences of the couple's lust: her pregnancy. Viewers' focus teeters between passion and physiology, foreshadowing Teresa's odyssey to a London abortion clinic, just before Italy passed the *Legge 194*, which only decriminalized abortion in 1978.[22]

Roses' 2007 theatrical release coincides with the reinvigoration of anti-abortion campaigns in the everlasting *dibattiti sull'aborto* (abortion debates), emboldened by Pope Benedict XVI's conservativism.[23] A review of *Roses* contextualizes the contemporaneous debates on abortion in Italy: "Marazzi's beautiful work came out in theaters in counterattack against Giuliano Ferrara's moratorium on abortion and in conjunction with the ever more insistent dictation of the Church's stance on defending life from the moment of fertilization. In recent days, then, more men and women from international and national media emphasize the backward leap for Italian women" (My translation).[24] That abortion continues to be the rope in Italy's moral and political tug of war is nothing novel. That control over women's bodies, health, and well-being are what is actually being debated is, sadly, still too novel.

Teresa's travails with pregnancy termination lead next into the 1970s and Italy's favorable connection between contraception and sexual liberation. Via images of a *fotoromanzo*, Marazzi splices together clips from the first discussions on "the pill," marketed as "The Secret to New Happiness" ("Il segreto della nuova felicità"). The troubles of the magazine's fictional couple seem to entirely vanish thanks to the pill—which the film's heavy-handed humor undeniably parodies. But the luster surrounding sexual liberation is demystified in a piece of footage from the Parco Lambro gathering in 1976 where a young woman being interviewed complains: "First, you have to be a virgin, you have to become a mother, and it is not true that in 1976 you no longer hear such things. Then you get into revolutionary Left-wing groups and you hear people saying that this is the sexual revolution: you're a woman, so open your pussy and fuck, because otherwise you are repressed, inhibited, you are not a revolutionary, you don't believe in class struggle, and you're even frigid . . . and you're an uptight bourgeoisie girl if you don't give it away to all the comrades."[25] The interviewee, thus, denounces sexual liberation as the newly accepted trend whose impartiality is clearly smoke and mirrors. The young woman's justified complaints follow the same intellectual wavelengths as Lonzi who found the most meaningful battle to be that of gaining women's corporeal sovereignty from male colonialism, as she writes, "Abortion is not a solution for the free woman, but for the woman colonized by the patriarchal system" (My translation).[26] It is the entrance of "the pill," in my view, that marks the beginning of the political fracture between lesbofemministe and feminists. As lesbian feminists argued, women's freedom does not come with the legalization of abortion nor with the pill but, in part, by laying claim to a sexuality that is disconnected from procreation.

Without quite raising the issue of compulsory heterosexuality, *Roses* seems in step with mainstream Italian feminisms. Since the dawn of feminist collectives, Liana Borghi explains,

> For lesbians, belonging to the "woman" category was limited by the necessity to hide or even deny one's desire and sexual practice. This was in a movement where hetero women realized that the type of free love flaunted by the new left and by counterculture (practiced also thanks to the invention of the pill in 1960) had negative repercussions for them, repercussions that no one was considering.[27]

By circumventing the "lesbian question," or in this case, the radical position that lesbian feminists were taking in their desire to change the lived reality for all women, the film extends the same side-stepping that feminists were doing at the time.

Teresa's abortion story—one with a "happier" ending than most others—instigates a conversation about the left's deceitful political agenda. Although a step closer to (some kind of) choice, women's corporeal policing moved from being legally disallowed from choosing abortion to being "liberated" by contraception. Yet, contraception is but a proverbial band-aid that only extends partiality in men's favor. In other words, men's sexuality remains untouched: now, *he* can enjoy her just as before without having to worry about the consequences. Meanwhile, *she* must take responsibility by pumping her body with synthetic hormonal drugs. Again, *Roses* reliably constructs an anti-heteropatriarchal critique and yet does not explicitly declare it.

The Case for Lesbian Separatism

But the "women" that *Roses* is mostly concerned with in discussing reproductive rights are, for the most part, heterosexual women, more specifically, a social understanding of woman in her reproductive and familial role. A woman's body is, thus, an instrument in the service of, as French lesbian philosopher Monique Wittig claimed, "the reproduction of heterosexual society."

As feminist movements coalesced around what was a primarily heterosexual concern, radical lesbian feminists adopted Wittig's now eminent statement, "lesbians are not women,"[28] as their mantra. Dating from 1976 to 1984, Wittig's essays encouraged a materialist perspective, in which she claimed that "the situation of lesbians . . . is located philosophically (politically) beyond the categories of sex."[29] The category of sex "is the product of a heterosexual society which imposes on women the rigid obligation of the reproduction of the 'species,' that is, the reproduction of heterosexual society."[30] Astutely, Wittig makes her mark by divorcing the heteronormative word "woman" from "lesbian" and defines the lesbian as an embodied subject whose desires are not and could not (con)figure into society at large. In so doing, she acknowledges that "[t]he ideology of sexual difference [functions] as censorship in our culture by masking, on the ground of nature, the social oppositions between men and women."[31] Wittig's militancy reverberated from northern France to Italy at the right moment of tension in feminist circles; it galvanized lesbian activists to see themselves not as different from, but different*ly*.

Italian lesbian feminists brought new meaning to the slogan "The personal is the political," in contrast to the *pensiero femminista* which more easily polarized personal (in this case sexual) and political action. Lesbians within feminist collectives fell into distinct categories: those who were willing to keep their private lives private, rather than part of their political missions; and radical lesbians who were not only unwilling to flout their private lives but for whom same-sex desire and intimacy informed their political activism. Unable to reconcile differences within feminist collectives, feminists (heterosexual and non-radical lesbians) parted ways from radical lesbian separatists between 1978 and 1979.[32]

But even lesbians who had taken their politics to gay collectives—whose activism made sexuality central—no longer felt welcome in those spaces either. By 1976, the women of FUORI! founded *Fuori donna*—a woman-only version of the original collective—which was inaugurated by a conference titled *The Lesbian in Masculine Heterosexual Society* (*La lesbica nella società maschile eterosessuale*). By the time of its second conference in 1978, *Fuori donna* had garnered hundreds of new members and formalized the scission between separatist lesbians and the original FUORI!'s feminists. The final straw, activist Maria Schiavo recounts, was the absence of lesbian-themed films in the collective's gay film festival that same year. After having dealt with segregations from within different groups from year to year, lesbian activists were unwilling to tolerate further excision from the social imaginary as well.

Separatism is complicated. Its configurations and motivations are as varied as each individual member of each collective. While *Roses* provides us with a representation of the realities of feminists fighting for reproductive rights, what lesbian activist history reveals is that such a struggle was far from a pro- or anti- stance. As I have argued, abortion is the issue that launched an enduring splintering within and between collectives. The final section of the film touches precisely on the experience of feminist collectives' fragility and their dispersal, which—as I will discuss—gave way to the fortification of lesbian collectives from the 1980s into the early 2000s.

VALENTINA'S DIARY 1979 ONWARD: WE WANT ROLE MODELS TOO

"November 6th 1979. We must find role models to follow"[33] begins the third and final diarist, Valentina (interpreted by actor, Valentina Carnelutti). She reflects on the act of writing in her diary—much like the prior two diarists—as a way to carve out her own private space when there seems to be none materially. She is anxious about the myriad images of herself in the world, "The real ones, the one's I can't quite say, the ones others throw onto me"[34] and expresses guilt for basking in the pleasure of writing instead of tending to her chores. Valentina is intrigued by "relationships with women" ("i rapporti con le donne") and admits to feeling privileged behind a typewriter or a photographic camera, nourishing her voyeurism, her epistephilia, her right to look, to capture. Valentina is profoundly insecure about herself, particularly about her sexuality: "I think I am just different sexually, incapable of coming."[35] In each such way—lack of space, lack of role models, being bombarded by prefabricated images of womanhood, unstable relations between women, and being anorgasmic—Valentina comprises *Roses*' major themes and brings the film full circle.

Valentina is active in the feminist community and her experiences become one more voice among the several I have mentioned thus far. She expresses her disillusionment with feminist collectives and, in a resentful tone, categorizes other participants as follows: "A. Honest mothers, B. Politicized extremists, C. True anti-revolutionaries."[36] Valentina's observations serve as situated knowledge (to borrow from Donna Haraway) on the dissonance between the politics of sexual difference, and the praxis: "When politics surface, we return to being an indistinct mass of women. Dissent is expressed only with horrible shouts over the microphone. Passivity is generalized with clapping for everything and the opposite of everything. It is as if everything new that had actually happened—that remained unpublished—had suddenly been erased."[37] In 1979, when collectives were progressively breaking apart, it makes sense that her anxieties find little alleviation in these groups. Instead, she searches for ways to understand herself in feminist philosophers like Carla Lonzi, who Valentina refers to as "una mente" ("a great mind"), and tries to explain her own sexual inadequacies via Lonzi's social archetypes.

Although not identified as a lesbian, Valentina's alienation from within the feminist movement is not dissimilar from the sense of exclusion decried by lesbian feminists. Her words reveal just how *il pensiero della differenza sessuale* had an intellectual monopoly over Italian feminist thought. The tenets of a movement set on giving women space, condemning social hierarchies and democratizing female voices, were actually starting to disintegrate beneath the force of individual differences.

The sounds of Valentina's final words hover over a vivid scene: a woman wearing a plain white mask, holding a red string between her hand and the hand of whomever is behind the camera. A clip from Adriana Monti's *The String of Desire* (*Il filo del desiderio* 1977), the masked actor moves across a public park, alternating between walking backward and looking into the camera and running away from the camera. And since both the actor's and the camera operator's faces are unseen, who leads and who follows remains ambiguous: a subtle reminder of cinema's seductive powers, of the power of the director to lead us on, and the power of the viewer to accept or refute the journey. One last question comes to mind in light of this sequence: *where* are we, as viewers, being led?

Curiously, the following scene includes a gallery of photographs of the Casa della Donna, whose walls are covered with text, where, finally, our graffiti in question appears: "Woman is beautiful, witch is better, lesbian is excellent." A lesbian feminist, if not a queer, reading of these cinematic moments suggests a "string of events" to come: the feminist movement's fracture and the rise of lesbian political activism. But while lesbian viewers like myself might find meaning in this graffiti, it will be lost to many. The danger in presenting the term without the proper context leaves the uninformed viewer to interpret "lesbian" as synonymous with being frivolously, rather than meaningfully, politically transgressive. For marginal communities the stakes are higher when it comes to naming. Naming means existing, and existing means gaining membership, or stepping out of the margins.

"Lesbian" Is Excellent

A central part of the lesbian feminist struggle—as the graffiti aptly encompasses—is language. In "To Call Oneself a Lesbian Today" ("Dirsi lesbica oggi"), Charlotte Ross and Silvia Antosa explore the history of silence surrounding lesbianism both as an identity and as a term in Italian culture more broadly. Deeply interdependent, terminology and identity have oscillated in the *secolo breve* (the short century) between dangerous and recuperative, depending on the decade. In the early part of the twentieth century, "lesbian" was introduced as a pejorative term connoting biomedical pathology; its stigma, of course, only worsened as the country headed into fascism. But the same period also saw a flourishing of underground networks of lesbian women who referred to one another in code like, "women who lived like that," "a woman with certain tendencies," "this thing," "this condition," "certain relations" (My translation).[38] Since the 1980s, "lesbian" has been recuperated as a positive political signifier by collectives, although it is still stigmatized (and barely utilized) in popular culture.

Unlike "queer" which was a derogatory term recovered by the LGBT community, "lesbian" has not yet enjoyed an analogous reclamation in Italy outside of lesbian collectives. While acknowledging all the problems that come with labeling in so far as labels are reductive or potentially essentialist, Ross and Antosa find that rejecting them entirely risks extending lesbians' invisibility and hindering self-acceptance.[39] Concomitantly, lesbian feminist philosopher Nerina Milletti argues that abstention from using the term is "a politically suicidal act, since having a shared collective identity is an indispensable prerequisite for the formation of any social movement to translate individual needs into group interests and common action" (My translation).[40] Lesbian is political, *punto e basta* (full-stop).

Arcilesbiche: The Private Is Political[41]

In the feminist periodical *DonnaWomanFemme* (*DWF*), lesbian feminist activist Simonetta Spinelli's "Je ne regrette rien"[42] examines the Libreria di Milano's 1983 publication in *Sottosopra Verde*, "More Women Than Men" ("Più donne che uomini"), which both recounts a history of the last decade and calls for new action to revive fragmented feminist collectives. The article attributes its participants' dispersal to separatism, which the authors consider to have strengthened women in private collectives but not in the public sphere, especially the workplace. Spinelli lauds the authors' desires to go beyond ideological uniformity but critiques the Milan Bookstore's (Libreria di Milano) dismissal of the milestones garnered from the years working in separatist collectives. As Valeria Mercandino writes: "The women of the Milan Bookstore, starting from these considerations, propose to cease the movement's separatism in favor of relations between women that empower women in all social fields" (My translation).[43] Instead, Spinelli reminds her readers that the practice of *autocoscienza* gave women the chance to define their own relationships and to respect one's own individuality starting from corporeality. Fearing another fracture in a new wave of feminism in the making, Ida Dominijanni insisted on keeping the private private—it was best for lesbians not to politicize same-sex desire. Spinelli's rebuttal, however, clarifies that the movement must consider the part and the whole: that it is impossible to separate one's desire for *a* woman and one's political investment in advancing the lives of *all* women.[44]

In the 1990 English translation of Italian feminisms' magnum opus, *Non credere di avere dei diritti* (translated in English as *Sexual Difference*, but whose direct translation is "Don't Think You Have Any Rights"), Teresa De Lauretis calls attention to the silence surrounding what may be called "the lesbian question," specifically censuring Dominijanni's dismissal of female homoeroticism, when, in the text's introduction she writes: "Living in a community of women was an extraordinary experience. The most amazing discovery was the intense eroticism present there. *It was not lesbianism, but sexuality no longer imprisoned in masculine desire*" (De Lauretis' emphasis).[45] Clearly anxious about being siloed as lesbian separatists, Dominijanni's intention was to reassure readers of *Non credere di avere dei diritti* that the Italian feminist movements were not founded on lesbian separatism. But, as De Lauretis specifies, the above is the only point in the text in which lesbianism is ever mentioned at all thereby achieving the opposite effect: the erasure of lesbianism altogether.

But lesbian feminist collectives enjoyed a strong presence in the 1980s and into the 1990s. In 1991 the first "lesbian week" ("settimana lesbica") took place: a lesbian-only retreat hosting approximately 1,000 women at a villa outside of Bologna. Still practiced today—as I myself have experienced—these week-long assemblies take place in spaces like a *masseria* or compound that can host a large number of women. Each day comprises presentations by group leaders, activists, speakers, poets, and includes discussion, writing, and performance. By the mid-1990s, however, lesbian feminism entered a crisis. Collectives were effective in creating spaces for women to congregate and discuss, but the undertow of a reinvigorated feminist movement left lesbians at the margins. Lesbian feminist leader Cristina Gramolini points out that lesbians were not so much *separatists* as they were newly being *separated* from feminist collectives—a kind of replay of scissions in the late 1970s. This kind of segregation only deepened as lesbian writers chose pseudonyms for themselves and avoided the press.[46] By 1996, lesbians moved from the reclusion of separatist groups to gay collectives, who were ironically—given past disagreements—more appreciative and supportive of their political struggle.

"Woman" Is Beautiful

Just before the credits roll, *Roses* punctuates its pedagogical mission with an outline of milestones for women's rights in Italian history: "1966—Italian law sees contraception as a crime against birth . . . 1970—Parliament approves the divorce law; 1971—the sale of birth control pills is legalized . . . 1978—abortion made legal: law 194 approved; 1996—sexual violence is declared a crime against a person not morality."[47] By closing with a list of dates, *Roses* invites us to think more deeply about women's rights in present-day Italy. It underscores how women and their bodies remain at the center of so many legal conversations. And although de jure women have rewritten the script, de facto—as it usually goes—achieving equity in respect, integration, and comportment is a much steeper hill to climb. In the last few years, Italy has taken a sharp turn toward hard-right politics. Right-wing politicians are weaponizing the rise in visibility and political activism of women and LGBTQ communities as imminent threats to the well-being of the nation. "Family Day," for instance, a day of protest organized by Catholic congregations opposing equal rights for people in same-sex relationships, made its first public appearance in May 2007—the same year of *Roses*' release. Specifically, they protested against the DICO law ("Diritti e doveri delle persone stabilmente conviventi" [Rights and duties of permanently cohabitating persons], my translation), which aims to legally recognize the rights of cohabitating couples (albeit this includes heterosexual couples!). The law was interpreted to be anti-heterosexual propaganda, and helped the Movimento Pro-Family (Pro-Family Movement) and Pro-Vita (Pro-Life) gain membership and political traction.[48]

The most recent conservative event, March 29–31, 2019, was the World Congress of Families (Congresso Mondiale delle Famiglie) in Verona—out to protect the "traditional" nuclear family. The event garnered an overwhelming oppositional response with feminist protesters flooding the streets of Verona and other major cities protesting in solidarity. This level of national assembly around a single issue can be credited to the nationwide feminist network, Non Una Di Meno.[49] The Congress of Families "is a major international public event that seeks to unite and equip leaders, organizations, and families to affirm, celebrate, and defend the 'natural family' as the only fundamental and sustainable unit of society."[50] Some of the themes included in its program were "The beauty of marriage"; "Children's rights"; "The woman in history"; "Women's dignity and health." The biological essentialist rhetoric suggests that much of their work focuses on preserving what they deem to be women's "natural" societal roles: as wives and mothers. Although Non Una Di Meno's massive influence is crucial and inspiring, their statement opposing the Congress is somewhat perplexing. They declare:

> We propose to build a space that rejects all forms of hierarchical thinking and its translation into discrimination such as racism and xenophobia, transmisogyny and sexism, LGBT * QIA-phobia (commonly abbreviated as lesbian / homo / trans-phobia), ableism, classism, ageism and adultism, which respects the emotional and physical boundaries of other people. Interactions between two people must be based on consent. Before establishing any form of physical contact, make sure that the other person agrees. NO MEANS NO and YES IS REVERSIBLE. (My translation)[51]

The word missing in this mission statement authored by a majority-woman network is, surprisingly, "women." Even in the portion of the statement specific to sexual violence (affecting women more than any other demographic), the network makes no mention of "woman." At the moment, feminist collectives are absorbing the queer political mission and progressively abandoning "woman" as an identity category in favor of attending to issues related to transgenderism. While political energies do well to shift their attention to the most pressing issues, here, the choice not to use the term "woman" in the long list of other targeted groups, seems like the wrong problem to solve. Women continue to exist and misogyny remains an all-too pervasive reality in Italy today,[52] a reality that is not in competition with transphobia (see figure 2.2).

Consider the poster in figure 2.2, reminiscent of *Roses'* graffiti. Of course, we should end violence against anyone altogether, and be particularly aware of the violence against the queer community as the "o" in "everyone"

Figure 2.2 Non Una Di Meno's "End Violence Against Everyone" Poster. This Image Is Posted on nonunadimeno.wordpress.com. *Source*: Screenshot.

implies.⁵³ But by crossing out "woman," the term is singled out as inherently exclusive and, in fact, eschews the very real problem of gender-based violence. The poster misses the point about denouncing violence against a group—women—that today remains disproportionally targeted. And so, the very power differentials the poster might appear to be combating—"women" as exclusionary and trans* as excluded—overlooks the very power imbalances that bring us to even make a poster about ending violence against women in the first place. Feminist and posthuman theorist Rosi Braidotti claims, "The fantasy of being 'beyond sex,' that is to say outside time, is one of the most pernicious illusions of our era."⁵⁴ The only other version of gender neutrality that we know is the patriarchal one that Irigaray denounces: the masculine as neutral and universal. Counterproductively, then, the omission of "woman" leads to its own replacement with queer/transfeminism, all the while men/patriarchy/heterosexuality remain untouched.

CONCLUSION

In "Compulsory Heterosexuality," Adrienne Rich warned, "A feminist critique of compulsory heterosexual orientation for women is long overdue."⁵⁵ Rich helps us see what is directly in front of us: a regime of desire that sustains itself, in part, through the normalization of its hierarchical logics, causing distracting schisms that inhibit feminists from working toward common goals—a classic "divide-and-conquer" tactic that leaves the heteropatriarchal system intact. Rich also explains that "feminist theory can no longer afford merely to voice a toleration of 'lesbianism' as an 'alternative life-style,' or make token allusion to lesbians."⁵⁶ *Roses'* fleeting shot of the graffiti, unfortunately, does just that. And so, if we juxtapose the graffiti with Non Una Di Meno's poster (figures 2.1 and 2.2), we can see that misogyny is constantly morphing rather than receding.

Ultimately, *Roses* aims to reconstruct a view on Italy's feminist history. But in studying the history of Italy's dreams of an alternative to heterosexual society, *Roses* unwittingly and inevitably captures a cultural imaginary about what feminism can be and do in Italy today. Regrettably, these dreams still lie within the ranks of heterosexuality. Perhaps engaging with the histories of lived alternatives to heterosexuality can not only help to reawaken our contemporary imagination but also inspire a shift in our critical approach.

NOTES

1. "Donna è bello, strega è meglio, lesbica è ottimo." *Vogliamo anche le rose*, directed by Alina Marazzi (Roma: Rai Cinema, 2007), DVD.

2. Heteronormative ideology presumes that women (read: heterosexual) are a biologically determined, cis-presenting standard, and lesbians (and bisexuals) are a deviation.

3. Heterosexuality, here, stands for more than a sexual preference and practice between members of opposite sexes (i.e., in the design of a binary understanding of sex and gender). I mean it as a political category that forms the bedrock of, and maintains, patriarchal power structures. It is *the* socially normalized affective dynamic that reinforces itself through mediatic messages, the law, religion, and socialization.

4. Some of the first lesbian-only collectives that formed included Rome's *Rifiutare*, *Artemide* and *Identità Negata*, Milan's *Donne Omosessuali*, and Torino's *Brigate di Saffo*.

5. "C'era un uomo di cui accarezzavo la schiena, l'unica cosa che ho visto fare nei film. E in sogno pensavo: 'Ecco, ora dovrei provare questo e quello; dovremmo fare questo e quell'altro.' Perché non succede niente? Non ho un briciolo di immaginazione visiva." *Vogliamo anche le rose*, Marazzi. All translations of the film's content throughout this chapter are taken directly from the film's impressed English subtitles. Any translations by myself will be marked as "my translation."

6. *Alice Doesn't: Feminism, Semiotics, Cinema* (Bloomington: Indiana University Press, 1984), 8.

7. One well-known attempt at breaking through the thick skin of this taboo was Pier Paolo Pasolini. In his documentary *Comizi d'amore* (*Love Meetings* 1965), the director interviews Italians from across the peninsula and across socioeconomic status about sex, virginity, prostitution, and homosexuality.

8. "Dice che . . . rifiuto di essere donna . . . un forte istinto sessuale, ma represso." *Vogliamo anche le rose*, Marazzi.

9. "Ma come si fa a vivere fuori dalle convenzioni sociali?" Ibidem.

10. In 1967, the Italian law on family rights specified that fathers have the exclusive right to *patria potestà*, that is, unquestionable authority and jurisdiction. Only in 1975 was this law changed to *potestà genitoriale*, commonly known as *responsabilità genitoriale*, thereby softening the authoritative qualifier and assigning responsibility for the family to both parents equally. Divorce became legal in 1970. The first time a divorce law had ever been introduced in Italy was in 1878 by Member of Parliament Salvatore Morelli, but his efforts and those of several men of Parliament in the years thereafter failed to produce legislation. Divorce became viable in 1902 in the case of adultery on the part of the wife, but the law fell shortly thereafter. World War I put a halt on civil legislation, and after the 1929 Lateran Pacts, divorce was no longer discussed. After being sanctioned, the divorce law continued being disputed, motivating a referendum in 1974 which failed to repeal it (Fiamma Lussana, *Il movimento femminista in Italia: Esperienze, storie, memorie, 1965–1980* (Roma: Carocci, 2012), 99–101). Regardless of the legal changes to the father's authority, long-standing cultural customs are less easily eradicated.

11. Lussana, *Il movimento femminista in Italia*, 173.

12. Ibid., 175.

13. That said, I am not sure there is such a thing as nontoxic patriarchal milieu.

14. *Il pensiero della differenza sessuale* (the theory of sexual difference) is considered the cornerstone of Italian feminisms. Major thinkers like those of Adriana

Cavarero, Luisa Muraro, and Carla Lonzi, as well as the plurality of voices in collectives like "Demau," "Diotima," "Rivolta Femminile," and the "Libreria delle donne di Milano," root their principles in the deconstruction of social, philosophical, and political paradigms. Indebted to the ideology of French philosopher Luce Irigaray, sexual difference ultimately exposes the ideological fallacy of Western philosophy's sexless, universal human subject. With the masculine perspective dominating all discourses, a female subject is but a nonsubject. In tandem with contemporaneous postmodernist and poststructuralist intellectual waves, Italian feminisms focused on deconstructing universalisms' inherent androcentrism and on constructing a female subject.

15. "[r]aggiungere la parità sul piano creativo definito storicamente dal maschio [e raggiungere la] liberazione autonoma della donna che recupera una sua creatività alimentata nella repressione imposta dal modello del sesso dominante." "La donna clitoridea e la donna vaginale," *Sputiamo su Hegel* (Milano: Gammalibri, 1982), 50.

16. "La donna vaginale è quella che, in cattività, è stata portata a una misura consenziente per il godimento del patriarca mentre la clitoridea è una che non ha accondisceso alle suggestioni emotive dell'integrazione con l'altro, che sono quelle che hanno presa sulla donna passiva, e si è espressa in una sessualità non coincidente col coito." Ibid., 67.

17. "hanno reso manifesta sia la violenza della colonizzazione patriarcale del corpo e della sessualità di tutte le donne attraverso l'eterosessualità obbligatoria, sia le diverse risposte politiche a questa evidenza da parte di un movimento complesso e maturo." Ibid., 48.

18. "Sexual Indifference and Lesbian Representation," *Theatre Journal; Washington, D.C.* 40, no. 2 (May 1, 1988): 155.

19. "Non si tratta soltanto di una minoranza in senso numerico. Il fatto è che noi non abbiamo all'interno del gruppo, in parte per colpa nostra, una fisionomia precisa in quanto lesbiche, una nostra autonomia. Siamo inglobate dal gruppo dei maschi. Non vogliamo dire che questo avvenga volontariamente da parte loro, ma è certo che rimane da percorrere molta strada prima che il processo alla fallocrazia si traduca in comportamenti concreti, in rapporti interpersonali veramente paritari." Daniela Danna, *Amiche, Compagne, Amanti: Storia Dell'amore Tra Donne*, Saggi. 1st. ed. (Milano: A. Mondadori, 1994).

20. "Se era difficile trovare spazio nel movimento omosessuale, monopolizzato da uomini che spesso le disprezzavano, quasi altrettanto faticoso era stare in un movimento di donne che considerava le relazioni lesbiche affari privatissimi di cui era meglio, forse, non parlare." *Fuori Della Norma: Storie Lesbiche Nell'Italia Della Prima Metà Del Novecento*, 1st ed. italiana, La Storia & Le Storie (Torino: Rosenberg & Sellier, 2007), 312.

21. "Care compagne, ci risulta che in certi gruppi femministi l'omosessualità di alcune militanti non solo non è ancora valutata come apporto rivoluzionario di altissimo potenziale, ma subisce oppressioni se non (orrore!) delle emarginazioni. [. . .] Il sistema maschile esercita ancora il suo potere attraverso i pregiudizi che servono ad ostacolare la nostra rivoluzione: lo provano le acrobazie compiute da alcune femministe per difendersi dalla stantia ma evidentemente sempre efficace accusa di lesbismo che il maschio rivolge allo scopo di ricacciarle al loro posto di femmine, sinonimo per lui di ubbidienza sessuale, culturale, ecc." *Fuori Donna ovvero*

femminismo e lesbismo [1974] Danna 1994. ("Dear friends, it has become evident that not only is some of our militant comrades' homosexuality in certain feminist collectives not valued. It also undergoes oppression if not (horrifyingly!) marginalization. The masculine system continues to exercise its power through prejudice that only serves to obstruct our revolution: proof of this is the ways in which some feminists bend over backwards in order to defend themselves from the outdated, yet still effective accusation of lesbianism that males use with the intent of putting them back in their place as females, a condition synonymous, to him, with sexual, and cultural obedience, etc.") (My translation).

22. Rights to the termination of pregnancy were granted on February 18, 1975, in a law that specified: "ricorrere all'aborto è conforme al diritto, non in assoluto ma nei casi indicati della legge." It was later refined in the Legge 194 of May 1978: "La 194 consente alla donna, nei casi previsti dalla legge, di poter ricorrere alla interruzione volontaria di gravidanza in una struttura pubblica (ospedale o poliambulatorio convenzionato con la Regione di appartenenza), nei primi 90 giorni di gestazione; tra il quarto e quinto mese è possibile ricorrere all'interruzione solo per motivi di natura terapeutica" ("To resort to abortion is in accordance with the law. It is not absolute but determined in the cases indicated by the law . . . Law 194 allows women, in the cases provided for by law, to be able to resort to the voluntary interruption of pregnancy in a public structure (hospital or polyclinic agreement with one's region of origin), in the first 90 days of gestation; between the fourth and fifth month it is possible to resort to interruption only for therapeutic reasons." "Ministero Della Giustizia-Pubblicazioni, Studi, Ricerche, Lavori Commissioni Di Studio" 2012 (My translation).

23. From the clerical side, Pope Benedict XVI declared: "Not only did allowing women to resort to the termination of pregnancy not solve the problems that afflict many women and families, it also inflicted a bigger wound on our societies, already sadly burdened by deep suffering" ("L'aver permesso di ricorrere all'interruzione della gravidanza, non solo non ha risolto i problemi che affliggono molte donne e non pochi nuclei familiari, ma ha aperto un'ulteriore ferita nelle nostre società, già purtroppo gravate da profonde sofferenze") (My translation). "Ai Membri Della Pontificia Accademia per La Vita," February 24, 2007.

24. "Il bellissimo lavoro di Marazzi è uscito nelle sale in piena offensiva di Giuliano Ferrara per la moratoria dell'aborto; in concomitanza con il sempre più insistito dettato della Chiesa a difesa della vita fino dalla fecondazione dell'ovulo. In questi ultimi giorni, poi, da media internazionali e nazionali più uomini che donne sottolineano il salto all'indietro delle donne italiane." "Server Donne—Recensione *Di Vogliamo Anche Le Rose* Di Alina Marazzi," April 7, 2008, http://www.women.it/.

25. "[P]rima devi essere vergine, devi fare la madre, che non è vero che nel 1976 non le senti più dire queste cose. Poi entri nei gruppi della sinistra rivoluzionaria e ti senti dire che la rivoluzione sessuale è questa: tu sei donna, apri la figa e scopa, perché se no sei repressa, inibita, non sei rivoluzionaria, non credi nella lotta di classe, e poi sei pure frigida."

26. "L'aborto non è una soluzione per la donna libera, ma per la donna colonizzata dal sistema patriarcale." Lonzi, *Sputiamo su Hegel*, 59.

27. "[Si] delineava per le lesbiche la appartenenza alla categoria 'donna' dove però era necessario nascondere o addirittura negare il proprio desiderio e la propria pratica

sessuale—in un movimento dove le etero si rendevano conto che il tipo di amore libero sbandierato nella nuova sinistra e nella controcultura (praticato anche grazie all'invenzione della pillola nel 1960) aveva ricadute negative per loro, ricadute di cui nessuno si occupava." Borghi 2001, 48.

28. "Lesbianism is the only social form in which we can live freely. Lesbian is the only concept I know of which is beyond the categories of sex (woman and man), because the designated subject (lesbian) is *not* a woman, either economically, or politically, or ideologically. For what makes a woman is a specific social relation to a man, a relation that we have previously called servitude." *The Straight Mind and Other Essays* (Boston: Beacon Press, 1992), 20.

29. Ibid., 47.

30. Ibid., 6.

31. Ibid., 2.

32. Milletti and Passerini, *Fuori Della Norma*.

33. "6 Novembre, 1979. Bisogna trovare un modello da seguire." *Vogliamo anche le rose*, Marazzi.

34. "[Q]uelle vere, quelle non-so-dire, quelle che gli altri mi buttano addosso." Ibidem.

35. "Sto pensando di essere una diversa sessualmente, incapace di godere." Ibidem.

36. "A. Oneste madri di famiglia, B. Politicizzate estremiste, C. Vere antirivoltose." Ibidem.

37. "Quando esce fuori la politica, si ritorna alla massa indistinta delle donne. Il dissenso non si esprime se non con orribili urla al microfono. La passività si generalizza con battimani su tutto e il contrario di tutto. È come se tutto quello che è successo di concreto, di nuovo, inedito nei vari corsi, fosse cancellato di colpo." Ibidem.

38. "ragazze che vivevano così"; "una ragazza che aveva queste tendenze"; "questa cosa"; "questa condizione"; "certe relazioni." "Although the label of 'lesbian' may be reductive for some, essentialist, if not even, binding, there is an inherent danger in trying to overcome it; in fact, there is the risk of making an identity even more invisible and dispersed, which has never really reached a level of (self) acceptance, recognition and socio-cultural visibility" (My translation). "Dirsi Lesbica Oggi? Lesbofobia Nei Media Italiani Tra Indicibilità e Invisibilità," *Donne+Donne. Prima, Attraverso e Dopo Il Pride*, 2014.

39. Ibid., 62.

40. "Un atto politicamente suicida, poiché avere un'identità collettiva condivisa è il prerequisito indispensabile alla formazione di qualsiasi movimento sociale per tradurre le necessità individuali in interessi di gruppo e azione comune." Milletti and Passerini, *Fuori Della Norma*, 301.

41. "Arci" is in Italian is an acronym for "Associazione Ricreativa e Culturale Italiana" ("Italian Cultural and Recreational Association"), but the word in itself is also used colloquially to mean "uber" or "extra." Thus, my subtitle can be understood as "Uberlesbians."

42. "Je ne regrette rien," *DWF: Donnawomanfemme; Roma*, Spring 1986.

43. "le donne della Libreria di Milano, a partire da queste considerazioni, propongono l'uscita dal separatismo del movimento in favore di relazioni tra donne

potenzianti che siano diffuse in tutti gli ambiti sociali." "Un'innominabile presenza: le lesbiche nel femminismo italiano tra nominazione, silenzio e conflitto. Elementi di un dibattito e considerazioni attuali" ("An Unmentionable Presence: Lesbians within Italian Feminism between Naming, Silence and Conflict"), n.d., 27.

44. "[The] private and the political are . . . so closely interrelated that one cannot be presumed to exist without the construction of women's freedom which is the foundation of the other. And this interrelation is not conceivable if at the same time it does not bring into play the necessity of thinking of oneself as a woman which is characterized by tenacity, because the awareness of existing as a body of desire depends on it" (My translation) "[Il] privato e il politico sono . . . così strettamente interrelati da non poter presumere l'uno senza la costruzione di libertà femminile che è fondamento dell'altro, e questa interrelazione non è concepibile se nello stesso tempo non mette in campo la necessità di quel pensarsi donna che è connotato di tenacia, perché da esso dipende proprio la consapevolezza di esistere come corpo di desiderio." Ibidem.

45. Libreria delle donne di Milano, ed., *Sexual Difference: A Theory of Social-Symbolic Practice*, Theories of Representation and Difference, MB 605 (Bloomington: Indiana University Press, 1990), 16.

46. "Arcilesbica perchè," *Lez Wiki* (blog), 2000, http://www.leswiki.it/cultura-lesbica/politica/2000-cristina-gramolini-arcilesbica-perche/.

47. "1966 la legge italiana considera ancora la contraccezione reato contro la stirpe . . . 1970 il parlamento approva la legge sul divorzio. 1971 viene permessa la vendita della pillola anticoncezionale . . . 1978 aborto legale, approvata la 194 . . . 1996 approvata la legge 66 sulla violenza sessuale: reato contro la persona, non più contro la morale." *Vogliamo anche le rose*, Marazzi.

48. Their objectives include defending "traditional" families from the downfall of society whose values are in jeopardy. For more on the Congresso Mondiale della Famiglie (World Congress of Families), see wcfverona.org/it/about-the-congress/.

49. I refer to Non Una Di Meno as a network because they are not a collective or single circumscribed group but a platform connecting various groups to common issues. We can think of it as comparable to the "Women's March" in the United States: their presence starts and evolves on social media.

50. Non Una Di Meno. wcfverona.org/en/about-the-congress/.

51. "Ci proponiamo di costruire uno spazio che rifiuti ogni forma di pensiero gerarchico e la sua traduzione in discriminazioni quali razzismo e xenofobia, transmisoginia e sessismo, LGBPT*QIA-fobia (comunemente abbreviata in lesbo/omo/trans-fobia), abilismo, classismo, ageismo e adultismo, che rispetti i confini emotivi e fisici delle altre persone. L'interazione tra due persone deve basarsi sul consenso. Prima di instaurare qualsiasi forma di contatto fisico, assicurarsi che l'altra persona sia d'accordo. NO SIGNIFICA NO e SÌ E' REVERSIBILE." Ibidem.

52. *Femminicidio* or, "femicide" is described as "Qualsiasi forma di violenza esercitata sistematicamente sulle donne in nome di una sovrastruttura ideologica di matrice patriarcale, allo scopo di perpetuarne la subordinazione e di annientarne l'identità attraverso l'assoggettamento fisico o psicologico, fino alla schiavitù o alla morte" (Sara Porco, stopfemminicidio.it.) ("Any form of violence systematically exerted onto women in the name of a patriarchal ideological superstructure, that intends to perpetuate their subordination and annihilate their identity through physical

or psychological subjugation, to the point of slavery or death.") (My translation). Stopfemminicio further contextualized: "La violenza di genere è purtroppo un problema strutturale della società che nonostante le lotte femministe dell'ultimo secolo continua ad essere di stampo patriarcale. Il femminicidio rappresenta l'estrema conseguenza della disparità di genere presente nel mondo. Per combattere il fenomeno della violenza sulle donne si deve partire da un'analisi piú profonda della società." ("Unfortunately, gender-based violence is a structural problem of a society that, despite the feminist struggles of the last century, continues to be patriarchal. Femicide is the consequence of gender disparity in the world. To combat the phenomenon of violence against women we must start from a deeper analysis of society in itself.") (My translation).

53. This is not unlike the "All Lives Matter" response from individuals who are overlooking racial power imbalances that spawn movements like "Black Lives Matter" in the first place.

54. *Nomadic Subjects*, 54.

55. "Compulsory Heterosexuality and Lesbian Existence," *Signs* 5, no. 4 (1980): 2.

56. Ibid., 49.

BIBLIOGRAPHY

Antosa, Silvia and Charlotte Ross. "Dirsi lesbica oggi? Lesbofobia nei media italiani tra indicibilità e invisibilità." Edited by Roberta Di Bella and Romina Pistone. In *Donne+Donne. Prima, attraverso e dopo il Pride, Femminile Oltre* (2014): 55–80.

Baeri, Emma. "Le femministe, le lesbiche, le storiche. Appunti per una storia da scrivere." In *Il movimento delle lesbiche in Italia*. Edited by Monia Dragone, Cristina Gramolini, Paola Guazzo, Helen Ibry, Evan Mamini, and Ostilia Mulas. Milano: Il Dito e La Luna, 2008.

Benedetto XVI. *Ai Membri della Pontificia Accademia per la vita*, Febbraio 24, 2007. http://w2.vatican.va/content/benedictxvi/it/speeches/2007/february/documents/hf_ben-xvi_spe_20070224_academy-life.html. Accessed 25 January, 2019.

Borghi, Liana. "Connessioni transatlantiche: lesbismo femminista anni '60–70." In *Ilmovimento delle lesbiche in Italia*. Milano: Il Dito e La Luna, 2010.

Braidotti, Rosi. *Nomadic Subjects*. New York: Columbia University Press, 2011.

Danna, Daniela. *Amiche, compagne, amanti: Storia dell'amore tra donne*. Saggi. 1st ed. Milano: A. Mondadori, 1994.

———. "La Partecipazione delle lesbiche al movimento omosessuale italiano: il caso del Fuori." August 7, 2015. http://www.danieladanna.it/wordpress/?tag=lesbismo.

De Lauretis, Teresa. *Alice Doesn't: Feminism, Semiotics, Cinema*. Bloomington: Indiana University Press, 1984.

———. "Sexual Indifference and Lesbian Representation." *Theatre Journal; Washington, D.C.* 40, no. 2 (May 1, 1988): 155–177.

———. *Technologies of Gender: Essays on Theory, Film, and Fiction*. Bloomington: Indiana University Press, 1987.

delle donne di Milano, Libreria, ed. *Sexual Difference: A Theory of Social-Symbolic Practice*. Theories of Representation and Difference, MB 605. Bloomington: Indiana University Press, 1990.

Dominijanni, Ida. "Doppio movimento." *DWF "Appartenenza"* no. 4 (1986): 7–26.

Gramolini, Cristina. "Arcilesbica perché." *Lez Wiki* (blog), 2000. http://www.leswiki.it/cultura-lesbica/politica/2000-cristina-gramolini-arcilesbica-perche/.

Lonzi, Carla. *Sputiamo Su Hegel: La donna clitoridea e la donna vaginale*. Milano: Gammalibri, 1982.

Lussana, Fiamma. *Il movimento femminista in Italia: Esperienze, storie, memorie, 1965–1980*. Roma: Carocci, 2012.

Marazzi, Alina. *Vogliamo anche le rose*. Rai Cinema, 2007.

Mercandino, Valeria. "Un'innominabile presenza: le lesbiche nel femminismo italiano tra nominazione, silenzio e conflitto. Elementi di un dibattito e considerazioni attuali (An Unmentionable Presence: Lesbians within Italian Feminism between Naming, Silence and Conflict)." n.d.

Milletti, Nerina and Luisa Passerini, eds. *Fuori della norma: Storie lesbiche nell'Italiadella prima metà del Novecento*. 1st ed. italiana. La Storia & Le Storie. Torino: Rosenberg & Sellier, 2007.

"Ministero Della Giustizia – Pubblicazioni, Studi, Ricerche, Lavori Commissioni Di Studio." February 2012. https://www.giustizia.it/giustizia/it/mg_1_12_1.page;jsessionid=k1xncyzqyo6y+GnC8Z++xTqu?facetNode_1=0_8&facetNode_2=0_8_7&facetNode_3=0_8_7_3&contentId=SPS995907&previsiousPage=mg_1_12.

Rich, Adrienne. "Compulsory Heterosexuality and Lesbian Existence." *Signs* 5, no. 4 (1980): 631–660.

"Server Donne – Recensione di *Vogliamo anche le rose* di Alina Marazzi." April 7, 2008. http://www.women.it/magazine-mainmenu-46/recensioni-mainmenu-82/420-recensione-di-vogliamo-anche-le-rose-di-alina-marazzi.html.

Spinelli, Simonetta. "Je ne regrette rien." *DWF: Donnawomanfemme; Roma*, Spring 1986.

Wittig, Monique. *The Straight Mind and Other Essays*. Boston: Beacon Press, 1992.

Chapter 3

A Queerer Road

Crossing Borders On and Off the Screen in Corazones de Mujer

Sole Anatrone

The 2008 film *Corazones de mujer* tells the story of two women on a road trip from Italy to Morocco. Zina (Ghizlane Waldi), a young woman of North African descent, raised in a Muslim community in Turin, is to be married to a man of her parents' choosing. Shakira (Aziza Amehri), a transwoman from Morocco, works as a seamstress in Turin and has been selected to prepare Zina's wedding clothes. When Zina confides her anxieties about her wedding night and the impending discovery that she has already been sexually active, Shakira proposes a road trip to a surgeon in Casablanca who will "restore" Zina's hymen, "reset her to kilometer zero," as Shakira puts it.[1] In this chapter, I propose a reading of *Corazones de mujer* as a film that imagines a queer utopian future in which not only rigid borders of gender and sexuality are destabilized but also nation-state, culture, and language are destabilized. I argue that this queered future is envisioned through a practice of cinematic citation; drawing primarily on Sergio Leone's spaghetti Westerns and Callie Khouri and Ridley Scott's *Thelma & Louise* (1991), this film challenges expectations and associations of linguistic, national, and generic coherence.[2]

This destabilization, this weakening of borders, is the consequence of migration. It is a redistribution of people and cultures across political and geographic boundaries that, the film suggests, brings with it a disruptive force enabling, making room for, the survival of queer bodies. The practice of rethinking boundaries is of particular relevance to the Italian context, where the question of political borders has been, and continues to be, at the forefront of questions about national identity both within the European Union, and with regards to surging numbers of migrants arriving on the Italian peninsula over the past fifteen years in response to increasingly unstable living conditions in Africa and the Middle East. Some of the loudest voices on the Italian left and right have sought to reaffirm coherent narratives about national identity that rely on notions of solid political borders; these narratives also invariably involve images of the Italian citizen as a participant in a particular formations of family, gender, and sexuality: these are almost always images based in hetero- (and occasionally homo-)normative ideals, that cast the queer / brown / other as part of the corrosive force eating away at the borders that protect the integrity of the Italian nation-state. José Muñoz describes queerness as "a structuring and educated mode of desiring that allows us to see and feel beyond the quagmire of the present," understanding queerness as "the rejection of the here and now and an insistence on potentiality or concrete possibility for another world."[3] It is my position that this film performs the queer practice of desiring that Muñoz describes, positing the expression of that "other world" in the increasing spaces of interaction among queer people.

When thinking about this kind of queer desiring in conjunction with cinema I am stressing the important role representation has in ensuring queer livability; films that depict queer bodies make precarious subjects visible and, as Schoonver and Galt write, "queer cinema enables different ways of being in the world and, more than this, [. . .] creates different worlds."[4] This work of representing other worlds is "a process that is active, incomplete, and contestatory and that does not presuppose a settled cartography."[5] In *Corazones* we see this cartographic destabilization both in terms of the production (which, as I will discuss, is profoundly transnational) and in terms of the narrative and genre.

Corazones is a hard film to place both thematically and generically because, on the one hand, it is a typical road trip, buddy movie, telling the story of two people who travel by car from Turin to Casablanca. It is also categorized as a "migrant" film, because, though the protagonists live in Italy, they have origins in Northern Africa. It is also very much a film about sexuality and gender norms as these motivate the journey. This blending of genres is part of an ethos of destabilization and nomadism that is, I argue, an inherent aspect of the precarity of queer migrant life.

The concept of nomadism at work in this chapter, and in Federica Mazzara's analysis of *Corazones* which I will discuss presently, comes from Rosi Braidotti's elaboration of nomadic thought. Braidotti proposes harnessing the concept of nomadism as a tool for producing more subtle understandings of the ways differently situated bodies move and are impacted by power structures within the new and changing context of our increasingly hybridized globalized world: "Thus nomadic thought amounts to a politically invested cartography of the present condition of mobility in a globalized world."[6] Nomadism becomes, in this way, a radical political practice that seeks to reconfigure the ways in which we understand ourselves in relation to geopolitical borders; it is an intentional divorcing of the subject from the fixity imposed by state structures. For the queer subject, nomadism, understood in this way, can become a survival strategy, a way of finding community and safety beyond and despite the sociopolitical systems that seek to link behavioral and identity norms to institutions of power and control; *Corazones'* two protagonists enact this nomadism as they perform a queer kind of journeying that travels through time and culture, as much as over land and sea. To borrow from Jasbir Puar, this film enacts "a queer praxis of assemblage that allows for a scrambling of sides that is illegible to state practices of surveillance, control, vanishment and extermination."[7] The traveler in *Corazones* is always looking toward specific sites and moments that are important and defining, but she is not bound to them in the way the typical hetero-hero is obliged to define himself by and aligning himself with the dominant principals (traits) of those locations. We see Zina's uneasy relationship to norms of femininity and heteronormative marriage, and we witness the sacrifice Shakira makes when, crossing the sea by ferry as they head from Europe to Morocco, she tosses aside her wig and dresses in male drag in an effort to shield herself from bigotry and violence. Zina's gender nomadism is inherently linked to her geographical nomadism thus embodying a performance of the contradictory and revolutionary position the queer body is forced to inhabit as a subject that is necessarily outside the logic of national borders. Throughout the film Zina embodies different expressions of gender, racial, and cultural and identity, refusing to align with any one fixed position, locating herself in the very ambiguity of these intersections. Her very being troubles the political and cultural borders that seek to police and organize lives and bodies, because she exists in a space beyond the identity categories these sociopolitical structures seek to force; by traveling and bonding with others that inhabit spaces of excess, she calls attention to this trouble-making. Zina and Shakira move toward Casablanca through a process of transformation that is nonlinear and nonprogressive in that it does not follow the traditional protagonist's journey of "evolving," but rather moves into and cycle backs through different modes of being. Shakira sheds the dresses and wigs she wears in Turin, and appears as masculine when visiting her hometown (and estranged son), but these identities are not fixed in these locations, nor are they presented as irreconcilable opposites; instead, Shakira carries both with her as she travels, allowing each place to infect, affect and be impacted by her multitude, maintaining her identity despite her shifts in gender performance. Zina also explores different embodiments of gender performance as they follow a path that is capped on each end by spaces that seem, at first, to be defined by the control they exert on Zina's (female) body, but which, in the end, are shown to be malleable because Zina's embodied gender is itself malleable.

In "Performing Post-Migration Cinema in Italy," Federica Mazzara argues, and I agree, that *Corazones*' plurality of genre speaks to a nomadic aesthetic, thus resisting a categorization of the film as a "migrant" film.[8] This is an important consideration in the Italian context because, in the thirty-odd years since Italy has become a migrant destination, Italian film (and Italian culture more broadly) has struggled to deal with the question of representing its new and changing demographic. By and large, Italian films that are classified as "migrant films" depict the non-Italian migrant as the object of the film, something to offer a homogeneous Italian public in a narrative that presents them as nonthreatening and eager to assimilate. As Vetri Nathan writes, migrant cinema in the Italian context "systematically follows a pattern of aligning the dominant gaze with that of the Italian characters (of national or racial construction) while allowing even so-called immigrant heroes to fall into becoming objects."[9] Mazzara sees *Corazones* as a film that foregrounds migration, but does so in a way that breaks from the (still new) canon of migrant films by presenting "the possibility for opening up an alternative discourse on migration. Here, the migrant characters are real negotiators of identities and cultures, and they offer a more credible window onto a more contemporary world, bringing to the fore issues other than integration and racism in the destination country."[10] But, where Mazzara suggests that—because the characters are not defined by their condition as immigrants, and the struggles the plot focuses on are not dependent on their being immigrants—this film can be described as an example of "post-migrant" cinema, I argue that their nomadic aesthetic works in conjunction with their immigrant status. Where "post-migrant" would suggest a concept and mode of being that is free of the concerns of geopolitical confines, this nomadism engages with, and very intentionally troubles, those borders and the identities and expectations with which they are associated. In other words, the nomadic aesthetic of their immigration works to disrupt a heteronormative narrative that is deeply tied up in preserving national boundaries.

This nomadism occurs not just on the narrative level, but also on the levels of form and production. In fact, the majority of the limited critical, academic work that has been done on this film has focused on the peculiar make-up of this film's production: it was directed by two Italian men, Davide Sordella and Pablo Benedetti, using the pseudo-Arabic screenname Kiff Kosoof; the dialogue is primarily in Arabic with Italian subtitles, though some key moments are in Italian (most discussion of sex is in Italian, and the narrative is frequently interrupted by Shakira speaking directly to the camera in reality TV-style asides that are exclusively in Italian); the title of the film is in Spanish though virtually no Spanish is spoken (the title translates to "the hearts of women," which speaks to the film's insistence on consistently reading Shakira as a woman, despite her dressing in male drag most of the time:

the portion of the story that takes place in Morocco); the film is shot in Italy, Spain, and Morocco; the music comes from a variety of cultural, linguistic, and temporal registers, and the funding and distribution are equally international as the producers chose to avoid state funding under the assumption that the storyline and characters would disqualify them.[11] The intensely and intentionally transnational composition of this film, on the level of production, rehearse the thematics of border destabilization and community building that inform the narrative and, in my view, speak toward an ethos of nomadism rather than migrancy, where migrancy has to do with moving from one national context to another in search of stability and permanency, and nomadism is understood as a political practice of living outside of—or in disruptive disregard of—imposed boundaries.

With this in mind, I argue against Mazzara's claim that, in this film, Italy is made to be the site of freedom, "where no resistance is expressed to minorities."[12] Mazzara's point, whether intentionally or not, echoes a neo-leftist Western liberal discourse that sees the West as the model of freedom, identity-based rights, and successful democracy; it is an ideal toward which everyone is presumed to be striving. According to this logic, the non-West can only ever be a more oppressive and less desirable space, regardless of the challenges faced in the West. Such reasoning inevitably falls into the trap of establishing an oppositional binary (us/them, West/Other, Italy/Morocco), in which each term is flattened and made to be homogenous, ignoring the fact that Italy and Morocco each contain contradictory differences. In the socially progress space of urban Italy, Zina faces oppression because she a sexually active woman (that this resistance occurs within the parameters of her religious community does not change the fact that it is in Italy, nor is an alternative accepting Italian community depicted in the film); in the restrictive rural space of Morocco she is empowered to make her own choices about transforming her body (or not). Shakira's experience is somewhat inverse; she is accepted and comfortable as a woman in Italy, while in Morocco she is rejected because of this same gender transgression, and beaten in response to her attempt to be intimate with a man (in an interaction when she is presenting as male). In other words, the sites of oppression are decidedly unmoored. Freedom is not presented as the opposite of oppression, but as a potentiality, as a possible condition of nomadism because, for both Zina and Shakira, the danger lies in stasis.

I see the nomadic behavior in this film as an expression of movement that responds to, and is in part fueled by, the formation of new queer kinships made possible through encounters with different places and times. In other words, what is represented here is an experience of freedom in communities formed through and made possible by migration, travel, and interaction across borders (national, cultural, linguistic). The political foundations behind this idea of community formation are reinforced by the intertextual play that occurs throughout the film.

This intertextuality occurs principally with Sergio Leone's Spaghetti Westerns and *Thelma & Louise*. Each operates in a variety of ways, serving both as representative of ideologies that make queer livability impossible and as sources of potentiality from which to draw material for the construction of other worlds. As I will discuss, we see echoes of these cinematic precursors in both direct and indirect ways; there are explicit restagings of scenes and dialogue, and there are distortions of narrative and aesthetics that work to insert *Corazones* into a cinematic canon that is grounded in mythologies of nation building and dismantling.

On the methodological level, *Corazones*' borrowing and thatching together of these disparate genres and sources is, itself, a style championed by Leone which, as Christopher Robé writes, is a "composite of several global influences that didn't always cohere: the Hollywood Western, the Japanese samurai film, neorealism, and the peplum, to name only a few."[13] In *Corazones* this non-coherence is self-aware, as form, content, and characters call attention to sources they draw from; the first stop on their road trip is one such example. At Shakira's insistence, the pair stop at a hotel in Spain where Sergio Leone stayed. The scene opens with a shot of a large black bull (what turns out to be a billboard-type cutout) atop a desolate, sandy hillside, looming over a highway. We shift to an aerial shot of the road and follow Shakira's red sports car, zooming along as she shares her excitement about visiting a place the great Italian director once patronized: "Just think, tonight we're going to be sleeping in the same hotel, the same room as Sergio Leone! And do you know what they said when I booked it?"[14] The audio shifts, and we are hearing her conversation with the hotelier: "Grand Hotel. Good morning! Oh yes, you're the one that called earlier to know about Sergio Leone's room. I asked management, but they said we can't release private information about a guest." "But he's been dead for twenty years!" "Even worse to do with a deceased person!" The phone clicks off and we're back in the car with Shakira and Zina. Shakira laughs and continues talking to Zina in Arabic, "Can you believe it?" "Yeah, but . . . who is this Sergio . . . Sergio?" "Just forget it."[15] The interplay that happens here, between Shakira's thrill at being in the same geographic, if not temporal, space as Leone, and Zina's total ignorance of the director, speaks to the ambiguous position *Corazones* occupies within the national and international filmscape. It is the same kind of ambiguous position Zina and Shakira occupy in relation to the national and cultural structures that seek to police and restrict them; this (mis)recognition of such an iconic figure in Italian cinema is a performance of a queer excess, where the queer narrative exists in relation to dominant narratives, but cannot be contained within the same generic confines; the film's queerness is always already an excess, a spillage, but that does not mean it is not related to or in dialogue with the canon. Leone functions as a historical marker of both absence and possibility; following Muñoz's discussion of queer readings of historical objects, Leone functions as "a mode of being and feeling that was then not quite there but nonetheless an opening."[16] In addition to this direct mention of Leone, the film is peppered with what I am calling "aesthetic citation," with the rehearsal of specific items of clothing, set, placement of colors and sounds. One such instance is the iconic cemetery scene *The Good, the Bad, the Ugly* (1966), in which Blondie (Clint Eastwood) says to Tuco (Eli Wallach): "See in this world there's two kinds of people my friend, those with loaded guns, and those who dig. You dig."[17] In *Corazones* we have an unmistakable repetition of both setting and dialogue. We are in a similarly arid, empty cemetery, only this time there is no tension between the two people in the scene. Shakira, in male drag, squats by an empty grave and talks to an old man digging:

Shakira: What are you doing?
Digger: Can't you see? I'm digging.
Shakira: What for?
Digger: In life, there are those who have guns and those who dig. I . . . dig.
Shakira: What does that mean?
Digger: I don't know. But I dig while I'm waiting.
Shakira: They already dug my grave even though I'm not dead yet.[18]

The call back to Blondie's menacing words is unmistakable, but here the violence has been removed, because the gun has been removed; the oppressor is unseen, all that is left is the one forced to dig in an empty cemetery as he waits for death. The line has shifted from being a threat to a bleak motto for survival. Shakira's question about the meaning of the phrase—a phrase she would surely recognize as an avid Leone fan—reinforces the ambivalent position this film occupies with respect (or disrespect) to the canon.

About midway through their road trip, the narrative is interrupted by a dream sequence; it is a surreal, semi-erotic, quasi-violent scene in which Zina dreams of possessing and being possessed by Shakira. The scene opens with Zina dressed in pants and a sporty top, with a scarf wrapped around her head, completely covering her face. She is running across a seemingly endless stretch of sandy dunes, the camera alternates perspectives, first behind her and then suddenly in front, to the side, conveying the dizzying, frenetic feeling of the chase we are witnessing. We see Shakira, in a nearly identical outfit (though the colors are darker) appear atop a dune, pursing Zina. But it is unclear who is pursuing whom, as the chase sequence is crosscut with a scene in which Zina is the aggressor. In this scene Zina and Shakira are outfitted with costumes typical of Leone's Westerns, with Zina in the male garb, and Shakira in the dress. Zina roughly pushes Shakira up against a dead tree and tears at her dress. "What do you want from me?" Shakira asks.[19] We cut back to the chase and the camera zooms in as the movement stops with the two collapsed in exhaustion. "What do you want from me?" Shakira repeats; and the crosscutting picks up the pace, jumping back and forth between these two scenes. "What do you really want from me?"[20] Shakira asks again, now wearing just a pearl necklace as Zina has ripped open the bodice of her dress. Zina responds by grabbing Shakira's head and forcing her into a kiss. In the final shot of the dream sequence, we cut to a new scene. The two women are fully clothed in their Western costumes and are posed in front of a false Western-style façade in what appears to be a standoff. But only Zina has a pistol. She aims at Shakira, who stands with outstretched arms; the shot wakes Zina up, returning us to the "real world" of the film (see figure 3.1).

All of this is a distorted mash-up of two scenes from two different Leone films; the chase sequence in the dunes is an echo of the scene in *The Good, the Bad, the Ugly,* in which Tuco is chasing a desperate Blondie across the sand dunes. The other half of the dream sequence recalls a confrontation in *Once Upon a Time in the West* (1968), in which Harmonica (Charles Bronson) corners Jill McBain (Claudia Cardinale) in the barn. As Harmonica walks toward Jill in the beginning of the scene, she asks, "What do you want?"[21] The same question Shakira will repeat. We see another echo in Shakira's dress in the dream sequence, which is a close copy of Jill's; both dresses are torn, exposing the chest, as both women are backed against wooden posts and forced into unwanted sex acts. I am reading this citational collage as part of the ethos of nomadism that pervades the film in that it refuses to participate in the monogamous structure of loyalty to a singular source (be in film or nation), adopting instead a citational pose that creates its own pastiche genealogy

Figure 3.1 Zina and Shakira in a Leone-Style Western Standoff, with Zina Masculine-Presenting on and Shakira-Feminine Presenting. *Source*: Screenshot.

in film history which in turn suggests the possibility of creating a similar queer genealogy off-screen. This practice of creating history is particularly urgent for queer subjects who have been violently and intentionally excluded from dominant narratives of the past; it is, as Muñoz explains, an expression of hope, where "hope [is used] as a critical methodology that can best be described as a backward glance that enacts a future vision."[22] *Corazones* shows us the work of this future-history building through the intentional, almost campy, citations of these other films.[23]

The aesthetic citations to *Thelma & Louise* also create a queerness, positioning *Corazones* in ambivalent relation to a tradition of films about outsiders (the road trip genre), and to a genealogy of films that confront and reject patriarchal control of non-hetero female sexuality.[24] The citations of *Thelma & Louise* are equally prevalent though never explicitly named in *Corazones*. Thematically the films are similar, both feature two women on a road trip propelled by a desire to escape a system of male dominance: Thelma and Louise drive away from an abusive, controlling (male) husband, an exploitative (male) employer, a (male) rapist, and a male police force; Shakira and Zina drive away from families and social structures that demands (female) virginity, heterosexuality, and marriage. Though the endings differ in significant ways, there are key moments of aesthetic citation worth reviewing. Within the first few minutes of both films, we have almost parallel scenes of two women packing the car. In *Thelma & Louise*, we see Thelma (Susan Sarandon) pull up to Louise's (Geena Davis) house in her flashy convertible. She pops the trunk and watches in shock as Louise begins to haphazardly fill the car with a ridiculous number of things before intervening to help pack the car in a more orderly fashion, all the while reassuring Louise that she is in good hands. Finally ready to leave, Thelma draws Louise close for a polaroid-selfie to mark the start of their journey. Shakira and Zina's journey begins in a nearly identical fashion, with Shakira pulling up in her flashy convertible. This is followed by a comical packing and repacking of the car, and Shakira's reassurances that Zina is in good hands. Finally ready to leave, Shakira draws Zina close for a polaroid-selfie to mark the start of their journey. The polaroid pictures featured in both scenes are an important symbol in *Corazones*, as Shakira takes a new one to mark each leg of their journey as they arrive closer to "kilometer zero." And, the polaroids feature as retroactive storytellers in the credits of *Thelma & Louise,* marking each leg of their journey.

Both films also make use of another marker: the elder witness, sitting and watching. Thelma and Louise's journey is peppered with these elderly watchers posted at gas stations, looking out from behind screens, perched on dusty chairs, observing, at times talking to one another, rarely interacting with the heroines. These dusty elder watchers reappear in *Corazones* when our pair is traveling in Morocco. Two men sit on overturned buckets in front of a small roadside building, eating seeds, spitting the shells, and watching the road. They are mostly silent, the audio filled with the sounds of sucking and spitting shells, the camera focusing on the flies that buzz about their eyes which remain fixed on mostly empty road. When they do break their silence it is to stress the fixity of their position, highlighting their remove from forces of change:

> In any case, we'll always be here. Until the Big Day.
> All this time we've waited will disappear that day too.
> Not if we tell each other our memories first . . . . Want to tell me one?
>   If you trust me with a memory . . . I'll keep it safe and bring it
>   with me to the Beyond. Doesn't that seem like a good deal?
> It seems like a good deal, but the memory I'd like to keep isn't easy to tell.
> So, you'll tell me?
> I'm afraid I'll lose it if I tell it.
> Why can't you tell it?
> It's a sin.
> A sin? At your age?
> It's a sin I committed a long time ago.
> So you'll tell me?
> It happened a long time ago, I don't remember it anymore.
> Okay, okay . . .
> My memory is no good anymore.
> It's fine. Don't worry. When you remember I'll be here to listen.
> In any case, we'll always be here.
> God willing.[25]

I agree with Giampiero Frasca's assertion that these elders embody "the immutability of tradition."[26] At the same time, I want to argue that the use of this particular form of witness (an elder sitting in the heat, by the edge of the road, watching the journey and its heroes pass by) is a mode of challenging structures of time and history that do not make room for, do not tell the stories of, do not record the histories of our protagonists because theirs are stories that tell of rejecting gender norms, defying rules of behavior based on (intentionally) oppressive notions of gender binarism.

Ultimately, however, the two films convey very different relationships to time and history, as demonstrated most clearly in their endings. *Corazones* ends with Zina deciding not to go through with her marriage. When she calls to convey her decision to her mother back in Italy, she is met with acceptance, and is freed from her obligation of marriage. Like Thelma and Louise, Zina and Shakira sit in a sporty, convertible car at the edge of the earth, but unlike the American women, they do not continue the forward movement of their journey. That the two will eventually return safely to Turin is implied by Shakira's retrospective, reality-TV-style asides which take place in Turin.[27] The contrast between this ending, and the ending of *Thelma & Louise*, with the two women hurtling toward an implicitly violent death at the bottom of the canyon, is striking and speaks to the queer utopianism that runs through *Corazones*. Thelma and Louise choose death because it is a mode of control in a world where violence is power. Their journey is propelled by violence and ends in violence.

Violence is, of course, also a defining feature Leone's work. Violence is, more specifically, the way the outsider asserts himself, taking the tools of civilization (represented by the violent battles for conquest and dominance in Leone's American West), and deploying them on the individual scale, thus bringing into focus the horror and ease with which notions of community and alliance can be shattered. As Timothy Campbell writes, "Order appears as the never-ending attempt to keep the outside apart, even as it continually appears that the outside can at any minute break through and threaten law and order." In Leone's Westerns, he continues, "we have porous borders and with it a violence that touches everyone."[28] What is often discussed as the "amoral" dimension of Leone's films is, in my view, a representation of the only means of survival available to those who are, in some way, outcast: in other words, those who are offered no entrance into community must and will resort to violence. For instance, the Stranger, the protagonist in the Dollars trilogies, is defined by belonging to no community in a world where everyone is understood in terms of his alliance with a particular group, family or gang: Confederate or Union army in *The Good, the Bad, the Ugly;* the Rojos or the Baxters in *A Fistful of Dollars*; townspeople and El Indio's gang in *For a Few Dollars More*. The Stranger asserts his identity with violence.

The violence in *Thelma & Louise* assumes a similar function, though here it is linked to gender in a way that is thematically more significant. Thelma and Louise live in a world where male dominance is the norm, and where women are defined by their submission to men. Violence in this film (regardless of who perpetrates it) is the only possible expression of women's attempt to assume control (over themselves, others, anything). The key example of this is Thelma's shooting a man outside a bar because he tries to rape Louise, who he considers his property; this event transforms their road trip from vacation to evasion, but it is not the first example of misogynist violence—Louise's husband is vocally abusive—nor is it the last: there is the trucker who harasses them; and the male police who pursue them with an armory of guns. Thelma and Louise respond to all of these assaults with violence of their own: holding a state trooper at gunpoint; setting the trucker's tanks on fire, and taking their own lives. The women's use of violence—and of guns specifically—has been a topic for debate in feminist readings of this film. Those who argue against a feminist reading of this film contend that, by taking up guns Thelma and Louise become phallic women, assuming the same tools and posture of the male system that oppresses them, and thus, rather than suggesting a possible revolution, they are a testament to the invincibility of the patriarchy.[29] While I do not share this view entirely, in large part because I think that reading all guns as phallic is unnecessarily limiting, I do agree with the conclusion that sees the use of violence in this film as indicative of its structuring philosophy that sees no outside to an oppressive patriarchy. By citing the violence of these earlier films, *Corazones* points to the precarious condition of the queer subject navigating through a world structured by patriarchy, but in this film those systems based in violence are shown to be porous in the same way nomadism reveals the possibilities of transgressing borders. The question of geopolitical, gender, and sexual borders is brought to the fore at a critical moment in the last scene of *Thelma & Louise:* the kiss between the two women. This kiss—immediately preceding their plunge over the edge of the canyon—is the mark of dystopian queerness; it is the impossibility of a non-heteronormative narrative, and as such it must be followed by their death. As Cathy Griggers writes,

> The kiss [. . .] exceeds the economy of both the film's dominant narrative (the road film) and of the dominant social body (heterosexual femininity). Thus it exacts a certain price in order to circulate within mainstream representation–the familiar death sentence demanded of characters when the subversive narrative generating them threatens to go too far.[30]

The queer logic of *Corazones*, on the other hand, refuses this kind of ontological progression. The ending of *Corazones* is a point on a circular journey: they depart from Turin and go to kilometro zero and then presumably return to Turin, bringing the mileage back to what it was when they left. But this does not suggest a meaningless journey; instead it is the story of producing a history that allows for a livable future. In restaging *Thelma & Louise, Corazones de mujer* highlights the perils and possibilities of queer migrations, and complicates the idea of the West as a safe haven for queer bodies, calling attention to the real and perceived violence that accompanies queer lives.

In *Corazones* there is both implicit and overt violence: Shakira is brutally assaulted in Morocco by a band of homophobes; the aforementioned dream scene depicts sexual aggression and gun violence; and Zina's "hymen-repair" procedure is a form of violence itself. However, violence plays a different role here than in the other films it dialogues with; the violence here is one that seeks to police queer bodies, attempting to force them into ill-fitting molds. Zina's sexually charged aggression and use of the gun are, importantly, within the dream sequence, occurring in the space of fantasy and the surreal;

they are also moments when Zina is casting herself in the role of particularly male-macho characters from Leone's repertoire, testing out a performance of masculinity that is subverted by virtue of her own malleable experience of gender, *and* because it is set in the realm of the fantastic. These are important considerations in that they point to the characters' attitude toward violence; unlike the characters in the other films considered here, who take up violence as their primary mode of expression, Zina and Shakira will not be transformed by it. This is ultimately a conversation about refusing to participate in the normative structures of surveillance and control. In *Thelma & Louise,* though the protagonists fight against the oppressiveness of their (female) gendered—and as such, submissive—positions, their struggles for freedom are thwarted. The struggle is queered in this movie. Zina and Shakira are confronted with the same forms of violent control Thelma and Louise encounter, but, where their American counterparts pose a head-on challenge to these forces that seeks to (re)cast them within the confines of the heteronormative narrative, *Corazones'* protagonists move to a narrative that exists in a space of excess, inhabiting a space beside and outside of the dominant script. Key to this mode of survival is a rejection to take up violence as a mode of communication and self-definition, and to focus instead of creating new ways of being and bonding. It is my view that, in this way, *Corazones* counters the dystopian vision that underlies both Leone's work and *Thelma & Louise,* with a specifically queer futurity. Drawing on Muñoz's discussion of queer utopianism as being both a movement forward and a (re)construction of an obfuscated past, "a mode of being and feeling that was then not quite there but nonetheless an opening," I argue that the past, here, is produced through the citation and rewriting of these different films, from different cultures and moments.[31] Muñoz writes: "Queerness exists for us as an ideality that can be distilled from the past and used to imagine a future."[32] I want to add a consideration of place and movement to this equation.

In other words, *Corazones* lives in a here and there *as well as* in a past and future because the positioned subject is always and necessarily in motion: nomadic. The survival of their queer selves (their bodies and their hopes) depends on movement.[33] However, and this is key, their travel does not proceed toward a predetermined destination, the destination is not the narrative outcome of the journey. This narrative ethos is most clearly conveyed when the final scene is read as a response to the final scene of *Thelma & Louise,* with the refusal of suicide as an act of queer political nomadism. This is a performance of queer futurity, in which queer futurity is, in this formulation, defined by—*enabled by*—movement: movement through genre as well as across different national and cultural spaces. *Corazones de mujer* embodies precisely the kind of transnational, transcultural, gender nomadism that is viewed as threatening to the endurance of the nation.

NOTES

1. "farla tornare kilometro zero." *Corazones de mujer*, directed by Kif Kosoof (Italy: Movimento Film, 2008). The dialogue alternates between Italian, Arabic, and Spanish throughout the film; when they speak Arabic or Spanish, Italian-language subtitles appear. I have transcribed the Italian subtitles for the sake of consistency. All translations are my own.

2. As many scholars have noted, cinema plays a fundamental role in the conceptualization of the Italian national imaginary. Derek Duncan writes that "cinema in Italy has been seen as the cultural form in which national identity is most securely located" (2008, 211). *Corazones'* citation of Sergio Leone, one of the most well-known auteurs of Italian film, is a way of commanding a place for itself within this national tradition. *Thelma & Louise* clearly does not participate in this same cultural sphere; released in 1991, a moment that marks a renewed flood of American film and television into Italy with the reorganization and revamping of Italian media. Additionally, in the time since its release *Thelma & Louise* has come to occupy a cult-like status in the cultural imaginary of many marginalized, "othered" groups which see it as telling the story of a revolt against the patriarchy.

3. José Muñoz, *Cruising Utopia: The Then and There of Queer Futurity* (New York: New York University Press, 2009), 1.

4. Karl Schoonover and Rosalind Galt, *Queer Cinema in the World* (Durham, NC: Duke University Press, 2016), 4.

5. Ibid.

6. Rosi Braidotti, *Nomadic Subjects: Embodiment and Sexual Difference in Contemporary Feminist Theory,* second ed. (New York: Columbia University Press, 2011), 4.

7. Jasbir Puar, *Terrorist Assemblages: Homonationalisms in Queer Times* (Durham: Duke University Press, 2007), 221.

8. Federica Mazzara, "Performing Post-Migration Cinema in Italy: *Corazones de mujer* by K. Kosoof," *Modern Italy* 3 (2013): 41–53.

9. Vetri Nathan, *Marvelous Bodies: Italy's New Migrant Cinema* (West Lafayette: Purdue University Press, 2017), 135. Two other useful resources on the topic of migrant cinema are *The Cinemas of Italian Migration*, edited by Sabine Schrader and Daniel Winkler (Newcastle: Cambridge Scholars Publishing, 2013), and Áine O'Healy's *Migrant Anxieties: Italian Cinema in a Transnational Frame* (Bloomington, IN: Indiana University Press, 2019).

10. Mazzara, "Performing Post-Migration Cinema in Italy," 46.

11. The directors explain this as a nondecision, necessitated by a desire to preserve the integrity of both the story and the form of the film they sought to make: "L'ultra indipendenza di questo film nasce da un motivo ovvio: se tu vai da un produttore e gli dici salve siamo due registi sconosciuti, vorremmo fare senza sceneggiatura, con degli attori non-professionisti di cui sappiamo l'inizio ma non la fine, credo che la risposta possa essere ovvia quindi per risparmiarci una serie di "no" abbiamo deciso di farlo e di scommetterci . . . il vantaggio è la libertà . . . era l'unico modo secondo noi di raccontare questa storia" ("The extreme independence of film is born of an obvious cause: if you go to a producer and say, 'Hi, we are two unknown directors,

we'd like to make a movie without a set, with non-professional actors; we know the beginning, but not the end.' I think the answer is obvious, so, to spare ourselves a series of "nos," we decided to take a gamble and make it . . . the advantage is freedom . . . it was the only way, we thought, to be able to tell this story") (from the director's commentary released with the DVD). The film's composer, Enrico Sabena, explains the intentionality of this musical nomadism: "il film ovviamente tratta di temi scontanti. La non-libertà della donna nel mondo arabo, la sessualità nel mondo arabo . . . Però di fatto tematiche universali . . . proprio perché le tematiche sono universali, proviamo a spaziare. Proviamo a fare una sorta di commistione di stili che però in realtà non fosse proprio una macedonia, ma andiamo a prendere dalle varie culture degli elementi diciamo peculiari, capillari. Proviamo a farle dialogare insieme . . . volevamo fare questa commistione orizzontale in termini geografici, usando stili diversi ma anche temporali" ("the film doesn't deal with easy topics, obviously. The non-freedom of women in the Arab world, sexuality in the Arab world . . . but they are universal topics . . . precisely because these are universal themes, let's try and broaden our scope. Let's try to make a sort of mixture of styles—not exactly a salad—let's take all these special, unusual elements from different cultures. Let's try to put them in dialogue with one another. . . . We wanted this to be a horizontal of geographic and temporal styles"). The soundtrack is almost entirely original or reworked pieces that combine traditional Moroccan and Occitan music; songs in ancient languages like Sephardic, Aragon Celtic; Chopin sonatas reinterpreted using the Arabic scale; and more contemporary pop songs interwoven with the folkloristic sounds commissioned by Sabena. From the commentary about the soundtrack released with the DVD. All translations are my own.

12. Mazzara, "Performing Post-Migration Cinema in Italy," 51.

13. Christopher Robé, "When Cultures Collide: Third Cinema Meets the Spaghetti Western," *Journal of Popular Film and Television* (2014), 163.

14. "Pensa che questa notte dormiremo nello stesso hotel, stessa stanza di Sergio Leone! E quando ho prenotato sai cosa mi hanno detto?"

15. "Gran Hotel. Buongiorno! Ah si, lei è quello che ha chiamato prima per sapere la stanza di Sergio Leone. Ho chiesto alla direzione, ma non possiamo dare informazioni riservate su un ospite." "Ma è morto da vent'anni!" "Peggio ancora su un morto!" The phone clicks off and we're back in the car with Shakira and Zina. Shakira laughs and continues talking to Zina in Arabic, "Ti rendi conto?" "Si ma . . . chi sarebbe questo Sergio . . . Sergio . . . ?" "Lascia perdere."

16. Muñoz, *Cruising Utopia*, 9.

17. *The Good, the Bad, the Ugly*, directed by Sergio Leone (Produzioni europee associati, 1966).

18. *Shakira:* "Cosa stai facendo?"
Digger: "Non vedi? Sto scavando."
Shakira: "Per cosa?"
Digger: "Nella vita c'è chi ha la pistola e chi scava. Io . . . scavo."
Shakira: "Cosa vuol dire?"
"Non lo so. Io nell'attesa scavo."
"A me hanno già scavato una tomba eppure non sono ancora morto."

19. "Cosa vuoi da me?"

20. "Cosa vuoi veramente da me?"

21. *Once Upon a Time in the West*, directed by Sergio Leone (Rafran Cinematografica, 1968).

22. Muñoz, *Cruising Utopia*, 4.

23. While I do not engage directly with the concept of camp in my reading of this film, camp has certainly been (and continues to be) a fruitful strategy and critical concept for queer survival. Many queerist thinkers and scholars have written about the topic, one useful place to start is Fabio Cleto's *Camp: Queer Aesthetics and the Performing Subject* (Ann Arbor, MI: University of Michigan Press, 1999).

24. For more on the way *Thelma & Louise* participates in, and plays with the road movie genre, see Carmen Indurain Eraso's "*Thelma & Louise*: 'Easy Riders' in a Male Genre," *Atlantis* 23, no. 1 (2001), 63–73.

25. "Tanto rimarremo sempre qui. Sino al 'gran Giorno.'" / "Quel giorno se ne andrà anche tutto il tempo che abbiamo aspettato." / "A meno che non ci raccontiamo i ricordi prima . . . Vuoi dirmene uno? Se mi affidi un ricordo . . . Io lo conserverò e lo porterò con me nell'aldilà. Non ti sembra una buona offerta?" / "Sembra una buona offerta, ma il ricordo che vorrei conservare non è facile da raccontare." / "Me lo racconti allora?" / "Se lo racconto ho paura di perderlo." / "Perché non puoi?" / "È un peccato." / "Un peccato alla tua età?"/ "È un peccato che ho commesso tanto tempo fa.'" / "Me lo racconti allora?" / "È successo tanto tempo fa', non me lo ricordo più." / "Va' bene, va' bene . . ." / "Non ho più una buona memoria." / "Non è un problema. Non devi preoccuparti. Quando te lo ricorderai io sarò qui per ascoltarti." / "Tanto rimarremo sempre qui." / "Se Dio vuole."

26. "l'immutabilità della tradizione." Giampiero Frasca, "In viaggio verso la consapevolezza: *Corazones de mujer* di Kif Kosoof," *Cineforum* no. 476 (2008), 23.

27. The documentary-like quality suggested by these asides is reinforced through the use of nonprofessional actors and a largely improvised script. This style is, of course, very much in line with neorealist film aesthetics which dominate the Italian film canon. I am choosing not to focus on those echoes here because, while they play out on the formal levels just mentioned, it is my position that the film dialogues with *Thelma & Louise,* and with Leone's work, in more consistent, engaging, and provocative ways.

28. Timothy Campbell, "The Corrupting Sea, Technology and Devalued Life in Sergio Leone's Spaghetti Westerns," *California Italian Studies* 1, no. 1 (2010), retrieved from https://escholarship.org/uc/item/22t992pn, April 12, 2016.

29. Yvonne Tasker offers a useful analysis of the different angles of this debate and the way *Thelma & Louise* fits into the genre of women-led action movies more generally in her book *Spectacular Bodies: Gender, Genre and the Action Cinema* (London: Routledge, 2014).

30. Cathy Griggers, "*Thelma and Louise* and the Cultural Generation of the New Butch-Femme," in *Film Theory Goes to the Movies*, edited by Jim Collins et al. (New York: Routledge, 1993), 133.

31. Muñoz, *Cruising*, 9.

32. Ibid., 1.

33. Throughout this chapter I have been referring to Zina and Shakira as "queer" despite the fact that the term is not used in the film. I use it here to describe the ways

their gender and sexuality remain ambiguous and shifting throughout the film, and as a critical lens through which we can consider a queer politics of their story.

BIBLIOGRAPHY

Braidotti, Rosi. *Nomadic Subjects: Embodiment and Sexual Difference in Contemporary Feminist Theory,* second edition. New York: Columbia University Press, 2011.

Campbell, Timothy. "The Corrupting Sea, Technology and Devalued Life in Sergio Leone's Spaghetti Westerns." *California Italian Studies* 1, no. 1 (2010). Retrieved from https://escholarship.org/uc/item/22t992pn. April 12, 2016.

Corazones de mujer. Directed by Kif Kosoof. Italy: Movimento Film, 2008.

Duncan, Derek. "Italy's Postcolonial Cinema and its Histories of Representation." *Italian Studies* 63, no. 2 (2008), 195–211.

Eraso, Carmen Indurain. "*Thelma & Louise*: 'Easy Riders' in a Male Genre." *Atlantis* 23, no. 1 (2001), 63–73.

Frasca, Giampiero. "In viaggio verso la consapevolezza: *Corazones de mujer* di Kif Kosoof." *Cineforum* no. 476 (2008), 21–24.

The Good, The Bad, The Ugly. Directed by Sergio Leone. Italy: Produzioni europee associati, 1966.

Griggers, Cathy. "*Thelma and Louise* and the Cultural Generation of the New Butch-Femme." In *Film Theory Goes to the Movies*, Jim Collins, Hilary Radner and Ava Preacher Collins, eds. New York: Routledge, 1993, 129–141.

Mazzara, Federica. "Performing Post-Migration Cinema in Italy: *Corazones de mujer* by K. Kosoof." *Modern Italy* 3 (2013), 41–53.

Muñoz, José. *Cruising Utopia: The Then and There of Queer Futurity.* New York: New York University Press, 2009.

Nathan, Vetri. *Marvelous Bodies: Italy's New Migrant Cinema.* West Lafayette: Purdue University Press, 2017.

Once Upon a Time in the West. Directed by Sergio Leone. Italy: Rafran Cinematografica, 1968.

Puar, Jasbir. *Terrorist Assemblages: Homonationalisms in Queer Times.* Durham: Duke University Press, 2007.

Robé, Christopher. "When Cultures Collide: Third Cinema Meets the Spaghetti Western." *Journal of Popular Film and Television* (2014), 163–174.

Schrader, Sabine and Daniel Winkler, eds. *The Cinemas of Italian Migration.* Newcastle: Cambridge Scholars Publishing, 2013.

Spivak, Gayatri Chakravorty. "Can the Subaltern Speak?" In *Colonial Discourse and Post-Colonial Theory: A Reader*, Patrick Williams and Laura Chrisam, eds. Hertfordshire: Harvester Wheatsheaf, 1994, 66–111.

Tasker, Yvonne. *Spectacular Bodies: Gender, Genre and the Action Cinema.* London: Routledge, 2014.

Thelma & Louise. Directed by Ridley Scott. USA: Pathé Entertainment, 1991.

Chapter 4

The Queer Potential of Mainstream Film

Dom Holdaway

Quo vado?, the 2016 Checco Zalone comedy that broke recent cinema-going records and fast became one of the most attended films at the cinema in Italy ever,[1] features a gay marriage around midway through the film. The event serves an ongoing irony in the film: that Norway, where the wedding takes place, is the vision of a modern, liberal country that contrasts "backward" Italy. And an intrinsic component of that modern society is built on multiculturalism, gender freedom, and equal rights: Checco's girlfriend Valeria is polyamorous and has a multiracial family; the bisexual father of one of the children is one of the grooms. The contrast between liberal attitudes toward sexuality and outdated homophobia therefore serve, in *Quo vado?*, to create humor through the "macro" irony around Checco Zalone's characteristic ignorance, and his role as an average Italian man.

Though brief, the presence of a gay marriage in this comedy is surprising, perhaps, for a national cinema that is often erroneously presumed to feature few LGBT characters.[2] In fact, this film continues a tendency in contemporary mainstream Italian film, starting in the late 2000s, to include queer characters in supporting roles or among choral casts. Moreover, these characters are depicted in positive or nuanced tones that are a far cry from either the homophobic stereotypes or tragic configurations of the queer characters in comedies and dramas from the previous century.[3]

These characters appear in a range of mainstream comedies, with different registers. As well as the blanket successes of ex-TV comic Zalone, paired with Nunziante (*Quo Vado?*, but also the earlier *Cado dalle nubi*, 2009), this includes choral comedies starring some of the most contemporary middlebrow actors (*Tutta colpa di Freud*, 2014 and *Perfetti sconosciuti*, 2016), to genre and star vehicles (*Io che amo solo te*, 2015; *Scusate se esisto*, 2014), and even slightly more offbeat, intelligent comedies (e.g., *Una piccola impresa meridionale,* 2013). Unlike certain other contemporary dramas—from the films of Ferzan Ozpetek to Maria Sole Tognazzi's *Io e lei* (2015), which thematize homosexuality more explicitly through lesbian and gay protagonists, these comedies normalize queer characters as a part of mixed social groups. As the films often find larger audiences than the "film a tematica LGBTQ," what make these characters interesting objects of study are the elements that are negotiated or sacrificed in order to allow their entrance into the mainstream. This is my focus in this chapter.

More specifically, I study first the construction of these characters in relation to anti-homophobic critiques of Italian society in two instances. I then situate the gay characters within broader cultural images of Italian society and its anxieties surrounding LGBT people: criticisms of racism and patriarchal masculinity, that never step outside of a normative representation of queer people (middle class, white, cis-gender), and reflect on the terms in which these prejudices are related to specific geographic spaces, that is, as an Italian phenomenon, but also ironically connected to a "backward" South. In the final section, my interest turns to the grey area that exists between positive images of lesbian, gay, and bisexual characters in mainstream films, and the potential of a theoretical queer spectator of such texts. With recourse to the work of Alexander Doty, the chapter concludes reflecting on the tensions between the problematic nature of these representations, and their ability nonetheless to activate oppositional spaces for interpretation.

With a focus on the tensions surrounding the presence of queer people in a cultural form that seeks first and foremost economic gain, there are some political issues that need to be addressed. First, there is a valid accusation that queer people are being enlisted into consumerism through self-representation. And yet, as the scholarship I turn to in the final section shows, queer people are not strangers in and around popular culture. The perhaps more pressing issue is how queer people are instrumentalized in a broad cultural process of identity normalization, serving a neoliberal society and economy.[4] Though the identification of queer people in these films as singularly economic subjects is not straightforward, there is certainly a process of identity restriction: there are practically no trans, asexual, intersex, or nonbinary characters in contemporary mainstream films, and the queers depicted are always white, and usually middle-class, native Italians. In order to represent more accurately this limited representational agenda, there is a temptation to refer not to queer characters, but, for instance, to LGBs or homosexuals. Nevertheless, I will continue to use the term "queer"[5] for two motives: to foreground the same presence that queer people have always had around popular culture, especially as interpreters of it, and to maintain the term as a space of resistance, even to restrictive representational codes.

ANTI-HOMOPHOBIA

Cado dalle nubi tells the story of Checco Zalone's attempt to become a famous singer, traveling from Puglia to Milan at the beginning of the film to attend auditions of a talent show. He stays with his cousin Alfredo (Dino Abbrescia), not knowing that he is gay and lives with his long-term boyfriend Manolo (Fabio Troiano). Fearful of his family's homophobia, Alfredo chooses not to come out, and urges Manolo to pose as his flat-mate. Feeling snubbed, Manolo enacts revenge at a dinner later on, betraying his sexuality through an exaggerated, camp performance. He makes a series of hyperbolic, effeminate noises to express his pleasures, affecting his gestures and theatrical intonations—for instance, exclaiming that the burrata is "like a cloud"—to the painful embarrassment of the other two (figure 4.1).

As with the gay wedding sequence in *Quo vado*, the humor of this sequence works on different levels: Manolo's slapstick actions are funny, but we also laugh at Checco's discomfort. This ties into a larger function of the comedy of the Zalone/Nunziante films, which Manzoli has interpreted in terms of a jarring divide between the character and a modernizing habitus:[6]

> Zalone uses the figure of a premodern social idiot, introduced into the globalized universe of the mass media, to demonstrate with affectionate irony the absolute inadequacy of the habitus through which most subjects seeks to protect themselves from the confusion into which standard distinctions of class, background, race, religion, political affiliation, gender, family role and so forth have fallen.[7]

Figure 4.1   Checco's Embarrassment about Manolo's Camp Behavior, in *Cado dalle nubi*. *Source*: Screenshot.

Checco's embarrassment in this sequence is an iteration of this same "inadequacy," an invitation to recognize and laugh (affectionately) at his outdatedness in a society in which, with globalization, homophobia ought to be considered absurd. The ironic, camp behavior therefore becomes a vehicle to mock the lingering homophobic attitudes of a particular social context.

The ironic criticism of homophobia in Italian social norms is a common motif in a number of mainstream films released over the last decade. One of the more pronounced and developed examples is *Perfetti sconosciuti*, winner of the David di Donatello for "Best Film" and "Best Screenplay." The film narrates the dinner party of a group of forty-something friends, where an innocent game of cellphone transparency (the characters have to read aloud any text messages that arrive during dinner, and respond to any calls on speaker-phone) descends into a series of dramatic revelations, among which the homosexuality of one character.

The coming out sequence in *Perfetti sconosciuti* is nonetheless built into a layered criticism of Italian society, which in part takes aim at the contradictory presence of homophobia among the liberal bourgeois. The film has two key sequences that develop this critique. In the first, gay character Peppe (Giuseppe Battiston)—the only attendee who came alone—reluctantly accepts to swap his identical iPhone with Lele (Valeria Mastandrea), present with his wife Carlotta (Anna Foglietta) but expecting an incriminating message from his (secret) online girlfriend. Shortly after, messages from Peppe's (also secret) boyfriend trigger the collective misidentification of Lele as gay. The revelation escalates, the group are shocked, and Lele scrambles to defend himself to Carlotta: he simulates anal sex, and asks, "Can you really see me like this?" The camera focuses on Peppe's reaction (figure 4.2), and immediately he realizes his mistake, and hurriedly adds "of course, there's nothing wrong with it, it's just not my thing."[8] Cosimo, who reacts more violently to

Figure 4.2 Lele Enacts Anal Sex but the Camera Focuses on Peppe, in *Perfetti sconosciuti*. *Source*: Screenshot.

the revelation, scrambles unconvincingly to place blame in his best friend's lack of transparency ("we've been friends since we were kids, don't you want to tell me who you are?"), while statements like "we slept in the same bed, we took showers together"[9] betray a more irrational, corporeal gay panic.

The mobilization of the gay character as a vehicle for this critique is made explicit in a second relevant sequence. Following a series of increasingly dramatic disclosures that culminate in further homophobic accusations from Lele's wife, Peppe reveals that he is the true recipient of Lucio's messages. When he tries to explain the reasons for the concealed truth, Lele interrupts in a revealing piece of dialogue:

Peppe: Why didn't I tell you sooner? Because I didn't know. Then when I worked it out . . .
Lele: Then when he worked it out, I'll tell you why he didn't tell us. I've been gay for two hours and that was enough. We're all modern here, right? We all want a gay friend. Well, now we have one too. And I guess we took it pretty well.[10]

This declaration therefore temporarily establishes a redemptive mea culpa for the straight character, quickly forgetting the fact that he, too, had departed from a space of homophobia. Lele's previous violence is elided, and he is provided redemption *through* a temporary (and therefore safe) queer positionality, moreover giving him priority within the narrative and establishing him as the symbolic, heterosexual "savior" of the queer.

The sequence does culminate in an ethical lesson from Peppe. He dismisses the others, telling them he is unwilling to introduce them to his boyfriend: "Because tonight you're the ones who came out. Not me. I won't let you meet him. Not because I'm afraid of your little jokes, but because any weird looks would make him suffer. And I don't want him to suffer, I want to protect him, because if you love someone you protect them, from everything."[11] It is certainly important and powerful for the queer character to articulate this moral judgment. However, his point is very much tied to the heteronormative experience rather than Peppe's own, queer, subjecthood: first, the space for his voice relies on Lele's own declarations taking precedence; second, the criticism is aimed at the universal experience of love, where anyone ought to know how to behave, gay or straight.

As these examples have shown, *Perfetti sconosciuti* and *Cado dalle nubi* demonstrate how queer characters serve a critique of homophobia in Italian society today, yet that this is often much more reliant on speaking to (and ultimately safeguarding) a heteronormative experience than a queer one. This tendency to tie homophobic attitudes to the shortcomings of contemporary Italian society in a globalized world is in fact connected to a series of broader cultural anxieties about the shifting status of Italian identity.

INTERCONNECTED PHOBIAS

As O'Leary has illustrated, representations of gay panic in the massively popular *cinepanettone* films[12] can be interpreted less as homophobic than as criticism of mainstream masculinity. Using the examples of muscular, black, gay men and Brazilian transvestites, and their interactions with straight men, he argues that stereotypes and the identification of these people as abject actually serve to laugh at straight, white, Italian men, who in turn are shamed for their inability to adapt appropriately to a new, multicultural society.[13] This kind of patriarchal masculinity is repeatedly the object of mockery in the comedies studied here, too, in contrast with the queer characters and in relation to other cultural anxieties.

One common scenario in which this arises is through relationships between lesbians and straight men. In *Tutta colpa di Freud*, for instance, when repeated heartbreak with women inspires Sara (Anna Foglietta) to search for a boyfriend, this leads to a handful of catastrophic dates. In the meeting with Roberto (Edoardo Leo), the film detaches and ridicules straight dating norms, by projecting male stereotypes onto Sara: for example, on arrival they both chivalrously hold out their chairs for the other, and she unthinkingly takes the wine list, even though the waiter offers it to Roberto. Discussing exes, and maintaining another straight-male stereotype, fear of commitment, she furthers the chaos when fumbling her attempts to pretend she was a man: "He was desperate to get pregnant."[14] While the humor emerges through the misunderstandings of both characters, exaggerated via a series of medium close-ups of embarrassed reactions and Sara's voice-over, there is also an important differentiation to be made here. We laugh with Sara because she parodies the peculiarities of common, normative behavior; we laugh at Roberto because he is completely unable to grasp that other situations might exist, that her ex could be a woman (figure 4.3).

Figure 4.3 Sara's Embarrassment and Roberto's Naive Incomprehension, in *Tutta colpa di Freud*. *Source*: Screenshot.

The 2010 comedy *Maschi contro femmine* plays with a similar motif. One of the film's many vignettes focuses on Marta (Chiara Francini) and Andrea (Nicolas Vaporidis), young flat-mates who compete for the affections of Francesca (Sarah Felberbaum). Here, too, Marta is represented through recognizable straight-male stereotypes, and her embodiment of a kind of *gallismo* provides the impetus to laugh at it. Again, it is Andrea rather than Marta who is the subject of lighthearted mockery. Though Francesca ultimately chooses Andrea, during their competition Marta is repeatedly depicted as more naturally capable and competent: engaging and sure of herself, unashamed to strip naked, able to ride horses. When contrasted to Andrea's shyness and shortcomings, these serve to make fun of the masculine norms that he struggles, unnecessarily, to enact.

In the alternative configuration—that is, relationships between gay men and straight women—it is once again traditional masculinity which bears the brunt of the humor, as in *Scusate se esisto*. As Hipkins has argued, the film deconstructs the tenets of "latin lover" masculinity, which are undermined as the film constructs its strong female lead, Serena (Paola Cortellesi).[15] This is further achieved in her connection with the gay character Francesco (Raoul Bova). In a revision of sexualized male gazes, the film "objectifies" Francesco from the perspective of Serena, building (empathetic) humor around her incomprehension of the futility of her crush on Francesco, even though she is an extremely intelligent and capable architect. This is further underlined through music, too, in a series of inter-referential sequences, from his first appearance, in an ironic slow-motion pan over a cover of Nina Simone's "Feeling Good," and a foot rub to "Unchained Melody" (lambasting *Ghost*), to Francesco's homoerotic performance to Blondie's "Call me," in a gay bar, when the coin finally drops. The film's main social comment, however, is on the lack of opportunities for young people and women in Italy, as embodied in the deep-rooted misogyny of Ripamonti (Ennio Fantastichini), Serena's future boss. The film presents a kind of resolution to this only when the heterosexual woman and the gay man work together (his body, her skills), illustrating the strength of unity among the victims of patriarchal masculinity.

While these films create considered negotiations of gender in relation to the nonnormative sexualities of such characters, the same cannot be said of class, race, or age. Though only implicitly and contextually, there are several instances of working-class characters that are always heterosexual and, more often than not, more explicitly homophobic than other, bourgeois characters (such as Cosimo in *Perfetti sconosciuti*). Similarly, these films rarely thematize race in relation to lesbian, gay, and bisexual characters in any concrete way. Italy's ever more relevant nonwhite communities are little considered in these films, unless implicitly in the depiction of racism, alongside nonwhite, straight characters.

A relevant example that intersects these tendencies is another Cortellesi and Bova vehicle, *Nessuno mi può giudicare* (2011). The romantic comedy focuses on Alice (Cortellesi), a bourgeois woman forced to reconstruct her life as an escort in a working-class, multicultural suburb of Rome, following the death of her wealthy husband. One of the (more offensive) supporting characters, the porter Lionello (Rocco Papaleo), is characterized as an unmitigated racist and homophobe. In one scene, he approaches one of the film's gay characters to ask how "you inverts" recognize one another, exclaiming then how much easier it is than for "us normals," who must wine and dine a woman, and so forth.[16] Denis' (Massimiliano Delgado) reaction provides unusually explicit account of gay sex ("I grab him, take him to a dark room, do him and don't even look at his face") that seemingly reveals his indifference, again signaling Lionello's "backwardness" as essentially harmless and laughable.

This anti-prejudice humor is rooted in a kind of tolerant average-ness, clear from the introduction of Papaleo's character by the narrator:

> *Narrator:* Frustace, Lionello, from seven generations of doormen. On these occasions he has three go-to statements, repeated in the same order for the past twenty years.
> *Lionello:* They come to Italy and think they can act like our bosses!
> *Narrator:* This is the first. The second is more considered.
> *Lionello:* Do they think they're in their own country, and can do whatever they want?
> *Narrator:* And with the third he'd win the elections.
> *Lionello:* I'd kick them out by the backside![17]

The dialogue and its accompanying visual and aural humor (Alice's embarrassed reaction, covering her child's ears, the non-diegetic applause after Lionello's third "go-to" declaration, Lionello's magisterial pose) attempt to dislocate the actual racism, and make fun of it. This is reliant on the off-screen narrator (Valerio Mastandrea), whose ironic interjections attempt to make the scene humorous and satirical, but ultimately never challenge the content of Lionello's words: it is laughed off. In fact, as a kind of irony that confirms this, in his final scenes the character (inexplicably) ends up in a romance with a black woman, and his adult son comes out as gay. Surrounding queers and people of color therefore serve to help make fun of his outdated attitudes, in an unthreatening and entirely unchallenging way.

GEOGRAPHIES OF PREJUDICE

As in a few instances mentioned above, in *Una piccola impresa meridionale* the lesbian characters Rosa Maria (Claudia Potenza) and Valbona (Sarah

Felberbaum) function, in part, to make fun of Rosa Maria's ex-husband Arturo (Riccardo Scamarcio). His masculinity is repeatedly dented, not only by the revelation of his *corna* (even the children of the local town chant "cornuto"), but, worse still, that his wife left him for a woman. Patriarchal homophobia and misogyny are spatialized, very insistently located in Puglia as a stand-in for the "backward" Italian south—the same thing occurs in *Cado dalle nubi* as well as Ozpetek's *Mine vaganti* (2010); in *Nessuno mi può giudicare* prejudice is located in Roman periphery. Ultimately the "piccola impresa" of the title creates a safe space for a group of social outcasts: a defrocked priest, a cuckolded man, a retired sex worker, precarious construction workers including a single father, and a lesbian couple. This is made most explicit for the latter, who are married at this hotel in a rebellious and symbolic act led by the ex-priest. However, when the invited guests all leave in resentment of the "sacrilegious" affair, it is clear that the safety of this liberal haven is limited.

These films have in common a tendency to contrast parts of the South to specific other cities, where queer people can exist more freely: Rome in *Mine vaganti*, Milan in *Cado dalle nubi*, even Bari in *Io che amo solo te*. There is evidently some irony in this regional prejudice about a regional prejudice: by presenting the South in this way, the films risk producing a kind of local scapegoat for a deeply rooted, nationwide problem.[18]

The tendency to depict the South as a space of heightened homophobic prejudice recurs across a few films, which, like *Una piccola impresa meridionale*, contrast the region with an idealization of equal, normative marriage. In the 2015 rom-com *Io che amo solo te*, the protagonist's brother Orlando (Eugenio Franceschini) is caught having sex in the bathroom by his own father, and subsequently comes out in an impassioned best man's speech:

> Today is a very sad day for me, because I'll maybe never have a day like it. Because I'm gay. Yes, dad, I'm gay. And you know, gays cannot have certain things. And you'll say "ooh, how dramatic, being gay in Puglia today," and you're right. But if someone is afraid to tell their father, their brother, well that is a drama. Sorry, I forgot—here's to the bride and groom.[19]

The speech therefore has a series of functions: it's an extremely emotional climax in the film—many of the characters are in tears, the music is similarly impassioned. This gives much weight to the message. Orlando's words offer a complex idea of homophobia where, on the one hand, it would be expected no longer to be an issue "today," but concretely it still is, in terms of rights, but also family relationships. He also spatializes homophobia to Puglia, and presents an implicit, utopian alternative in an accepting family, and the possibility to have his own wedding day. Thus, the film ties homophobia into its macro narrative about the truth of love. In the words of one reviewer, "This is the only merit of the film: the invitation to narrate yourself, without the fear of how others might react, thinking only of the true aim of our journey, the happiness that nobody can deny"[20]—a sentiment in fact repeated to Orlando by his father Don Mimì (Michele Placido) at the end of the film: "I'm happy, honestly, because you're trying to be what you really are."[21]

Referring to a controversial TV film *Il padre delle spose*, screened on RaiUno in 2006 and also set in Puglia, Dines and Rigoletto note a Puglia that appears forward-thinking and liberal, having shaken off its image of backwardness thanks to the guidance of then president of the region Nichi Vendola and reforms to the regional government.[22] Puglia evidently recurs very commonly in these films: from *Cado dalle nubi* to *Io che amo solo te* and *Una piccola impresa meridionale*. In all three, though we have some acceptance of—normalized—queer people (Checco, Don Mimì, and Rosa Maria's brother openly accept their gay relatives), this remains limited: in particular the mothers of Alfredo, Orlando, and Rosa Maria are visibly shaken and do not find clear peace by the film's end. In *Una piccola impresa*, there is no clear sense of resolution after the negative reaction to the wedding. As such, it is possible to speculate that these films represent a kind of "backlash" to the idea of a liberalized Puglia, where, by now, full acceptance is to be expected; but reality has proven the process is slow and by no means complete.

Dines and Rigoletto moreover illustrate how foreign countries are invoked as counter-points to Italy (they refer to Zapatero's Spain, where gay marriage had already been legalized). As the authors illustrate, the comparison with international countries makes explicit the anxieties in *Il padre delle spose*, both the liberal "desire for reform" and the conservative "threat" to Italy's traditions.[23] In the more recent mainstream comedies released after *Il padre dello sposo*, this element has remained consistent. In *Puoi baciare lo sposo* (2018) Antonio (Cristiano Caccamo) and Paolo (Salvatore Esposito) live an openly gay life in the liberal city of Berlin; *Tutta colpa di Freud* begins with Sara returning to Italy from New York City, where she had lived openly as a lesbian; in *Come non detto* (2012), the closeted Mattia (Josafat Vagni) has an openly gay, Spanish boyfriend Eduard (José Dammert) who lives in his home country, where the couple plan to go and live together. In the same way, therefore, the films make explicit the "Italianness" of the same homophobia that they ridicule, therefore introducing a national element to their lighthearted social criticism.

It is curious, as such, to compare Italian filmmaking to a few other instances of global queer cinema. Working specifically on popular cinema, Rosalind Galt and Karl Schoonover have illustrated how certain cinematic traditions mobilize nationalist resistances to globalization via homophobic representation. In the Nollywood "homo cycle" in particular, as they demonstrate, blatant homophobia works to fight off "a Gay International as an agent of globalization and exemplar of the foreign forces that threaten the integrity of Nigeria's autonomous national culture."[24] In Italy, conversely, "Gay International" is present, yet is almost unanimously a force that inspires embarrassment about backwardness, and the need to make playful fun of those traditional identity models that are struggling to modernize.

"E SE FOSSE BISEX?": QUEER POTENTIAL

As the analysis so far has sought to illustrate, these films contain some interesting critiques of contemporary Italian society and identity that tie homophobia to other prejudices in order to ridicule the country's backwardness. Queer characters therefore serve as tools to this broader purpose, and in this process are normalized; more authentic or radical images of queer subjectivity are denied. Nevertheless, as this final section will try to illustrate, these products are simultaneously "open" texts, which can be interpreted in contrasting and even contradictory ways according to the experience and expectations of the spectator. Following the representation schema of *Maschi contro femmine*, for instance, Marta is legible as a male stand-in, where the adoption of stereotypically straight, masculine behavior signals a simplistic, binary notion of lesbian identity. This makes this plotline a simple variation of a straightforward homosocial story, a "bromance:" at the end of the film, when Francesca ultimately picks Andrea, he decides that it is not worth risking his friendship with Marta, and the pair return to a norm of (separate) competitive macho conquests. Nevertheless, the film *also* provides a liberal criticism of patriarchal masculinity and heteronormativity, in how we laugh at Andrea's failings, and this moreover accompanies repeated, explicit vocalizations of lesbian desire by Marta. The film also verbalizes the potential for characters to be bisexual or fluid (Marta and Andrea's third flat-mate wonders about Francesca "e se fosse bisex?" though the question is never answered). By eschewing simple definitions in favor of anti-normative sex and relationships, the film can therefore be seen as nuancing its image of desire and allowing its queer characters to appropriate it. And, not by chance, the film's comedy of errors is unveiled at the gay pride in Rome, where Francesca's sexual orientation is contemplated. This subplot therefore centralizes gay pride (literally) and connects the manifestation to a freedom and fluidity of sexuality.

This fluidity of interpretation creates the potential for queer readings, even in this perhaps unlikely space of popular comedies. The crux of this question remains something I hinted at in opening this chapter: what negotiations must be made to allow queer to enter the mainstream?

As Galt and Schoonover write,

> There is a difficulty in thinking about the popular as a modality of queer cinema, because queerness is often seen to confound the category of the popular. [. . .] As a category and practice, queerness defines itself against cultural normalcy: by rejecting the status quo, it seems like an awkward fit with the dominant forms of Bollywood, Hollywood, or Nollywood.[25]

This precarity is a commonplace in queer theory, too. As Heather Love observes, in her study of queer historiography *Feeling Backwards*, queer identity in the past is chained to negative emotions and experiences of violence, to "the corpses of gender and sexual deviants."[26] As Love illustrates, tying ourselves to these "earlier forms of feeling" is vital, both to excavate queer experiences of the past and to identify the forms of inequality today. Nevertheless, in her view, this is incompatible with advances in rights and the mainstream experiences of gays and lesbians: "The invitation to join the mainstream is an invitation to jettison gay identity and its accreted historical meanings."[27]

The films that I have mentioned here represent mainstream, often homonormative identities. They depict a cultural normalcy (or an idealized normalcy) in contemporary Italy; they represent the kinds of advances of which Love is critical, such as gay marriage; their lesbian, gay, and bisexual characters are universally white, bourgeois, cis-gender and they exist in homosocial relationships. Previous scholarship demonstrates the possibility to interpret them queerly nonetheless—with no intention on my behalf of somehow redeeming these representations—in two ways. First, there is always the subversive potential for queer transcodings of texts, as the work of Alexander Doty, Richard Dyer, and Vito Russo has most famously illustrated.[28] Nowhere is this better put to use than in popular culture, and especially filmmaking. Second, these films can be aligned with a tendency of queer film identified by Schoonover and Galt, that is, "a queer popular," that is, mainstream cinema that represents, even problematically, queer people. Nevertheless, as they illustrate, this mode "draws on the forms, modes of production and address, and sensual pleasures of popular genres to produce queer counter publics within the circulatory systems of world cinema."[29]

Despite these important examples of queer readings, the idea of interpreting contemporary Italian popular comedies as "queer" is still the cause for some hesitation. This is for a series of reasons: first, Italian popular cinema since the 1970s and, particularly, 1980s has (like Italian television) established a reputation as an exploitative medium that sacrifices politically correct representation for financial profit.[30] Thus, the chance to identify any radical or interesting identity models feels particularly problematic. Second, queer appropriation has a very rich history in its application to cinema of the past: gay culture is very firmly rooted in classical Hollywood—suffice it to think of divas like Bette Davis, Marlene Dietrich, and Judy Garland.[31] Though this has evolved and updated, the major works of transcoding have nevertheless continued to focus on past cinemas—in a highly productive way, in order to demonstrate not only that LGBT people "do exist," but that we always have done.[32] As Doty observes, the political project of transcoding is both an act of resistance but also something that is deeply nostalgic and romantic, rooted to Western representations of childhood (also in view of the own critic's experience).[33] However, this perhaps leads to a critical hesitation to queer readings of today's cinema. Third, the contemporary comedy in particular is rarely the object of such interpretative work, which has typically found more fruitful objects of study in genres like the melodrama or horror film.[34]

Another motive for this third—the lack of subversive queer readings in (contemporary mainstream) comedies—is perhaps the uncomfortable legacy of lesbian and gay stereotypes in this genre, in Italy and internationally. In fact, this problematic tradition can help to illustrate one example of a queer reading of these films, in the aforementioned dinner sequence in *Cado dalle nubi*. Manolo enacts revenge on Alfredo, who had closeted his boyfriend, camping up his behavior at the dinner with Checco. In view of the history of camp that made fun of homosexuality (from comedies like the British *Carry On* series to the queer men in the Italian *polizieschi* filone, such as *Delitto al blu gay*),[35] this sequence can assume an enriched meaning. In *Cado dalle nubi*, the gay character reappropriates and manipulates a visual agenda that was once used violently, in order to take advantage of the situation and mock Checco for his homophobia.

This interpretation therefore makes Manolo an interesting, subversive agent within the narrative of the film;[36] a relevant shift in agency, but one that will likely go unperceived to the majority of spectators. Of course, to paraphrase Doty, who cares? As the critic notes, any perceived insubstantiality of this kind of interpretation does nothing to undermine its relevance. After all, queerness is always already present in mass cultural texts, and these textual readings only illustrate and help to dismantle a "closet of connotation" that exists only as long as we (mistakenly) "keep thinking within conventional, heterocentrist paradigms."[37] The potential "queer discourses" of these mainstream films exist in a complex and varied relationship with the intentions and representations of the text itself, working both textually but also relying on external experiences, at times in blatant contradiction of the ideological agenda of the film. Let us consider some examples.

First and foremost, we can review those humorous functions that criticize, implicitly or explicitly, patriarchal masculinity and heteronormative behavior. Though the queer characters are instrumentalized to this aim, this does not preclude our capacity to enjoy the humor. In fact, queer spectators are perhaps quicker off the mark to identify queer characters, certainly before the straight characters (and perhaps straight spectators) do. And this can occur even when the films include gender red herrings (the references to Rosa Maria's lover in the masculine in *Una piccola impresa meridionale*; Francesco's reference to his wife in *Scusate se esisto*; the rechristening of Lucio as Lucilla in *Perfetti sconosciuti*, Orlando's insistence that his "girlfriend" Daniela exists, and that "we love each other to death" in *Io che amo solo te*). Queer subject positions actually enable us to centralize the same identification processes within the film's critiques of the habitus, often in intersectional ways. For example, transvestitism is central to *Scusate se esisto*'s denunciation of misogyny (Serena Bruno disguises herself as Bruno Serena in order to win an architecture competition, Francesco eventually plays the role). In *Una piccola impresa meridionale*, it is all of the other characters who have to closet and uncloset themselves at various stages, as priests, escorts, shamed mothers, or cuckolded men, while the lesbian couple remain steadfastly open. And in *Tutta colpa di Freud*, the playful re-closeting of the lesbian sister serves as an ironic counterpoint to the falsehoods of the other sisters' relationships.

A useful example of queer readings that emerge alongside the text thanks to a larger queer experience is Manolo's appropriation of camp, which is essentially textual but *also* relies on a previous queer experience. *Cado dalle nubi* in fact contains several more personal and emotional instances of queer complicity too. As an example, the film treats Alfredo's difficulty in coming out to his family with bittersweet humor throughout. When his parents visit, leading to a girlfriend posing as his fiancée (a similar motif occurs in *Io che amo solo te*), there are several visual and verbal gags that re-signal the closeting to the viewer. One point is his mother's compliment to the kitchen, saying "You can feel a woman's touch."[38] This is followed by a quick cut to Alfredo who forces a laugh before casting down his eyes, melancholically (figure 4.4). In simple narrative terms, it is a step toward Alfredo eventually coming out; from the perspective of a queer viewer, this gaze can just as easily be read as the frustration, humiliation, and above all sadness that accompanies such quotidian moments of an imposed closet. The film therefore perhaps unknowingly captures some of the real complexity of queer life in heteronormative Italian society.

As a final example, and a queer discourse that is more dislocated from the text's own intentions, let us return instead to *Perfetti sconosciuti*. The film is ambiguous about the function of secrets, where some—such as Lele and Carlotta's online flirtations—appear harmless, at best they seem to maintain an equilibrium for the couple. And while its denunciation of homophobia is unwavering, the same ambiguity is applied to the question of whether or not Peppe ultimately *should* come out to his friends.

Peppe is the only character to leave the party alone. As in Alfredo's reaction to his mother's words, his solitude at the end of the film enacts a poignant

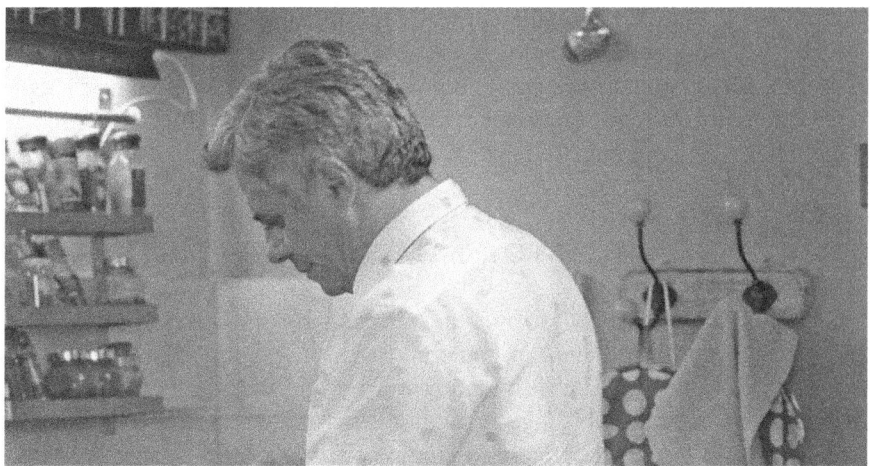

Figure 4.4 Alfredo's Melancholic Reaction to His Closeting, in *Cado dalle nubi*. *Source*: Screenshot.

representation of shame and marginalization—the same negative feelings that Love underscores as characteristic of the queer experience in *Feeling Backwards*, again familiar to many queer spectators. In the film's very final sequence, Peppe pulls his car over alongside a bridge and gets out, perhaps allowing a flicker of concern from the viewer for what he might be considering, over somber music on the soundtrack. This sentiment quickly vanishes when he starts doing jumping jacks, as guided by his spontaneous exercise app, in a returning joke. The melancholy of his queer position is therefore undermined by humor, and more relevantly still by an act of self-care.

This can be interpreted actually quite radically, as Peppe's choice to focus on himself and refuse the shame and homophobia that belongs to his "closeting" friends and not to him. It is possible, in other words, to suppose that Peppe is *choosing* not to come out to his friends, and to some extent freed by that choice to live a more content life, without the oppression of his friends; indeed that the need for action is *theirs*, not his. This finds affirmation in his earlier speech: "Tonight you're the ones who came out;" in the same way, he also actively chooses not to present Lucio to them: it is not a refusal of his own sexuality, but a refusal of their violence, even a refusal to present himself and Lucio as a homonormative couple, in line with the others. Of course, this appears contradictory to those of us who are well aware of the political value of coming out utterances (and its rooted history in queer cinema[39]). Nevertheless, in a time of greater visibility in Western countries, the significance of coming out has mutated, and it is possible to start to question the limits of this declaration and its Anglo-American-centric notion of gay identity. In Italy in particular, this radical questioning echoes reflections that Rigoletto raises in relation to cinema and indeed in the Italian public and private queer experience.[40] Following his observations, this potential reading could similarly help to problematize "an interpretative framework in which homosexuality should be, by default, publicly acknowledged and made visible through a confessional mode of unequivocal verbalization."[41]

POTENTIALITY

This chapter has sought to illustrate the unexpected complexity of the lesbian, gay, and bisexual characters in contemporary Italian popular comedies. As the first parts illustrate, the films present a pro-gay rights image by poking fun at those uncomfortable figures who are left behind in a fast globalizing Italy. This is often closely tied to a complex image of that "habitus," where homophobia is tied to patriarchal masculinity and sometimes racism, while gay experiences culminate in a utopian idea of marriage. It has also sought to demonstrate that the images of gay, lesbian, and bisexual people, despite their clear limitations, can be subjected to more radical interpretations that defy the mainstream audience's expectations.

This representation allows us to align this tendency in contemporary Italian filmmaking with Galt and Schoonover's notion of the "queer popular." Though the scholars emphasize this mode as something international, something which we cannot say of Italian popular cinema (again, especially comedies, which are very rarely transnational in production or circulation terms), aside from an implicit international comparison. Nevertheless, as the examples collected here seek to show, the very mainstream or popular elements of the films converge with their radical potential, which in turn, quoting Galt and Schoonover, make them "capable of articulating both the political anxieties of being queer in the world and the aspirations of a queer critique."[42]

The films have what I have repeatedly referred to as the "potential" for queer readings. The use of the term in particular seeks to emphasize both the multi-stable nature of the texts, which can be manipulated for different uses, but, to return to Doty, represent "the complex range of queerness that has been in popular culture texts and their audiences all along."[43] If anything, the activation of that potential means merely the deactivation of the assumed heteronormative praxis that define the interpretation of a film. This "potentiality" moreover raises some other interesting provocations about the form of queer spectatorship and interpretation. As the examples provided in the last section hope to illustrate, though these texts are ideologically hetero- and homonormative, there are small, perhaps unintended gestures and gazes that unlock very complex notions of queer experience. Notions that at times disavow strict labels, as in the case of Francesca, or indeed the tenets of gay rights, such as Peppe's coming out: notions that, therefore, can challenge that same normativity from within.

NOTES

1. The film fell a little short of the record box-office takings for *Avatar* (2009) in Italy—€65.3m and €65.7m, respectively—though Nunziante's film sold 9.3 million tickets, over 1.8 million tickets more than Cameron's film. Data taken from Cinecittà Luce (http://news.cinecitta.com/IT/it-it/cms/42/box-office.aspx) and the Lumière Audiovisual Observatory (http://lumierepro.obs.coe.int/).

2. Derek Duncan, "The Queerness of Italian Cinema," in *A Companion to Italian Cinema*, ed. Frank Burke (Chichester: John Wiley & Sons, 2017), 467–483.

3. Cf. Mauro Giori, *Homosexuality and Italian Cinema: From the Fall of Fascism to the Years of Lead* (London: Palgrave MacMillan, 2017); Vincenzo Patanè, "Breve storia del cinema italiano con tematica omosessuale," in *Lo schermo velato*, ed. Vito Russo (Milan: Baldini e Castoldi, 1999), 449–468. Anecdotally, I refer to characters that would for the most part pass the "Vito Russo" test, that is, be clearly defined as LGBT, not singularly characterized by that status, and a relevant element of the plot. Cf: https://www.glaad.org/sri/2014/vitorusso, accessed September 28, 2018.

4. Cf. Rosemary Hennessy, *Profit and Pleasure. Sexual Identities in Late Capitalism*, 2nd edition (New York; London: Routledge, 2018); Donald Morton, ed., *The Material Queer: A LesBiGay Cultural Studies Reader* (Boulder: Westview, 1996); Lisa Duggan, *The Twilight of Equality? Neoliberalism, Cultural Politics and the Attack on Democracy* (Boston: Beacon Press, 2003).

5. My understanding of the term is based on the critical notion, whereby a sexual identity is a space of resistance against normativity. Cf. Judith Butler, "Critically Queer," *GLQ: Gay and Lesbian Quarterly* 1 (1993): 17–32.

6. Pierre Bourdieu, *The Logic of Practice* (Cambridge: Policy Press, 1992).

7. "Zalone ha utilizzato questa figura di idiota sociale premoderno, calato nell'universo globalizzato dai mass-media, per dimostrare con affettuosa ironia l'assoluta inadeguatezza degli habitus con cui la maggior parte dei soggetti cerca di ripararsi dalla confusione nella quale sono ormai cadute le consuete distinzioni di classe, ceto, razza, religione, schieramento politico, gender, ruolo familiare, cultura, e così via" [all translations are my own]. Giacomo Manzoli, "Habitus," in *Lessico del cinema italiano: forme di rappresentazione e forme di vita*, ed. Roberto De Gaetano, vol. II (Milan: Mimesis, 2015), 7–68, (67). Cf. Gianni Canova, *Quo chi? Di cosa ridiamo quando ridiamo di Checco Zalone* (Vimercate: Sagoma Editore, 2016).

8. "Mi ci vedi così?," "che poi non ci sarebbe niente di male...solo che non sono i miei gusti."

9. "Siamo amici da quando siamo ragazzini, me lo vuoi dire chi sei?," "abbiamo dormito insieme, abbiamo fatto la doccia insieme."

10. Peppe: Perché non ve l'ho detto prima? Perché prima non lo sapevo. Poi quando l'ho capito . . .

Lele: Poi quando l'ha capito ve lo dico io perché non ce l'ha detto. Perché sono stato frocio due ore e m'è bastato. Qui siamo tutti moderni, no? Ci piace a tutti avere un amico frocio. Ecco adesso ce l'abbiamo pure noi. Mi sembra pure che l'abbiamo presa abbastanza bene."

11. "Perché questa sera avete fatto voi outing. Non io. Non ve lo farò conoscere. Non perché abbia paura delle vostre battutine [. . .] ma perché so che al primo sguardo strano ci starebbe male. E io non voglio che lui stia male, lo voglio proteggere, perché se vuoi bene a una persona la proteggi, da tutto."

12. The term "cinepanettone" or "Christmas cake film" is used to refer to a series of popular, vulgar comedies made in Italy predominantly between the 1990s and especially 2000s. Released every Christmas, the films repeatedly obtained extremely high box-office takings, despite being critically derided year on year.

13. Alan O'Leary, *Fenomenologia del cinepanettone* (Soveria Manelli: Rubbettino, 2013), 58–63.

14. "Lui smaniava della voglia di rimanere incinta . . . incinto." The wordplay, in Italian, relies on Marta changing the gendered adjective for the word "pregnant" (incinta/incinto).

15. Danielle Hipkins, "Paola Cortellesi: Fragmenting the *Latin Lover* in Italian Romantic Comedy," *L'avventura*, special issue on "The Latin Lover," 2018, 83–98 (90–91).

16. "Voi invertiti," "Noi normali," "io me lo acchiappo, me lo porto dentro a una dark room, me lo faccio e manco lo guardo in faccia."

17. *Narrator:* Frustace Lionello. Portiere per sette generazioni. Per queste occasioni in repertorio ha tre frasi cult che ripete nello stesso ordine da vent'anni.
    Lionello: Questi vengono in Italia e pensano di fare i padroni!
    Narrator: E quest'era la prima. La seconda è più ricercata.
    Lionello: Che credono, che stanno al paese loro e possono fare quello che gli pare?
    Narrator: E con la terza vincerebbe le elezioni.
    Lionello: Io li caccerei a calci nel culo!

18. See, for instance, the report in *L'espresso* about homophobia across the country: Simone Alliva, "'Frocio, ti spacco le ossa': viaggio nel Paese dell'omofobia," *L'espresso*, February 8, 2019, online: http://espresso.repubblica.it/plus/articoli/2019/02/06/news/frocio-ti-spacco-le-ossa-viaggio-nel-paese-dell-omofobia-1.331399, accessed July 1, 2019.

19. "Oggi per me è un giorno molto triste. Perché io forse un giorno così non lo vivrò mai. Perché sono gay. Sì papà sono gay. E sai come i gay certe cose non le possono fare. E tu mi dirai 'ooh che dramma essere gay oggi in Puglia,' ed è vero. Ma se uno ha paura di dirlo a suo fratello, e a suo padre, beh quello sì che è un dramma. Scusate, dimenticavo. Viva gli sposi."

20. "Ecco l'unico pregio di questo film: l'invito a raccontare se stessi, senza avere paura di come gli altri potrebbero reagire e pensando solo all'obiettivo del nostro cammino, la felicità che nessuno ci può negare." Claudio Iannone, "Io che amo solo te: Leggerezza a secchiate," *Mondo Film*, October 16, 2015, http://www.mondofilm.it/2015/10/16/io-che-amo-solo-te-leggerezza-a-secchiate/, accessed December 27, 2018.

21. "Io sono felice, ma te lo dico col cuore, perché tu stai provando ad essere quello che sei."

22. Martin Dines and Sergio Rigoletto, "Country Cousins: Europeanness, Sexuality and Locality in Contemporary Italian Television," *Modern Italy* 17, no. 4 (2012): 479–491 (484–5).

23. Dines and Rigoletto, "Country Cousins," 484.

24. Rosalind Galt and Karl Schoonover, *Queer Cinema in the World* (Durham-London: Duke University Press, 2016), 174.

25. Galt and Schoonover, *Queer Cinema in the World*, 167; to these I would add popular Italian cinema.

26. Heather Love, *Feeling Backwards Feeling Backward: Loss and the Politics of Queer History* (Harvard University Press, 2007), 1.

27. Love, *Feeling Backwards*, 30.

28. Cf. Alexander Doty, *Making Things Perfectly Queer: Interpreting Mass Culture* (Minneapolis: Minnesota University Press, 1997) and *Flaming Classics: Queering the Film Canon* (New York: Routledge, 2000); Richard Dyer, *Now You See It: Studies on Gay and Lesbian Film* (London: Routledge, 1990); and *The Culture of Queers* (London: Routledge, 2002); Vito Russo, *The Celluloid Closet: Homosexuality in the Movies* (New York: Harper and Row, 1987).

29. Galt and Schoonover, *Queer Cinema in the World*, 170.

30. Cf. Louis Bayman and Sergio Rigoletto, eds, *Popular Italian Cinema* (Basingstoke: Palgrave Macmillan, 2013); Sergio Rigoletto, *Masculinity and Italian Cinema: Sexual Politics, Social Conflict and Male Crisis in the 1970s* (Edinburgh: Edinburgh University Press, 2014).

31. David Halperin, *How to Be Gay* (Cambridge, MA: Harvard University Press, 2012); Richard Dyer, *Heavenly Bodies: Stars and Society* (London: Routledge, 2013), in particular "Judy Garland and Gay Men," 137–191.

32. Russo, *The Celluloid Closet*, xii.

33. Doty, *Making Things Perfectly Queer*, 4; cf. also Doty's Introduction to *Flaming Classics*, 1–21, which begins with a nostalgic account of his own "investment."

34. Doty, *Making Things Perfectly Queer*, 14.

35. Cf. Patané, "Breve storia del cinema italiano con tematica omosessuale."

36. The same process occurs shortly after in the film, when, thanks to Manolo, Checco is given the chance to perform in a gay bar (he sings his infamous song, "gli uomini sessuali"). Here, too, the character's bigotry is inverted, and the gay music manager that Checco was trying to impress instead sends the offensive singer to a gathering of a thinly disguised Lega Nord, inviting him to sing about Calabrian pride. Here, too, the queer characters are not only assuming narrative agency and defining the humor, but moreover they are subverting homophobia and directing it into a political joke.

37. Doty, *Making Things Perfectly Queer*, xii.

38. "si sente la mano della femmina."

39. See Michele Aaron, ed., *New Queer Cinema: A Critical Reader* (New Brunswick, NJ: Rutgers University Press, 2004); David M. Jones and JoAnne Juett, eds, *Coming Out to the Mainstream: New Queer Cinema in the 21st Century* (Newcastle: Cambridge Scholars Publishing, 2010).

40. Sergio Rigoletto, "Against the Teleological Presumption: Notes on Queer Visibility in Contemporary Italian Film," *The Italianist* 77, no. 2 (2017): 212–227.
41. Rigoletto, "Against the Teleological Presumption," 217.
42. Galt and Schoonover, *Queer Cinema in the World*, 170.
43. Doty, *Making Things Perfectly Queer*, 16.

BIBLIOGRAPHY

Aaron, Michele, ed. *New Queer Cinema: A Critical Reader*. New Brunswick, NJ: Rutgers University Press, 2004.

Alliva, Simone. "'Frocio, ti spacco le ossa': viaggio nel Paese dell'omofobia." *L'espresso*, February 8, 2019. http://espresso.repubblica.it/plus/articoli/2019/0 2/06/news/frocio-ti-spacco-le-ossa-viaggio-nel-paese-dell-omofobia-1.331399.

Bayman, Louis and Sergio Rigoletto, eds. *Popular Italian Cinema*. Basingstoke: Palgrave Macmillan, 2013.

Bourdieu, Pierre. *The Logic of Practice*. Cambridge: Policy Press, 1992.

Butler, Judith. "Critically Queer." *GLQ: Gay and Lesbian Quarterly* 1 (1993): 17–32. https://doi.org/10.1215/10642684-1-1-17.

Canova, Gianni. *Quo chi? Di cosa ridiamo quando ridiamo di Checco Zalone*. Vimercate: Sagoma Editore, 2016.

Dines, Martin and Sergio Rigoletto. "Country Cousins: Europeanness, Sexuality and Locality in Contemporary Italian Television." *Modern Italy* 17, no. 4 (2012): 479–491.

Doty, Alexander. *Flaming Classics: Queering the Film Canon*. New York: Routledge, 2000.

———. *Making Things Perfectly Queer: Interpreting Mass Culture*. Minneapolis: Minnesota University Press, 1997.

Duggan, Lisa. *The Twilight of Equality? Neoliberalism, Cultural Politics and the Attack On Democracy*. Boston: Beacon Press, 2003.

Duncan, Derek. "The Queerness of Italian Cinema." In *A Companion to Italian Cinema*, edited by Frank Burke, 467–483. Chichester: John Wiley & Sons, 2017.

Dyer, Richard. *Heavenly Bodies: Stars and Society*. London: Routledge, 2013.

———. *Now You See It: Studies on Gay and Lesbian Film*. London: Routledge, 1990.

———. *The Culture of Queers*. London: Routledge, 2002.

Galt, Rosalind and Karl Schoonover. *Queer Cinema in the World*. Durham-London: Duke University Press, 2016.

Giori, Mauro. *Homosexuality and Italian Cinema: From the Fall of Fascism to the Years of Lead*. London: Palgrave MacMillan, 2017.

Halperin, David. *How to Be Gay*. Cambridge, MA: Harvard University Press, 2012.

Hennessy, Rosemary. *Profit and Pleasure. Sexual Identities in Late Capitalism*, 2nd edition. New York; London: Routledge, 2018.

Hipkins, Danielle. "Paola Cortellesi: Fragmenting the *Latin Lover* in Italian Romantic Comedy." *L'avventura*, special issue (2018): 83–98. http://doi.org/10.17397/90662.

Iannone, Claudio. "Io che amo solo te: Leggerezza a secchiate." *Mondo Film,* October 16, 2015. http://www.mondofilm.it/2015/10/16/io-che-amo-solo-te-leggerezza-a-secchiate/.

Jones, David M. and JoAnne C. Juett, eds. *Coming Out to the Mainstream: New Queer Cinema in the 21st Century.* Newcastle: Cambridge Scholars Publishing, 2010.

Love, Heather. *Feeling Backwards Feeling Backward: Loss and the Politics of Queer History.* Harvard University Press, 2007.

Manzoli, Giacomo. "Habitus." In *Lessico del cinema italiano: forme di rappresentazione e forme di vita,* edited by Roberto De Gaetano, vol. II, 7–68. Milan: Mimesis, 2015.

Morton, Donald, ed. *The Material Queer: A LesBiGay Cultural Studies Reader.* Boulder: Westview, 1996.

O'Leary, Alan. *Fenomenologia del cinepanettone.* Soveria Manelli: Rubbettino, 2013.

Patanè, Vincenzo. "Breve storia del cinema italiano con tematica omosessuale." In *Lo schermo velato,* edited by Vito Russo, 449–468. Milan: Baldini e Castoldi, 1999.

Rigoletto, Sergio. "Against the Teleological Presumption: Notes on Queer Visibility in Contemporary Italian Film." *The Italianist* 77, no. 2 (2017): 212–227.

———. *Masculinity and Italian Cinema: Sexual Politics, Social Conflict and Male Crisis in the 1970s.* Edinburgh: Edinburgh University Press, 2014.

Russo, Vito. *The Celluloid Closet: Homosexuality in the Movies.* New York: Harper and Row, 1987.

Chapter 5

An All Italian *Game of Thrones*
A Social Media Investigation of Maria de Filippi's Gay Male Version of the Trash, Dating Show Uomini e Donne

Luca Malici

> We joke about it, but when the housewife from a small southern town finds out that THESE FAGGOTS ARE ACTUALLY NICE it will be a real cultural revolution #tronogay.[1]

Italian mainstream television programming in 2016–2017 was hailed as "more 'rainbow' than previous seasons"[2] because, thanks in part to the newly recognized *unioni civili* (civil unions, also known as the Cirinnà Law),[3] Italian channels saw a surge of more programs with BGILQT[4] themes and characters. However, the pot at the end of the rainbow is not always filled with gold. Italian public service broadcasting (*Radiotelevisione Italiana*, or RAI) produced more progressive television in this period, such as *Stato Civile: l'amore è uguale per tutti*[5] (Civil state: love is equal for all), a docu-reality about Italian same-sex couples registering their civil unions. The program won the Italian Association of Homosexuals' Parents and Relatives (AGEDO) award as well as the Italian Diversity Media Award, yet it was also harshly criticized by right-wing politicians for its low ratings and for the change in its time of broadcast from a late-night slot to prime time.[6] Concurrently, there have also been instances of resistance toward representing more explicit examples of sexual dissidence[7] on RAI channels during peak viewing times in this period, similar to what had already happened in 2008 to the broadcasting of Ang Lee's *Brokeback Mountain*.[8] This time around, too, RAI preemptively censored gay male kisses and gay sex scenes during the prime-time airing of the US series *How to Get Away with Murder* which raised complaints and remonstrations from Italian viewers and even by some of the original actors and the series' scriptwriter on Twitter.[9]

Observing these contrasting examples, it appears as if not much has changed since my research findings on the representation, circulation, and reception of sexual dissidence on Italian mainstream television from 1990 to 2012.[10] My previous work on BGILQT and heterosexually identified samples of Italian viewers had gestured toward their willingness to watch more Italian, true-to-life, varied representation of sexual dissidence on mainstream television without censorship and at more accessible times of the day. To some degree, the popular, daytime program analyzed in this chapter appeared to have moved toward these trajectories. Despite this, I suggest that Italian BGILQT mainstream televisibility remains a site of discursive struggle in the country. My contribution is a social media investigation of the gay male version of *Uomini e Donne* (men and women, 1996 to present), aired daily on the commercial channel Canale5, part of Silvio Berlusconi's family mass media company, Mediaset. The program is a blend of TV genres at the intersection of dating, reality, and talk shows—comparable to the US TV series *The Bachelor*[11]—created and hosted by the very influential Italian presenter Maria De Filippi.[12] In this taped-for-broadcast program, main participants sit on a throne and wait for interested suitors, all recruited through castings. In this chapter, I scrutinize in particular the September–December 2016 season, in which same-sex participants were allowed on the program for the first time.

As in the afore-cited tweet, several social media users, bloggers, and journalists welcomed this event enthusiastically, considering it nothing less than a "cultural revolution"[13] in Italy. I am a bit skeptical about this, as the *trono gay* (gay throne) served as yet another normalizing, desexualized representation of exclusively gay male identities. I maintain that the real mediatic novelties—rather than revolution—of the trono gay in Italy were that openly gay male participants, and consequent discourses surrounding male homosexuality, have been regularly included in a very popular, afternoon program,[14] which commentators have often considered "the temple of Italian trash TV."[15] Moreover, the show appealed to a vast assumed viewership often perceived as less educated, coming from the South, of a certain age, and who must be educated about sexual diversity through the program (as per the case of the above-mentioned housewife).

Before moving any further, I would like to express my feeling of being "off-topic" presenting this research within this queer collection. In my research, the word "queer" appeared only twice, and the program was not at the forefront of Italian BGILQT associations' debates. Furthermore, the TV program analyzed here does not seem to be an instance of "queer TV" able to challenge heteronormativity at large[16] but is rather an example of homonormative portrayal: neoliberal, domesticated representations of sexual dissidence, which do not help to trouble viewers' expectations but instead eclipse the possibilities for other kinds of sexual subjects and relationships.[17] Besides, *Uomini e donne* is popular, mainstream, and considered "trash," and these adjectives are not often associated with queer inquiries and audience research.[18] Despite this, I find the trash concept theoretically captivating. Research in other fields—namely cinema, media, and feminist studies—have ascribed academic significance to trash artifacts and pleasures.[19] In my study, I draw on the claims of Alan O'Leary, who—while discussing the tacit distinction between "us" critics, academics, and persons of tastes and "they," the "duped," passive public—maintains that, although it would be easy to dismiss the taste of this public and to denounce the appeal of "trash," "we can try to explain a phenomenon in all its complexity, not exempting ourselves from its pleasures."[20]

More direct and available representations of dissident sexualities on daytime trash TV, even within such a normalizing and hegemonic platform, could potentially speak to specific sections of the viewing public of mainstream Italian television which would not necessarily engage with such representations otherwise. For example, Michele Pananari describing *Uomini e donne's* "estetica tamarrissima e coatta" (very trash and lout aesthetic) maintains that for viewers "devianza ed ex marginalità vengono elette a paradigma e si fanno [. . .] normalità" (deviancy and ex-marginality become a model and, hence, normality).[21] Crucially, the potential for enhancing queer visibility does not only rest with the trash televisual text itself but also within the array of discourses, debates, and the social commentary around it. After all, *Uomini e donne* is a popular convergent text[22] and Stefania Carini even maintains that it is an "origin text"[23] from which flows of information, materials, and narratives constantly depart and develop in a plurality of on- and offline media platforms (e.g., magazines, other TV programs, websites, social media), propagating, extending, and altering the content and messages of the program (e.g., from gossips to fan-generated conversations, art, and videos).

To understand and scrutinize this program and phenomenon, I further examine the concept of trash, the show and its audience, and move to an analysis of the public reaction to the announcement of a trono gay and its subsequent broadcasting. Methodologically, I have watched all the episodes of the show. In addition to academic scholarship, I have examined information related to the program in the press, tabloids, blogs,[24] and social media; I decided to analyze in detail all the tweets posted to Twitter—nearly 3,000 in all—which have included the thematic hashtag #tronogay (from its original appearance in 2013 until July 30, 2017). To do this, I have followed a qualitative methodology, using the grounded theory which looks at the Twitter data in search of possible discourses and relations without imposing predetermined categories of codification.[25] Despite acknowledging methodological limitations of research on Twitter,[26] results have highlighted several significant themes, such as the presence of considerable normalizing and assimilationist discourses around the trono gay. There is a greater presence of homophobia on specific social media platforms which remains, however, relatively small when compared to the general enthusiasm and engagement of many users. Discourses on the need to educate the public about sexual diversity, BGILQT civil rights, questions of public and private queer visibility, and the protection of minors from the danger of "trashy" programs with BGILQT themes are among the heterogeneous nodes discovered in the granular data analyzed in this chapter.

TRASH

According to the Oxford English Dictionary, together with its denotative meanings of waste material and refuse, the Anglophone term "trash" can generally refer to "cultural items, ideas, or objects of poor quality" as well as "a person or people regarded as being of very low social standing."[27] In Italian, this Anglicism caught on around 1986, coinciding with the popularization of the first nationalized commercial broadcasting channels, and the term started to refer to tacky, distasteful mass media products.[28] Julie Manga argues that trash TV is akin to other historical forms of lowbrow entertainment with a mass appeal which engaged lower classes and marginalized groups but have been routinely criticized by intellectuals and the dominant class of their time.[29] In fact, trash is inevitably tied to classed,[30] localized, and racialized discourses. For example, Laura Grindstaff argues that the US phrase "white trash" suggests that "color, poverty, and degenerate lifestyles go together so naturally that, when white folks behave this way, their whiteness needs to be named."[31] Similarly, with reference to the old continent, "Eurotrash" has also been coined and used to affirm, often derogatorily or jokingly, a US and UK supremacy of taste over other continental EU countries considered more exotic.[32] By invoking the term "trash" there are clear issues of cultural politics at stake that determine which form is regarded to be "legitimate."[33]

All these discussions resonate strongly with my understandings of queer and normativity. Quintessentially, trash can bring about an array of distinctions relevant to most queer revindications. It is perhaps no accident that the term was also recently reclaimed by the Anglo-Italian queer/feminist artistic group, CUNTemporary, in the title of their fundraiser nights, Deep Trash Italia.[34] Tommaso Labranca, theorist of Italian trash, maintains that trashiness transcends any form of critique or self-awareness, otherwise it develops into *kitsch*—when trash is refuted—or camp—when it is willingly accepted and embraced.[35] Labranca also sees a theoretical interconnection between trash and "trans(sexual)" concepts, as both appear to celebrate different forms of "failed emulation" which ultimately overcome canons and conventions.[36]

I agree with Milena Stanoeva who says that historically, trash TV "has often served as stepping-stones for women, people of color and sexual minorities seeking a spot in the media and public discourse."[37] Even nowadays, in some Middle Eastern countries, trash reality TV and talk shows can represent a platform for potential subversion with respect to sensitive subject matter.[38] BGILQT communities and trash TV have historically had a mutually beneficial and exploitative relationship.[39] Bringing intimate issues into the public sphere of daytime television has helped challenge stereotypes associated with sexual dissidence and, while normalizing behaviors previously perceived as deviant, these shows have gradually pushed the boundaries of prescriptive morality and what is deemed representable. Yet privileging more conventional members of minoritized sexualities as spokespersons has also served to further stigmatize those queer identities who do not fit that mold. At the same time, the popularity and profitability of these low-cost and accessible kinds of shows have arguably reshaped the landscape of television, exploiting subject matter considered "scandalous."

Despite it being criticized as controversial, devalued, and damaging,[40] there are millions of people watching trash TV. A host of studies have revealed some reasons behind this conflicted engagement where viewers' motives and reactions range from fascination, embarrassment, voyeurism, disgust, and even "hate-watching."[41] Charles McCoy and Roscoe Scarborough[42] distinguish between viewers who watch a trash program as a guilty pleasure (i.e., when they feel ashamed but they cannot help it), those who consume the show ironically (i.e., viewers who mock a program from an emotional distance, feeling superior compared with those represented), and viewers with a "camp sensibility" (those who enjoy an extravagant and exaggerated cultural object while celebrating its failed seriousness). Talk shows have been described as "a trashy forum for trashy people to act trashy."[43] In addition to the people represented on TV, the viewer, by association, is often assumed to be trash, too (as opposed to the "good TV" sophisticated viewer). This discussion helps to further understand the program, its audience and the reactions to the trono gay.

THE PROGRAM AND ITS PUBLIC

Uomini e donne is one of the Italian shows most often cited and mocked through memes,[44] video excerpts, and comments on various popular Italian Facebook pages like "Trash italiano by Andrea Cosimi," which has a following of over 14,000 users.⁴⁵ I now present the program and its public in more detail as well as some of the possible reasons behind the trash label.

Massimiliano Panarari believes that "behind its postmodern features, the program allows a glimpse of considerable traditionalism in the understanding of gender relations."⁴⁶ Salvatore Patriarca sustains that even the studio mise-en-scène of *Uomini e donne* linguistically and semiotically resembles a medieval court: everything revolves around the thrones and the *tronisti*⁴⁷ (those who sit on the throne) who are flanked by the *opinionisti*, in-studio commentators, halfway between jester and court counselor figures.⁴⁸ In this patriarchal setting, however, I believe the undisputed "queen" and strategist of the program remains Maria De Filippi—humbly seated on the stairs in front of the thrones with the in-studio audience members on both sides of her (arguably representing another symbolic throne).

Through castings, the TV program production team (also known as *la redazione* or *la produzione*) selects two to four main tronisti, a mix of women and men between the ages of eighteen to thirty-five; up until 2015, contestants were exclusively heterosexual. Potential admirers (*corteggiatori/corteggiatrici*) meet the tronisti in the studio first and, if chosen, during off-site, pre-recorded, one-on-one romantic dates (*le esterne*) which are then commented on during the program. Suitors generally verbally fight with each other and with the *opinionisti* to stand out; overall, the program is very loud, with foul language and lots of bleeped swearing throughout most of the airing. This certainly contributes to the program's trash label.

In terms of the participants, the program feeds on stereotypes and specific ideals of white beauty: tanned, well-built, inked, muscular bodies which show meticulousness about their grooming and appearance. According to Alessio Cicchini, the program "has always staged a psychodramatic little scene where the actants are, in the majority of cases, fresh-faced, buff men, darkly tanned from using a UVA sunbed, together with wannabe *veline* (showgirls) who exploit the program as a springboard into the entertainment world."⁴⁹ Once one of the tronisti is ready to make their choice (*la scelta*) among the suitors, the chosen person has the option to accept or reject their invitation to start a relationship in the real world. In some cases, as provided for by the format and the game itself, the courtship is faked, as some participants are more in search of fame and a career in show business.⁵⁰ This show, given its popularity, regularly feeds the Italian gossip machine and the circulation of numerous tabloids and rumors which I do not intend to analyze, as this has also been the case of the gay edition of the show.⁵¹

Simone Alliva seems to agree with other journalists and bloggers maintaining that the gay throne is "a carbon copy" of the original heterosexual *Uomini e donne* in terms of the kinds of participants represented, but he goes so far as to say that this particular aesthetic—to an extent discriminatory—mold "already features prominently within the Italian LGBT community itself."[52] Manuel Peruzzo claims that the program serves to finally celebrate the right of gay males to be *tamarri* (louts or white trash), and suggests that Maria De Filippi intentionally aims to cast these people to appeal to a particular audience of the program.[53] In a way, Simone Zeni seems to agree with this view, affirming that "What viewers see in the program is what they are or what they know: good-looking men who like teased quiffs, the gym, UVA sunbed tans and the tweezers for their eyebrows."[54] This demonstrates that some commentators, as well as a considerable number of Twitter users, have in mind an implied viewership for this program, as previously discussed, skewed toward white trash.

The program is generally a leader in the early afternoon time slot ratings.[55] Between 2010 and 2016, the average number of viewers oscillated from 2,600,000 to almost 3,000,000 per episode, with a mean share of 20 and 23 percent.[56] Zeni sums up, I believe accurately, the kind of public that regularly watches the program: "Maria De Filippi has found the key to speak to a varied humanity who, in the afternoon, is in front of the TV set, made up of poorly paid freelancers, but mainly retirees, sleepy housewives, and students back from school."[57] This description and the one in the introduction to the chapter appear to be corroborated by the statistics available on the composition of the audience of *Uomini e donne*. AUDITEL data[58] show that 29 percent of the program's audience is male and 71 percent is female. Their schooling levels are mainly low: over 71 percent of the audience members appear to have no advanced degree, with only a primary or a lower secondary degree. Over half of the total number of viewers (54 percent) belongs to a lower or middle class, and 55 percent of the audience is aged over forty-four, with almost 23 percent over sixty-five. Conversely, viewers who are aged between twenty-five and forty-four are almost 30 percent of the total. Data related to the geographical provenance of the audience reveal that the Italian regions with the highest shares percentage-wise are those in the South (namely Calabria, Basilicata, and Puglia), whereas the regions with the smallest following are in the North (specifically Friuli Venezia Giulia and Liguria).[59]

A timeline and some examples of key episodes[60] and ratings data of the trono gay are shown in table 5.1, and they demonstrate that the number of viewers increased over the course of the season but not tremendously. Initially, some bloggers and social media users often said that the introduction of gay participants in the program might have been a cunning expedient of this commercial program to boost ratings and profitability. Francesco Dell'Acqua interprets the missed ratings soar as a potentially positive outcome, since he understands this as a "peaceful indifference" on the part of the—heterosexual—public toward the televisibility of gay men and their conquest of a new kind of "different normality;"[61] that is, a sort of re-normalization. This

Table 5.1   Main Events, Dates, Audience Ratings of Key Episodes

Event	Date	Number of viewers	Share (%)
Trono gay is announced	March 30, 2016	–	–
Castings opening	May 31, 2016	–	–
"Il quartetto" ("The quartet," the first episode of trono gay)	September 14, 2016	3,043,000	23.9
"Il bacio non visto" ("The unseen kiss")	November 22, 2016	2,715,000	21.7
"Il bacio e il bivio" ("The kiss and the bifurcation," the hidden kiss)	December 13, 2016	3,106,000	24.1
"Un giorno speciale" ("A special day," final episode with Senator Cirinnà)	December 16, 2016	3,282,000	24.6

Source: Copyright Luca Malici, 2018.

journalist seems to imply that perhaps televised male homosexuality is no longer perceived as scandalous, as it was in the past. Yet, as we will see, not all the Twitter data confirm this view. Overall, the series achieved good results in terms of audience ratings[62] and the program unquestionably had an impact on the public opinion and discourses of sexuality in Italy.

RESULTS AND ANALYSIS OF THE TWEETS BEFORE THE BEGINNING OF THE PROGRAM

Having introduced and analyzed the program, its trashy nature, and its audience, I now examine the results of my research on Twitter. Between February 2013 and February 2016—that is, before the official announcement of the trono gay—the first 100 of tweets with the hashtag #tronogay started to appear from Spain, with comments on the rumors of a possible trono gay in *Mujeres, hombres y viceversa*.[63] This is the TV format exported to the TV channel Telecinco—still part of Mediaset Spain—which, at the moment of writing (December 2018), has yet to hold a version with same-sex participants. On January 25, 2016, an Italian Twitter user first included the hashtag and the program *Uomini e donne* in relation to the national mobilization *Svegliatitalia!* (wake up, Italy!), an initiative launched by the main BGILQT Italian associations concomitantly with the parliamentary discussion of the bill on civil unions, in the following comment: "For a better world #civilunions in Italy and #tronogay at #uominiedonne #svegliatitalia."[64] As we will see from this point on, trono gay and unioni civili became a recurrent pairing on Twitter.

On March 30, 2016, just a month before the Cirinnà law was passed, Maria De Filippi announced in the tabloid *Chi* her intention to open her afternoon show to same-sex participants for the very first time in September 2016. The news immediately echoed on the web and in the major national press. On the occasion, Maria De Filippi herself explained: "I'm not looking for scandals, but for the normality of a love story lived in everyday life,"[65] thus inaugurating the use of a normalizing vocabulary shared by many commentators. The hashtag #tronogay on Twitter went viral, and in just a few hours became number one of the national trends on the platform, remaining there for over two days with a total of 1,147 tweets (i.e., as much as 39% of the total tweets posted and analyzed in this chapter). From the point of view of my research, these early tweets, for quantity and concentration, are the most interesting, as they present several nodes and specific discourses that I wish to further analyze and interpret.

Looking at figure 5.1, 77 percent of these tweets are clearly favorable comments on the program. Among them, 50 percent of the total are informative tweets reporting and retweeting the news, or citing parts of the interview with De Filippi, without expressing any kind of view on it. For 5 percent of these posts (sixty tweets), the users comment on the fact that, even though the program is regarded as a trash program, they will start to watch it for the first time just because of the new trono gay. One tweet says that trash entertainment "does not discriminate"[66] and as such evens out differences. There is even someone who writes that "#tronogay achieves real parity, and gays become an integral part of #trash"[67] while another user states: "So we finally realize that sexuality is independent of everything, idiocy included."[68]

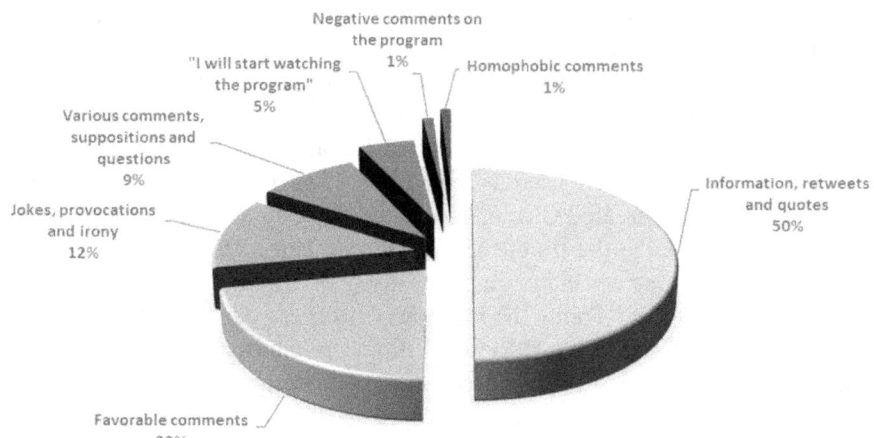

Figure 5.1 Graph of the 1,147 Tweets with #tronogay Posted between March 30 and 31, 2016. *Source*: Created by Luca Malici, 2018.

Ultimately, these posts seem to celebrate the right for gay people to be part of this kind of entertainment which once was perceived as a heterosexual prerogative.

Another 22 percent of tweets which followed the announcement of the *trono gay* (250 posts) explicitly gave a positive judgment on the event and talked of the possible normalizing effect on the audience. Many of them included the word "finally," while other users seemed not to believe the news. Many, at least twenty tweets, show approval and appreciation toward the program's host, who is often humorously associated with redeeming religious figures, being described with devout metaphors such as: "Queen Mary who hears our prayers;"[69] "Saint Mary Mater gay;"[70] "sainthood now;"[71] "beatified;"[72] "Maria who moves the sun and other stars"[73] (quoting the last verse of Dante Alighieri's *Divine Comedy, Paradise* XXXIII, 145).

Around fifteen tweets highlighted the magnitude of her decision to host a *trono gay*, commenting even that "Italy is a country where progress is promoted by a TV host,"[74] or "If Maria has decided to hold a #tronogay it must mean the time is ripe for marriage equality,"[75] whereas many others also claimed that Maria De Filippi does more for Italy "than the entire parliament,"[76] or the "Cirinnà law."[77] However, there are two Twitter users who try to bring the discussion back to political rights: "#tronogay? I would rather know what happened to #unionicivili. Or should we go to *C'è posta per te*[78] to find it out?" or even "Ok the #tronogay, but in the meantime the #unionicivili got lost in hell?"[79] In fact, the discussion of the law regarding civil unions—named after Democratic Party senator Monica Cirinnà, who promoted the initiative—would finally be adopted a month after the announcement of the *trono gay*, on May 11, 2016. In an interview, Maria De Filippi herself revealed that "the law on the civil unions contributed considerably to the decision" to have a *trono gay*,[80] but elsewhere she had also said that "society is ahead of laws" and she does not think a *trono gay* is a revolution as "TV must reflect reality and could not leave anybody out."[81] I will return to this last point toward the end of my chapter, but I would like to highlight how the program was subsequently used as a springboard to discuss and, to an extent, publicize the newly created Cirinnà law, as well as its promoter, and the affiliated party in charge at the time (the Democratic Party, PD). Senator Cirinnà has been an involved spectator in that season of *Uomini e donne*, tweeting after the first episode: "Today the #tronogay becomes part of #uominiedonne with normality. Thanks to #MariaDeFilippi for showing courage against #homofobia."[82] She also prerecorded a video message broadcast during the last episode of the series in which, once again, she used assimilationist language such as "normality," "acceptance," and "a love identical to ours" (i.e., heterosexuals').[83] Assimilationist, affirmative, or what I call "apologetic" language have attempted to show a "positive" normalizing image of sexual dissidence and to construct a sense of ordinariness and sameness comparable to traditional understandings of heterosexuality. The main issue with this is that discourses of assimilation, inclusion, and tolerance underline and take for granted an assumed asymmetry of power that sees heterosexual people in a more favorable and superior position.

Going back to the reactions to the announcement of a trono gay, another 12 percent of the tweets are characterized by jokes, provocations, and attacks on certain conservative figures such as Mario Adinolfi. Founder of the party *Popolo della Famiglia* (People of the family) and often at the forefront of the Italian Catholic anti-gender and anti-BGILQT "propaganda,"[84] Adinolfi is mocked in forty-five tweets and memes in which users imagine his possible reactions to the program, and its effects on minor viewers.[85] Given the specific content of certain other comments, some tweets seem to be tweeted by gay male users. For example, some jokes are linked to a gay culture and jargon related to mobile apps like Grindr.[86] A sizable number of users (forty-five tweets) imagined that the very same host and one of the *opinionisti*, Gianni Sperti, both perceived as closeted homosexuals, would be the first gay tronisti. In fact, almost 9 percent of the tweets posted after the announcement by Maria De Filippi encapsulated various speculations, questions, and predictions on the names of possible gay tronisti, and on the program. Sixteen users asked whether the title of program would change because of the new format, while two users propose new problematic titles on the verge of homophobia such as "uomini e donne mancate"[87] (men and quasi-women) and "uomini e gonne"[88] (men and skirts), also playing on the original title. Other Twitter users proposed "uomini e uomini"[89] (men and men) or "uomini, gay e donne"[90] (men, gay, and women), demonstrating very little understanding of the difference between sex, gender, and sexuality.

In relation to my previous work on the audience, it is interesting to note that twelve people discussed the possible reactions that elder family members, friends, and more generally perceived "bigots" might have while watching this program. Lastly, they often imply that this program will challenge their preconceptions toward sexual difference, yet they might still react negatively or with disgust to the portrayals in the program. Elsewhere, I have already discussed this "Third Person Perception" which happens when media messages and portrayals are not perceived as normatively and socially acceptable, potentially leading individuals to overestimate media influence on the attitudes and behaviors of others.[91] As it will be further discussed in the following section, which looks at social media reactions during the airing of the trono gay, however, there were instances when watching the program with other family members productively challenged some preconceptions.

The remaining 2.4 percent of tweets—that is, less than thirty posts in total—negatively commented on the news of the introduction of gay participants in *Uomini e donne*. Half of these tweets (1.2% of the total 1,149 posts) considered the program "trash," with users suggesting that they would not watch it as a result. Conversely, the other half of these posts made clear homophobic attacks which call into question long-standing problematic discourses on the fact, for example, that same-sex couples cannot procreate on their own and, as one post reads, "without science we'd have discovered how mankind could become extinct."[92] There is also pure verbal violence coming from a limited number of tweets by people presenting themselves as male users ("disgusting," "assholes," "faggots," or "do you call it #gaythrone because there is a stake/picket at the center of the seat?").[93] Finally, there is somebody who requests preventive censorship to protect minors who could be negatively affected by watching the program. As well as the already mention Third Person Perception, this discourse evokes a form of politics of substitution for which adults seem to use the rhetoric of the protection of minors to avoid more explicit representations which adults themselves might perceive as problematic.[94] Other Twitter users have reposted similar comments and attacks in response to this matter. One user asks, for example, "Trono gay? In the afternoon? And how do I explain it to my children?"[95] and receives a very direct response: "Your fucking problem. They are not my children";[96] other tamer comments, supported by numerous likes and retweets, underline the fact that children should not be watching this program regardless of its gay content because of the language frequently used and the themes previously discussed. In fact, even in the past, the *Movimento Italiano Genitori* (Moige)—the Italian conservative and Catholic parents' association which monitors Italian media for the protection of children—had already accused the program of being a "counter-educational model" for minors.[97]

The remaining comments reveal that in the face of heavy homophobic attacks, which account only for 1.2 percent of the total comments analyzed on Twitter, there is a conspicuous number of other users who criticize, shame, and fight back against these conservative and phobic positions. It is obvious that most Italians with a homophobic view would not necessarily go to Twitter to express their disapproval of the program, and would not use a thematic hashtag such as #tronogay. As per the view of other commentators,[98] I have also noticed that homophobia on Twitter seems contained; on the contrary, this social medium is often used to report homophobic discourses and to attack said positions often present on other platforms. The situation is different on other more open social networks with different demographics, such as Facebook and Instagram, where haters and homophobes also have at their disposal more than the 140 characters available on Twitter. Homophobic comments on the official Facebook and Instagram pages of the program made some headlines, particularly in relation to the post announcing the castings for the trono gay,[99] the first same-sex kiss broadcast on the program,[100] and the video posted of the final episode in which the gay male tronista chose his partner and kissed him.[101] I must say that usually these homophobic attacks never exceeded 4–5 percent of the total comments in a post, and for every intolerant message, I have observed an average of twenty replies which attack, insult, or try somehow to convince the intolerant user to change their mind. These users are perhaps BGILQT individuals, but would also include some queerophiles and allied heterosexuals. From my analysis, it would seem then that the fight to combat homophobia on social media creates more noise and discussions than anything else including the actual mainstream representation of BGILQT subjects, or better, in this case, of gay male individuals on TV. Overall, the announcement of the trono gay attracted a majority of positive, yet normalizing, commentaries online, as well as some homophobic remarks contrasted in novel ways.

TWEETS DURING THE TRONO GAY

After the announcement of the trono gay, the initial excitement died down a little, and the remaining tweets followed the development of the program as it was unfolding. I do not find most of these comments particularly interesting as they often refer to gossip, scandals, spoilers of some episodes, and users who support one or another courter. Due to the limited space of this chapter, I now want to focus on some nodes coming from the remaining tweets which I have found to be of significance, and which deal mainly with various discourses around BGILQT visibility in Italy and how different viewers have engaged with the program.

Some Twitter users have taken a critical position themselves toward the television representation of the trono gay. For example, the paucity of same-sex kisses, frequent in the heterosexual version of the program, has created some polemics as per the comment: "In real life they would have made out after 24 hours."[102] The program was initially accused of obstructing this kind of representation, but Maria De Filippi herself stated that this depended on the participants themselves, who had a problem in "letting themselves go in front of the cameras."[103] Because of this, or perhaps due to cases of internalized homophobia, the series saw only two same-sex kisses aired: one happened off-camera and the other recorded but hidden by the suitor.[104] Some Twitter users immediately noticed this and reacted saying, "They self-censor the kiss,"[105] "hypocrisy #censorship #notfair #missedchance."[106] The only visible kiss was the one which attracted homophobic responses online and took place during the last episode of the series.[107] These events might mean that although the representation of gay males on TV is growing in terms of quantity, quality, and time of broadcast, the visibility of same-sex affection might still represent a problem for some, including those who participate in the representation. This view is corroborated by recent findings in another European country, where a YouGov and Stonewall study claimed that more than half of gay men in Britain do not feel comfortable holding hands with a partner in public.[108] Another example linked with this in the program, which called into question matters of visibility of BGILQT subjects in Italy and the critical spirit of some Twitter users, is linked to the in-studio broadcast of the last *esterna*,[109] a recorded romantic date in Naples during which a huge crowd warmly welcomed the two men. If, on the one hand, a tweet proudly reads: "Could somebody alert #Adinolfi?"[110] involving yet again the already-mentioned conservative figure, another user demonstrates knowledge of the difference between television and real life, tweeting: "Everybody is happy only because there are cameras . . . had they been on their own, they would have received insults unfortunately."[111] Still today, particularly in southern Italy, attitudes toward homosexuality and same-sex couples are problematic, with news of homophobic violence in public places often making headlines in a country where discrimination based on sexual orientation and gender identity has yet to be legally recognized.[112]

Among the tweets, I have also found some examples of "Queer TV moments," instances of confrontation with BGILQT portrayals and narratives on TV in which individuals who watch television together reconcile contrasting opinions through discursive elaboration of the representations.[113] In some cases, the trono gay raised strong reactions on the part of the public and led some of them to action. For example, one male user confessed on Twitter that thanks to the program, he managed to come out to his family while watching it. Besides, as many as four online fan fictions—amateur novels written by viewers of the program who imagine how the relationship between the protagonists of the trono gay might evolve[114]—had almost 32,000 online readers. Another Twitter user cited her grandmother who said, "oh well, a boy and a boy dancing is cute, after all,"[115] and another girl who hyperbolically states, "my mom, who always wanted a boy, would now like to have a gay son,"[116] demonstrating that they have watched the program together, and that their perception of male homosexuality might have changed. The strongest and more numerous responses on Twitter came during the last episode of the season, during which, thanks as well to the aforementioned video message by Senator Cirinnà broadcast during the show, out of 190 comments, 30 people (16 percent) write on Twitter to express their emotions and to confess that they cried while watching the show. Among these comments, 68 percent of them appear to come from women, but I have also recorded that during the whole season, many female users seemed particularly enthralled by the trono gay, commenting enthusiastically on the various episodes and talking often of "emotions," "feelings," and the "sweet" representations. Perhaps this is simply because they have been gripped by the love story regardless of the discourse on sexuality, or maybe the transgender spokesperson for BGILQT people in Italy, Valdimir Luxuria, was right when, in an interview before the start of the trono gay, she claimed: "If Maria places a beautiful muscly hunk on the program, he'll become the women's idol too!"[117]

The selection of participants in the program is clearly influenced by the program's production decisions and preestablished models of beauty. De Filippi herself answered the question on her views about "placing perhaps participants who are not good-looking? I have thought about it, but the bummer is that suitors wouldn't come forward to pursue them."[118] On Twitter, at the dawn of the series, users had tweeted a great deal on the importance of castings, predicting the appearance of gay participants, as in the tweet: "I only hope they won't fill the program with stereotypes such as effeminate dudes and butch women;"[119] and there were many jokes and references to the masculinity and the metrosexuality of past heterosexual participants, such as: "The gay tronisti will be super fashionable, plucked, and with a massive ego. . . . PRACTICALLY like the hetero ones!"[120] At the start of the program, another female user also noted that "they are manlier than the hetero participants. I'm glad that they are people far from the stereotype of the fairy."[121] These comments might recall discourses of "Campophobia,"[122] or the rejection of effeminate models of masculinity, which often materializes even within the very same BGILQT communities. These same discourses emerged even in the program when a suitor left the show because he considered the gay tronista "unmanly [:] accusations which make the person inadequate, unworthy of attention or of living a love story,"[123] as Dario Accolla later commented.

As already mentioned, the word "queer" did not appear on the tweets analyzed but perhaps the "queerest" posts that I have read are those that, between the announcement and the end of first trono gay, critically questioned the representational limits of the program. Out of twenty tweets, almost one-third of users would like to see a lesbian throne next, despite their predictions that it will bring in lower audience ratings. Another user even ventures a wish to see more varied gay male subcultures represented, saying: "I want bear, otter, twink, wolf, hunk, jock tronisti. I want them effeminate and masc4masc."[124] There are those who would like a program with older bears, or even bisexual participants, admitting that this might productively disorient the putative heteronormative audience even more. Another user states: "So then will there be a black,[125] Asian, transsexual, pansexual, asexual, bisexual throne now? Just to avoid distinctions,"[126] yet in this case it is not totally clear from the context whether the tweet's author is being polemic, ironic or taking for granted that once there has been a gay male version of the program, this could now function as a gateway to open up the program to "all" multifarious identarian differences. The already-mentioned Valdimir Luxuria joins all these rhetorical questions with irony while returning to address the host with religious metaphors in this tweet: "Maria please after the #tronogay give me the #tronotrans: I'm looking for a living and patient husband! Perhaps you are the one who can perform the miracle."[127]

We must agree with those journalists and bloggers who said that this trono gay cannot and should not represent the BGILQT communities at large.[128] The very same first gay tronista, Claudio Sona, during the last episode made a disclaimer saying: "I want to point out that I never claimed nor wanted to represent any category."[129] In relation to this, Alliva observed that the program has not represented "gay twinks, blacks, boys next door, nor queers,"[130] and this is one of the two occurrences of the term queer found in my study. This term was called into question exactly when representational absences were discussed. In all the mostly normalizing debates on this event, "queer" passed almost as invisible. By the same token, the debate within Italian BGILQT associations in relation to this particular "gay" season of this trash program has been mostly absent.[131] In the meantime, another season of the program took place[132] and among the newly chosen tronisti (three boys and one girl), there was a gay male participant who, once again, largely reflected the discussed canons of the program.

SOME CONCLUSIONS AND CONSIDERATIONS

In 2016, together with important political and legislative advancements, there were some changes in the ways in which sexual dissidence is represented on Italian mainstream TV, yet not tremendous ones. The trono gay provided perhaps a "constructed," true-to-life representation of specific versions of Italian gay male sexuality, relationships, and linked discourses around homosexuality in the afternoon scheduling of a very popular channel. The portrayals offered in the program were of a rather homonormative and mostly normalizing nature and so were many of the enthusiastic comments and discourses surrounding the event on Twitter. Conversely, there were also several homophobic reactions and remarks to the program, but they quantitatively differed depending on specific social media platforms, with Twitter being the one with fewer negative comments. Some users very often challenged these homophobic views, exhibiting in their posts a critical stance in relation to the situation of BGILQT discourses, subjects, and their visibility in Italy. Despite this, I believe that "we" (scholars, critics, and persons of taste) must engage, analyze, and understand these kinds of available representations of dissident sexuality, even when the representation might be considered trash, homonormative, and assimilationist. By doing this we might be able to challenge the representational limits of sexuality on TV, revealing its mechanisms and trying to intervene to promote a democracy of desires and queer representations. I believe we should confront professionals behind the camera, those in charge of selecting who and what can be aired on mainstream TV. Future scholarship might also concentrate on researching the "second class" audience of trash TV, as well as the traditionally implied, and rather maligned, Italian TV audience, often assumed to be unprepared and uninterested in seeing more unapologetic, sexualized, varied nuances of sexuality and relationships on the small screen. Finally, it would also be interesting to understand whether Italian BGILQT subjects, academics, and activists are even willing to infiltrate, engage with and take part in mainstream representations and debates. All of this to make programs like *Uomini e donne* and queer visibility not just a guilty pleasure for some: "them."

NOTES

1. Kellakiara (@Kellakiara), "Noi scherziamo ma quando la casalinga di Gela scoprirà che STI FROCI ALLA FINE SO' BRAVI, sarà davvero una rivoluzione culturale #tronogay," Twitter, March 30, 2016, http://www.twitter.com/kellakiara. Unless otherwise noted, all translations are my own. I would also like to thank the QuIR organizers and those who participated in the Italian Queer Media Workshop in New York, particularly Charlotte Ross, Giancarlo Lombardi, and Julia Heim for their suggestions and insights into my research, as well as Brian DeGrazia for proofreading this chapter.

2. Francesco Dell'Acqua, "Da Maria De Filippi a Nonno Libero: la nuova stagione arcobaleno della televisione italiana," *Il sole 24 ore.com*, November 7, 2016, http://www.alleyoop.ilsole24ore.com/2016/11/07/da-maria-de-filippi-a-nonno-libero-la-nuova-stagione-arcobaleno-della-televisione-italiana/.

3. The Law 76 signed on May 20, 2016 represents the first Italian law providing for same-sex civil unions.

4. I employ the acronym BGILQT—bisexual, gay male, intersex, lesbian, queer, transgender—to jointly name marginalized sexualities in an alphabetical and linear order so that to avoid normative and hierarchical discourses. There have been often debates about the letters that should be included in this acronym and their disposition. In Italy, the form "GLBT" was initially preferred to LGBT. Playing on a set of presumptive bon-ton etiquettes, Teresa de Lauretis controversially and ironically noticed that "ladies should go 'first!'" (1991, v). If language is one of the primary forms of representation, it can reiterate and reinstate problematical imbalances of power and visibility. I willingly use the BGILQT acronym "improperly" because I am aware that these are just limited examples of sexual dissidence, subjects, and identities.

5. *Stato Civile: l'amore è uguale per tutti*, directed by Giampaolo Marconato (Italy: RAI 3, 2016).

6. Luca Romano, "Teoria gender e ascolti flop, la Bignardi si dimetta," *Il giornale.it*, December 27, 2016, http://www.ilgiornale.it/news/spettacoli/teoria-gender-e-ascolti-flop-bignardi-si-dimetta-1346249.html. Additionally, the first two women on the show received considerable harassment and threats on social media and they pressed charges toward fourteen individuals, see "Simona e Stefania: denunciano chi ha offeso la loro unione su Facebook!" https://www.lezpop.it/simona-stefania-unione-civile-denuncia-offese-facebook/, accessed May 22, 2018.

7. This term was first employed by Jonathan Dollimore in *Sexual Dissidence: Augustine to Wilde, Freud to Foucault* (Oxford: University Press, 1991) to reveal "the complex, often violent, sometimes murderous dialectic between dominant and subordinate cultures, groups, and identities" and "those conceptions of self, desire, and transgression which figure in the language, ideologies, and cultures of domination, and in the diverse kinds of resistance to it" (p. 21). In this term I loosely read an equivalence with "queer subjects" and "queerness."

8. See Luca Malici, "Queer in Italy: Italian Televisibility and the 'Queerable' Audience," in *Queer in Europe: Contemporary Case Studies*, ed. Lisa Downing and Robert Gillett (London: Ashgate, 2011), 113.

9. See Domenico Naso, "Rai Due censura il sesso in 'Le regole del delitto perfetto' Ma solo quello gay," *Il fatto quotidiano.it*, July 9, 2016a, http://www.ilfattoquotidiano.it/2016/07/09/rai-due-censura-il-sesso-le-regole-del-delitto-perfetto-ma-solo-quello-gay/2893053/. The censorship involved the first three episodes of the first season, namely the "Pilot," "It's All Her Fault," and "Smile, or Go to Jail," *How to Get Away with Murder*, created by Peter Nowalk (USA: ABC, 2014). The series, titled in Italian *Le regole del delitto perfetto*, premiered on RAI2 in July 2016. Following the complaints, the network aired again the full version of the three episodes. See also Roberto Proia, "'Le regole del delitto perfetto', Raidue si scusa e manda in onda la versione integrale," *Il fatto quotidiano.it*, July 10, 2016, https://www.ilfattoquotidiano.it/2016/07/10/le-regole-del-delitto-perfetto-raidue-si-scusa-e-manda-in-onda-la-versione-integrale/2894951/.

10. See Luca Malici, "Italian S-queer Eyes: Surveying and Voicing Television Representations," in *Queer Crossings: Theories, bodies, texts*, ed. Silvia Antosa (Milan: Mimesis, 2012), 105–122; Luca Malici, "Queer TV Moments and Family Viewing in Italy," *Journal of GLBT Family Studies* 10, nos. 1–2 (2014): 188–210; and Luca Malici, "Watching Queer Television: A Case Study of the Representation, Circulation and Reception of Sexual Dissidence on Italian Mainstream TV from 1990 to 2012" (PhD diss., University of Birmingham, 2015).

11. *The Bachelor*, created by Mike Fleiss (USA: ABC, 2002).

12. Maria De Filippi and her programs have been the subjects of written philosophical and academic treaties, monographs, as well as PhD dissertations (see, for example, Marina D'Amato, "Le donne dello schermo. Uno studio di caso," *Storia delle donne*, no. 3: 61–76 (Firenze: University Press, 2007); Emanuele Krashaar, *Iconoclasti. Maria De Filippi* (Padova: Alet edizioni, 2011); Salvatore Patriarca, *Il mistero di Maria. La filosofia, la De Filippi e la televisione* (Milano-Udine: Mimesis Edizioni, 2012); Nicolò Barretta and Maria Elisabetta Santon, *La signora della tv. Fenomenologia di Maria De Filippi* (Milano: Unicolpi, 2013); Pasqua Legrottaglie,

Una telespettatrice particolare: una counselor alla corte di Maria (PhD diss., Accademia per la Riprogrammazione, 2013); Irene Capatti, *Le donne in televisione. Analisi degli stereotipi sul corpo e sui ruoli attraverso il programma Uomini e donne* (PhD diss., Università di Bologna, 2015). Maria De Filippi's TV debut was in 1992 and three years later she married the famous Italian journalist and TV host, Maurizio Costanzo, becoming his fourth wife. Together with her brother Giuseppe, De Filippi founded Fascino PGT S.r.l., a television production company owned in part by Mediaset. Hostess and creator of over twenty TV programs and formats for the Mediaset scheduling, in 2016 she obtained great success cohosting the very popular Sanremo music festival on competitor network, RAI. Commentators have often defined Maria De Filippi the "Queen" or "Lady of commercial TV" (e.g., Patriarca, *Il mistero di Maria*; Barretta e Santon, *La signora della tv*) as well as a 'gay icon' (Domenico Naso, "Uomini e Donne, da settembre arriva il 'trono gay'. E così Maria De Filippi sdogana le coppie omosessuali in tv," *Il fatto quotidiano.it*, March 31, 2016b, http://www.ilfattoquotidiano.it/2016/03/31/uomini-e-donne-da-settembre-arriva-il-trono-gay-e-cosi-maria-de-filippi-sdogana-le-coppie-omosessuali-in-tv/2595468/) as she has occasionally hosted gay themes and guests within her programs, but also because there have been a number of rumors and gossip on her own and her husband's assumed closeted dissident sexual identities (see, for example, Bitchyf 2018).

13. See Andrea Cominetti, "Il trono gay fa bene all'Italia," *Letteradonna.it*, September 30, 2016, http://letteradonna.it/263475/trono-gay-uomini-e-donne-parer i-politici-personagg; Naso, "Uomini e Donne"; and Simone Zeni, "Trono gay, perché quella di Maria De Filippi è una rivoluzione culturale," *Wired.it*, September 14, 2016, https://www.wired.it/play/televisione/2016/09/14/trono-gay-uomini-donn e-omosessuali/.

14. Although the new millennium saw the appearance of some gay, lesbian, and transgender people and characters in prime-time and access prime-time reality TV shows, Italian-made films and soap operas, sexual dissidence has historically been largely marginalized in the TV schedules at the periphery of late-night slots (see Malici, "Queer in Italy," 120; Malici, "Queer TV Moments").

15. Naso, "Uomini e Donne"; Alessio Cicchini, "La parte per il tutto: ecco perché il trono gay di Uomini e Donne non può (e non deve) rappresentare tutta la comunità LGBT," *Gay.it*, October 1, 2016, http://www.gay.it/televisione/news/uomini-e-d onne-trono-gay-stereotipi-lgbt; and Massimiliano Panarari, "Dal costume al coattume nazionale: Maria De Filippi 'arbitra' *elegantiarum* della neo-Italia," in *L'egemonia sottoculturale: L'Italia da Gramsci al gossip* (Turin: Einaudi, 2010), 73–88.

16. Samuel A. Chambers, *The Queer Politics of Television* (London; New York: I. B. Tauris, 2009), 22; Glyn Davis and Gary Needham, *Queer TV: Theories, Histories, Politics* (London: Routledge, 2009), 5.

17. Lisa Duggan, "The New Homonormativity: The Sexual Politics of Neoliberalism," in *Materializing Democracy: Toward a Revitalized Cultural Politics*, ed. Russ Castronovo and Dana D. Nelson (Durham, NC: Duke University Press, 2002), 179, 175–194.

18. One exception being perhaps Joshua Gamson, *Freaks Talk Back: Tabloid Talk Shows and Sexual Nonconformity* (Chicago: University of Chicago Press, 1998).

19. Julie Manga, *Talking Trash: The Cultural Politics of Daytime TV Talk Shows* (New York: New York University Press, 2003); Jane Arthurs, *Television and Sexuality: Regulation and the Politics of Taste* (New York: Open University Press, 2004); Helen Wood and Beverly Skeggs, *Reality Television and Class* (New York: Palgrave Macmillan, 2011); Alan O'Leary, "The Phenomenology of the Cinepanettone," *Italian Studies* 66, no. 3 (2011): 431–443; and Alan O'Leary, *Fenomenologia del cinepanettone* (Soveria Mannelli: Rubbettino, 2013).

20. O'Leary, "The Phenomenology," 443.

21. Panarari, "Dal costume al coattume nazionale," 77.

22. On convergent texts, together with the seminal work by Henry Jenkins, *Convergence Culture* (New York: New York University Press, 2006), and for up-to-date investigations on Italian television and social media, see also Aldo Grasso and Massimiliano Scaglioni, *Televisione convergente. La tv oltre il piccolo schermo* (Milan: RTI, 2010); and Pierluigi Erbaggio, "*#GomorraLaSerie*: Convergin Audience and Enhanced Authorship on Twenty-First-Century Italian Screens," *Modern Italy* 20, no. 4 (2015): 335–349.

23. Stefania Carini, "Uomini e donne," in *Televisione convergente. La tv oltre il piccolo schermo*, ed. Aldo Grasso and Massimiliano Scaglioni (Milan: RTI, 2010), 148.

24. In contrast with what is deemed "good television," official and more credible media outlets rarely comment on trash TV. This kind of television is mainly discussed in tabloid media and blogs and this is why these are some of the secondary sources informing this chapter. See also Milena Stanoeva, *Hate Watching Trash TV: Intersections of Class and Anti-Fandom* (PhD diss., York University, Toronto, Ontario, 2016).

25. Dhiraj Murthy, "The Ontology of Tweets: Mixed-Method Approaches to the Study of Twitter," in *The Sage Handbook of Social Media Research Methods*, ed. Luke Sloan and Anabel Quan-Haase (London: Sage, 2017), 559–572.

26. Twitter population is amply unknown and although there are some strategies to determine some demographic attributes, researches cannot know who is represented and who says what with certainty (Luke Sloan, "Social Science 'Lite'? Deriving Demographic Proxies from Twitter," in *The Sage Handbook of Social Media Research Methods*, edited by Sloan Luke and Anabel Quan-Haase (London: Sage, 2017), 90–104). For example, we know that in Italy Twitter is used by 11.2 percent of the Italian population: almost one-third is aged fourteen to twenty-nine, and only 1.7 percent of Twitter users is over sixty-five (CENSIS, *I media tra élite e popolo, 13° Rapporto Censis-Ucsi sulla comunicazione*, September 28, 2016, http://www.censis.it/7?shadow_comunicato_stampa=121073). For what concerns gender, my sample of Twitter is made up of men (32%) and women (29%) but 26 percent remains unknown, whereas the remaining 13 percent represents collective accounts of associations, groups, or blogs. The difficulty to decode and interpret with certainty the irony and sarcasm of individual posts of 140 characters without knowing the demographic of the user is another important limitation of a Twitter analysis (Murthy, "The Ontology of Tweets").

27. *Oxford Dictionaries*, s.v. "trash," accessed May 22, 2018, https://en.oxforddictionaries.com/definition/trash.

28. *Sabatini Coletti*, s.v. "trash," accessed May 22, 2018, http://dizionari.corriere.it/dizionario_italiano/T/trash.shtml.

29. Manga, *Talking Trash*, 4.

30. See the seminal work of Pierre Bourdieu, *Distinction: A Social Critique of the Judgement of Taste* (London: Routledge, 1984).

31. Laura Grindstaff, *The Money Shot: Trash, Class and the Making of TV Talk Shows* (Chicago: University of Chicago Press, 2002), 263.

32. An example of this might be the homonym UK program *Eurotrash*, created by Peter Stuart (London: Channel 4, 1993–2004), in which in-studio commentators mocked a collage of surreal European TV excerpts.

33. Manga, *Talking Trash*, 2.

34. Since 2014, these are one-night art exhibition and performance platform, within the context of a club night "to bring together a community of people interested in the themes of sexuality, gender, creativity and politics, with an intersectional and transnational approach" (see https://cuntemporary.org/deep-trash-manifesto/). One of the organizers said that they initially employed "trash" to "queer Italian and 'Eurotrash' culture," but subsequently reclaimed the term to "dismantle the ideas that there is a determined space and time to experience culture" and to "criticize the high/popular art/culture tension within a queer/feminist spectrum" (Giulia Casalini, private email conversation, May 5, 2018).

35. Tommaso Labranca, *Andy Warhol era un coatto. Vivere e capire il trash* (Rome: Castelvecchi, 2004), 31.

36. Ibid., 29–30.

37. Stanoeva, *Hate Watching*, 3.

38. Brian Whitaker, "The Value of Trash TV," *The Guardian*, May 22, 2007, https://www.theguardian.com/commentisfree/2007/may/22/thevalueoftrashtv.

39. There is a shared consensus, for example, among Gamson, *Freaks Talk Back*; Manga, *Talking Trash*; Arthurs, *Television and Sexuality*; Stanoeva, *Hate Watching*.

40. In more recent research, Italian entertainment and trash TV has been accused of being a weapon of mass distraction from more crucial political matters and even of having duped the audience-electorate into voting for a series of populist leaders in the last thirty years. See Ruben Durante, Paolo Pinotti, and Andrea Tesei, "The Political Legacy of Entertainment TV," *American Economic Review* 109, no. 7 (July 2019): 2497–2530; and Andrew Van Dam, "How Trashy TV Made Children Dumber and Enabled a Wave of Populist Leaders," *The Washington Post*, July 20, 2019, https://www.washingtonpost.com/business/2019/07/20/how-trashy-tv-made-children-dumber-enabled-wave-populist-leaders/?utm_term=.a34ab8a1933f.

41. Stanoeva, *Hate Watching*; Grindstaff, *The Money Shot*; Charles McCoy and Roscoe Scarborough, "The Guilty Pleasure of Watching Trashy TV," *The Conversation*, May 20, 2015, https://theconversation.com/the-guilty-pleasure-of-watching-trashy-tv-40214.

42. McCoy and Scarborough, "The Guilty Pleasure."

43. Grindstaff, *The Money Shot*, 22.

44. An image, video, and/or piece of text typically humorous in nature, that is copied and spread rapidly by users and among social media platforms.

45. "Trash Italiano" di Andrea Cosimi's Facebook page, accessed May 28, 2018, https://www.facebook.com/Trash-Italiano-di-Andrea-Cosimi-409394790547/.

46. Massimiliano Panarari, "Maria De Filippi, critica della ragion televisiva," *La stampa.it*, March 3, 2012, http://www.lastampa.it/2012/03/10/cultura/maria-de-filippi-critica-della-ragion-televisiva-RMWc1oRltXwv74lVwCj0eJ/pagina.html.

47. Given the program's popularity, the neologism "tronista" has even been made an entry in Italian dictionaries (La Stampa, "Tronista e Subprime entrano nello Zingarelli 2009," *La Stampa.it*, October 7, 2008, http://www.lastampa.it/2008/10/07/societa/tronista-e-subprime-entrano-nello-zingarelli-RB66uO6whsxVGtzY8cH3QN/pagina.html).

48. Patriarca, *Il mistero di Maria*.

49. Cicchini, "La parte per il tutto."

50. See Carini, "Uomini e donne." From March 2018, Maria De Filippi's company now publishes a dedicated weekly tabloid, *Uomini e donne magazine*. See "Nasce Uomini e Donne Magazine," accessed March 31, 2018, http://www.mondadori.it/media/news-comunicati-stampa-e-social/anno-2018/nasce-uomini-e-donne-magazine.

51. Among the celebrities involved in the rumors and the tabloids there are the popular fashion designer Stefano Gabbana; the talent-scout involved with the *vallettopoli* scandal, Lele Mora (see Danielle Hipkins, "'Whore-ocracy': Show Girls, the Beauty Trade-Off, and Mainstream Oppositional Discourse in Contemporary Italy," *Italian Studies* 66, no. 3 (2011): 413–430; Danielle Hipkins, "Who Wants to Be a TV Showgirl?: Auditions, Talent and Taste in Contemporary Popular Italian Cinema," *The Italianist*, no. 32 (2012): 154–190; and Erik Gandini, *Videocrazy*, DVD, directed by Erik Gandini (New York: Lorber Kino, 2009); and Giulia La Torre, daughter of Massimiliano La Torre, one of the two Italian marines (*Marò*) prosecuted in the Enrica Lexie case, an ongoing international controversy about a shooting that happened off the western coast of India in 2012.

52. Simone Alliva, "'Uomini e donne' e il trono gay: i ragazzi stanno bene," *Gaypost.it*, September 14, 2016, http://www.gaypost.it/uomini-donne-trono-gay-i-ragazzi-stanno-bene.

53. Manuel Peruzzo, "Uomini e Donne gay, così Maria De Filippi non fa altro che seguire il suo pubblico," *Il foglio.it*, March 31, 2016, http://www.ilfoglio.it/cultura/2016/03/31/news/uomini-e-donne-gay-cosi-maria-de-filippi-non-fa-altro-che-seguire-il-suo-pubblico-94414/.

54. Zeni, "Trono gay."

55. Over time, the "trono classic" or "giovane," the classic game opened to youth under thirty-six years of age, has progressively changed to face up to the ratings battles and the counter-scheduling of the public service broadcasting. From 2010, the production company introduced a rather more heated "trono over," whose participants are aged between forty and eighty. This version is aired on alternate days and has a slightly different format and rules.

56. AUDITEL data 2012, "Composizione del pubblico di Uomini e Donne (Canale 5)," *Tvblog.it*, accessed May 30, 2018, http://www.tvblog.it/post/36635/uomini-e-donne-maria-de-filippi-bilancio-ascolti-auditel; AUDITEL data 2015–2016, "Bilancio stagione 2015–2016 Uomini e Donne (Canale 5)," *Tvblog.it*, accessed

May 30, 2018, http://www.tvblog.it/post/1327931/focus-ascolti-tvblog-bilancio-stagione-2015-2016-uomini-e-donne-canale-5.

57. Zeni, "Trono gay."

58. AUDITEL data 2012, "Composizione"; AUDITEL data 2015–2016, "Bilancio."

59. Ibid.

60. *Uomini e donne*, "Il quartetto," created by Maria De Filippi (Italy: Canale 5, September 14, 2016), http://www.wittytv.it/uomini-e-donne/mercoledi-14-settembre-il-quartetto/. *Uomini e donne*, "Il bacio non visto," created by Maria De Filippi (Italy: Canale 5, November 22, 2016), http://www.wittytv.it/uomini-e-donne/martedi-22-novembre-il-bacio-non-visto/. *Uomini e donne*, "Il bacio e il bivio," created by Maria De Filippi (Italy: Canale 5, Decembre 13, 2016), http://www.wittytv.it/uomini-e-donne/martedi-13-dicembre-il-bacio-e-il-bivio/. *Uomini e donne*, "Un giorno speciale," created by Maria De Filippi (Italy: Canale 5, Decembre 16, 2016), http://www.wittytv.it/uomini-e-donne/venerdi-16-dicembre-un-giorno-speciale/.

61. Francesco Dell'Acqua, "Da Maria."

62. Davide Maggio, "Auditel: Ascolti TV del giorno," accessed May 30, 2018, www.davidemaggio.it/archives.

63. *Mujeres, Hombres y Viceversa*, created by Maria De Filippi (Spain: Telecinco, 2008–present).

64. Giulia Di Girolamo (@giugidigir), "Per un mondo migliore: #unionicivili in Italia e #tronogay a #uominiedonne al posto del Trono Classico #svegliatitalia," Twitter, January 25, 2016, http://www.twitter.com/ giugidigir.

65. Martina Pennisi, "Uomini e Donne, Maria De Filippi ha deciso: da settembre il trono gay," *corriere.it*, March 30, 2016, http://www.corriere.it/spettacoli/16_marzo_30/uomini-donne-trono-gay-ufficiale-maria-de-filippi-921fe566-f656-11e5-b728-3bdfea23c73f.shtml.

66. Mavih (@mavih), "Il trash non discrimina #tronogay," Twitter, March 30, 2016, http://www.twitter.com/mavih.

67. FiglieDellaServa (@FigliedelaServa), "Col #tronogay si realizza la vera parificazione, i gay diventano parte integrante del #trash," Twitter, March 30, 2016, http://www.twitter.com/FigliedelaServa.

68. Marco Maietta (@MaiettaMarco), "Sono contento del #tronogay Così ci rendiamo conto che la sessualità prescinde sempre da tutte le cose, anche quando si parla di idiozia," Twitter, March 30, 2016, http://www.twitter.com/MaiettaMarco.

69. Gretaebasta (@greta_pittana), "Queen Mary che ascolta le nostre preghiere e finalmente farà il #tronogay!! Era ora!!!" Twitter, March 30, 2016, http://www.twitter.com/greta_pittana.

70. COTINO 5 (@cotiedp), "Santa Maria mater gay #tronogay," Twitter, March 30, 2016, http://www.twitter.com/cotiedp.

71. Ilenia (@Ilenia_aca), "#MariaDeFilippi SANTA SUBITO #uominiedonne waiting for #tronogay," Twitter, March 30, 2016, http://www.twitter.com/Ilenia_aca.

72. Tina Grazioli (@TinaGrazioli), "È una vergogna che nessuno abbia ancora aperto un processo di beatificazione per Maria #tronogay," Twitter, March 30, 2016, http://www.twitter.com/TinaGrazioli.

73. Kellakiara (@Kellakiara), "Maria De Filippi che move il sole e l'altre stelle," Twitter, March 30, 2016, http://www.twitter.com/Kellakiara.

74. il Maschilista (@MaschilistaITA), "L Italia quel paese dove il progresso è promosso da una conduttrice tv #tronogay," Twitter, March 30, 2016, http://www.twitter.com/MaschilistaITA.

75. Emanuele_DottorGay (@dottor_gay), "Se Maria ha deciso che deve esserci il #tronogay vuol dire che è tempo di matrimonio egualitario. E i bigotti muti," Twitter, March 30, 2016, http://www.twitter.com/ dottor_gay.

76. I Diari del Disagio (@diaridelisagio), "Rendersi conto che per la comunità gay, in materia di uguaglianza, #mariadefilippi fa più dell'intero Parlamento. #uominiedonne #tronogay," Twitter, March 30, 2016, http://www.twitter.com/diaridelisagio.

77. fraciaraffo (@fraciaraffo), "Farà molto di più #MariaDeFilippi per #gay che legge #Cirinà #unionicivili #tronogay," Twitter, March 30, 2016, http://www.twitter.com/fraciaraffo.

78. Cathy La Torre (@catlatorre), "#DeFilippi lancia #tronogay. Io invece vorrei sapere che fine hanno fatto #unionicivili. O dobbiamo andare a C'è posta per te per scoprirlo?" Twitter, March 30, 2016, http://www.twitter.com/catlatorre. Literally translated as "there is mail for you," *C'è posta per te*, created by Maria De Filippi (Roma: Canale 5, 2000–present) is another very popular Saturday-night program created and presented by Maria De Filippi. Its premise involves reuniting guests with long-lost loved ones and estranged family members.

79. Elevctraheart (@elevctraheart), "Va bene il #tronogay, ma le #unionicivili se ne sono andate a fanculandia?" Twitter, March 30, 2016, http://www.twitter.com/elevctraheart.

80. Titta, "Maria De Filippi a 'Tv Talk' parla del Trono gay di Uomini e Donne: 'È stato giusto e pacato. Baci censurati? No, uno deve ancora andare in onda!,'" *isaechia.it*, December 4, 2016, http://www.isaechia.it/2016/12/04/maria-de-filippi-a-tv-talk-parla-del-trono-gay-di-uomini-e-donne-e-stato-giusto-e-pacato-baci-censurati-no-uno-deve-ancora-andare-in-onda/.

81. Silvia Fumarola, "Basta esclusioni Uomini e donne adesso si apre al tronista gay," *Repubblica.it*, September 2, 2016, http://ricerca.repubblica.it/repubblica/archivio/repubblica/2016/09/02/basta-esclusioni-uomini-e-donne-adesso-si-apre-al-tronista-gay41.html.

82. Monica Cirinnà (@MonicaCirinna), "Da oggi il #tronogay entra con normalità a #uominiedonne. Grazie a #MariaDeFilippi per il coraggio contro #omofobia," Twitter, September 14, 2016, http://www.twitter.com/ MonicaCirinna.

83. *Uomini e donne*, "Un giorno speciale."

84. See Michela Marzano, *Papà, mamma e gender* (Novara: UTET, 2015); Lorenzo Bernini, "La 'teoria del gender,' i 'negazionisti' e la 'fine della differenza sessuale,'" *AboutGender* 5, no. 10 (2016): 367–381; Giovanni Dall'Orto, "I turbamenti del giovane Gender," *H-ermes: Journal of Communication* 7 (2016): 33–60; Chiara Lalli, *Tutti pazzi per il gender* (Roma: Fandango, 2016); and Sara Garbagnoli and Massimo Prearo, *La crociata "anti-gender." Dal Vaticano alle manif pour tous* (Torino: Kaplan, 2018).

85. See, for example, _DottorGay (@dottor_gay), "@marioadinolfi Dopo i 2 papà su kung fu Panda 3 adesso anche il #tronogay in fascia protetta. Faccia qualcosa," Twitter meme, March 30, 2016, https://twitter.com/dottor_gay/status/715152184338419717.

86. Geosocial networking mobile applications geared toward gay and bisexual men and designed to help them meet other men in their area, often for sex.

87. francesco (@macheansia), "Si dice che il nome del programma cambierà in: Uomini e Donne mancate. #tronogay," Twitter, March 30, 2016, http://www.twitter.com/macheansia.

88. P. L. (@PieroLatino), "A Settembre trono gay a Uomini e Donne. Ed è subito 'Uomini e Gonne,'" Twitter, March 30, 2016, http://www.twitter.com/PieroLatino.

89. Luca Fabb (@luca_fabb), "Grazie per questa orrenda ed ulteriore spettacolarizzazione del sesso. Ci mancava. #tronogay #uominieuomini," Twitter, March 30, 2016, http://www.twitter.com/luca_fabb.

90. Paolo Napolitano (@NapolitanoPaul), "Quindi si chiamerà Uomini, Gay & Donne? #tronogay," Twitter, March 30, 2016, http://www.twitter.com/NapolitanoPaul.

91. Malici, "Queer TV Moments"; and Malici, "Watching Queer Television."

92. enrico (@ENRICO_V), "#tronogay immagino quanti diventeranno gay x le telecamere, nulla contro i gay se nn ci fosse la scienza avremmo scoperto cm ci estingueremo," Twitter, March 30, 2016, http://www.twitter.com/enrico_v.

93. Alberto Colli (@MrTurtelen), "Ma lo chiamate #tronogay perché c'è un puntello al centro della seduta?" Twitter, March 30, 2016, http://www.twitter.com/MrTurtelen.

94. David Buckingham and Sara Bragg, *Young People, Sex and the Media: The Facts of Life?* (Basingstoke: Palgrave Macmillan, 2004), 4.

95. radio_zek (@radio_zek), "Sono partiti i casting per il #tronogay di #uominiedonne. -Trono gay? Al pomeriggio? E come lo spiego a mio figlio?" Twitter, May 31, 2016, http://www.twitter.com/MrTurtelen.

96. Michele Imberti (@MicheleImberti), "'Cosa dico ai miei figli?!' Cazzi tuoi. Mica sono i miei. #uominiedonne #tronogay," Twitter, August 27, 2016, http://www.twitter.com/MicheleImberti.

97. Adnkronos, "Moige boccia 'Gf Vip', 'Uomini e donne' e 'Dalla vostra parte,'" *Adnkronos.com*, June 22, 2017, http://www.adnkronos.com/intrattenimento/spettacolo/2017/06/22/moige-boccia-vip-uomini-donne-dalla-vostra-parte_BM0bpRQThYMlKk3X9GiqYN.htm.

98. For example, Francesco Dell'Acqua, "Da Maria."

99. Beatrice Gentili, "Uomini e Donne, trono gay: sui social commenti omofobi contro il casting," *Lineadiretta24.it*, June 1, 2016, http://www.lineadiretta24.it/tv-costume/arriva-ufficialmente-il-trono-gay.html; Lezpop.it, "Uomini e Donne trono gay: arriva l'annuncio ufficiale e i commenti omofobi!" *Lezpop.it*, May 31, 2016, http://www.lezpop.it/uomini-donne-trono-gay-arriva-lannuncio-ufficiale-commenti-omofobi/.

100. Bitchyf, "Trono gay: pioggia di commenti omofobi contro il bacio di Claudio e Mario," December 13, 2016, http://www.bitchyf.it/trono-gay-pioggia-commenti-omofobi-bacio-claudio-mario/.

101. See Gay.it, "'Che schifo', 'malati', 'gente aberrante': la scelta di Claudio Sona al Trono Gay presa di mira dagli omofobi," *Gay.it*, December 17, 2016, http://www.gay.it/televisione/gallery/commenti-omofobi-claudio-sona.

102. Luca P. (@tznlucas), "Nella vita reale avrebbero limonato dopo 24 ore E a #uominiedonne fanno le esterne filosofiche #tronogay #uominiedonne," Twitter, October 21, 2016, http://www.twitter.com/tznlucas.

103. Titta, "Maria De Filippi."

104. *Uomini e donne*, "Il bacio non visto"; *Uomini e donne*, "Il bacio e il bivio."

105. Michele (@xMikele87), "Si auto-censurano il bacio #uominedonne #tronogay," Twitter, December 13, 2016, http://www.twitter.com/xMikele87.

106. Christian Bianca (@XiaNb82), "Ipocrisia Sovrana...#uominedonne #uominieuomini #tronogay #tronoclassico #censura #bacio #primobaciogay #nonvale #peccato," Twitter, December 13, 2016, http://www.twitter.com/XiaNb82.

107. Gay.it, "Che schifo"; *Uomini e donne*, "Un giorno speciale."

108. Chaka Bachmann and Becca Gooch, *LGBT in Britain: Hate Crime and Discrimination, 2017*, accessed May 30, 2018, https://www.stonewall.org.uk/comeoutforLGBT/lgbt-in-britain/hate-crime.

109. *Uomini e donne*, "Un giorno speciale."

110. Vieneskifo (@stoabestemmia), "Qualcuno avvisa #adinolfi di cosa trasmettono ora a #uominiedonne ? Esterna a Napoli con bagno di folla pro #tronogay #clario," Twitter, December 16, 2016, http://www.twitter.com/stoabestemmia.

111. Mister G (@MisterG1991), "Solo perchè ci son le telecamere tutti contenti. se fossero stati soli sarebbe volato qualche insulto purtroppo #uominiedonne #tronogay," Twitter, December 16, 2016, http://www.twitter.com/MisterG1991.

112. See, for example, Gay.it, "Un'estate all'insegna dell'omofobia," *Gay.it*, September 2, 2009, http://www.gay.it/attualita/news/un-estate-all-insegna-dell-omofobia; and the Arcigay Report on Homo-Transphobia 2017: *Report Omotransfobia*, *Arcigay.it*, May 17, 2017, https://www.arcigay.it/wp-content/uploads/2017/05/Reportomofobia2017.pdf.

113. Malici, "Queer TV Moments"; and Malici, "Watching Queer Television."

114. See, for example, Clariofanfiction, *Love is Love*, accessed May 30, 2018, https://www.wattpad.com/story/91862078-loveislove/parts.

115. LO SFIGATTO (@TheSfigatto), "Però so carini maschio e maschio che ballano (cit. mi nonna) #uominiedonne #tronogay," Twitter, October 25, 2016, http://www.twitter.com/TheSfigatto.

116. Simona Bastioni (@SimonaBastioni), "Mia mamma, che ha sempre voluto un maschio, adesso vorrebbe un gay. Grazie Maria! #uominiedonne #mammina #tronogay," Twitter, November 2, 2016, http://www.twitter.com/SimonaBastioni.

117. Franci, "Vladimir Luxuria dice la sua sull'eventualità di un trono gay a Uomini e Donne: 'Finalmente si parlerebbe d'amore a prescindere dal sesso!,'" *isaechia.it*, April 2, 2016, http://www.isaechia.it/2016/04/02/vladimir-luxuria-dice-la-sua-sulleventualita-di-un-trono-gay-a-uomini-e-donne-finalmente-si-parlerebbe-damore-a-prescindere-dal-sesso/.

118. Titta, "Maria De Filippi."

119. Zia enri (@louisstrawberry), "Spero solo non lo riempiano di 'steriotipi' tipo solo tizi effemminati o donne macho #tronogay," Twitter, March 30, 2016, http://www.twitter.com/louisstrawberry.

120. Alessandro (@critico87k), "I tronisti gay saranno super fashon,,,spinzettati, con un ego pazzesco,,,PRATICAMENTE come quelli etero,,,,#tronogay," Twitter, March 30, 2016, http://www.twitter.com/critico87k.

121. Barbara Diamanti (@barbaradiamanti), "#tronogay sono molto più virili dei concorrenti etero. Fa piacere che siano persone molto lontane dallo stereotipo della checca. Ci piace," Twitter, September 14, 2016, http://www.twitter.com/barbaradiamanti.

122. West Andy, "The Rise of Campophobia. Why Does There Seem to be Such an Increase in Rejecting Campness?" *The Independent*, December 18, 2012, http://www.independent.co.uk/voices/comment/the-rise-of-campophobia-8422628.html.

123. Dario Accolla, "E al trono gay va in onda lo stereotipo sui gay poco maschili," *Gaypost.it*, October 1, 2016, http://www.gaypost.it/trono-gay-stereotipo-ma schile-scorrano.

124. Bageisha (@SaintPoppy), "Voglio tronisti bear, otter, twink, wolf, hunk, jock. Voglio tronisti effeminati e tronisti masc4masc #uominiedonne #tronogay," Twitter, March 30, 2016, http://www.twitter.com/SaintPoppy.

125. Despite having had some corteggiatori and corteggiatrici of various ethnic backgrounds and second-generation Italians, the program is yet to host a black or Asian male tronista.

126. Sad fluffy grinch (@hemmoschannel), "Quindi poi avremo anche il trono black, asiatico, transessuale, pansessuale, asessuale, bisessuale. Giusto per non fare differenze #tronogay," Twitter, March 30, 2016, http://www.twitter.com/hemmoschannel.

127. Vladimir luxuria (@vladiluxuria), "#uominiedonne Maria please dopo il #tronogay dammi il #tronotrans: cerco marito vivo e paziente! magari il miracolo lo fai tu.... :))))" Twitter, September 14, 2016, http://www.twitter.com/vladiluxuria.

128. See Cicchini, "La parte per il tutto"; Alliva, "Uomini e donne"; and Rosario Coco, "Trono gay: Maria De Filippi riempie il vuoto Rai," September 15, 2016, http://www.anddos.org/trono-gay-maria-de-filippi-riempie-il-vuoto-rai/.

129. *Uomini e donne*, "Un giorno speciale."

130. Alliva, "Uomini e donne."

131. I only found an event organized by DELOS (Italian acronym for Rights, Equality and Freedom for Sexual Orientation) an association in Vicenza since 2011. On October 5, 2016 they held a meeting titled "Trash & TV: Trono gay. I gay nell'universo Defilippico" (http://www.delosvicenza.it/eventi) to discuss the impact of mainstream TV, and this program in particular, on Italian gay, lesbian, bisexuals, transgender, heterosexual, and queer individuals (they use the acronym "GLBTEQ").

132. The first two seasons with gay participants both took place during the winter season (September to December 2016 and 2017) whereas the following spring seasons (January to May) remained exclusive to heterosexual contestants, as crucially, did the following three seasons of the program between January 2018 and June

2019. The trono gay so far appears to be an unpredictable, special event and remains perhaps an experience that the production company must carefully consider, or from which they must take a break.

BIBLIOGRAPHY

Accolla, Dario. "E al trono gay va in onda lo stereotipo sui gay poco maschili." *Gaypost.it*, October 1, 2016. http://www.gaypost.it/trono-gay-stereotipo-maschile-scorrano.

Adnkronos. "Moige boccia 'Gf Vip', 'Uomini e donne' e 'Dalla vostra parte'." *Adnkronos.com*, June 22, 2017. http://www.adnkronos.com/intrattenimento/spettacolo/2017/06/22/moige-boccia-vip-uomini-donne-dalla-vostra-parte_BM0bpRQThYMlKk3X9GiqYN.htm.

Alessandro. "I tronisti gay saranno super fashon,,,spinzettati, con un ego pazzesco,,,PRATICAMENTE come quelli etero,,,,#tronogay." Twitter, March 30, 2016. http://www.twitter.com/critico87k.

Alliva, Simone. "'Uomini e donne' e il trono gay: i ragazzi stanno bene." *Gaypost. it*, September 14, 2016. http://www.gaypost.it/uomini-donne-trono-gay-i-ragazzi-stanno-bene.

Arcigay. *Report Omotransfobia. Arcigay.it*, May 17, 2017. https://www.arcigay.it/wp-content/uploads/2017/05/Reportomofobia2017.pdf.

Arthurs, Jane. *Television and Sexuality: Regulation and the Politics of Taste*. New York: Open University Press, 2004.

AUDITEL data 2012. "Composizione del pubblico di Uomini e Donne (Canale 5)." *Tvblog.it*, accessed May 30, 2018. http://www.tvblog.it/post/36635/uomini-e-donne-maria-de-filippi-bilancio-ascolti-auditel.

AUDITEL data 2015–2016. "Bilancio stagione 2015–2016 Uomini e Donne (Canale 5)." *Tvblog.it*, accessed May 30, 2018. http://www.tvblog.it/post/1327931/focus-ascolti-tvblog-bilancio-stagione-2015-2016-uomini-e-donne-canale-5.

Bachmann, Chaka, and Gooch, Becca. *LGBT in Britain: Hate Crime and Discrimination,* 2017. Accessed May 30, 2018. https://www.stonewall.org.uk/comeoutforLGBT/lgbt-in-britain/hate-crime.

Bageisha. "Voglio tronisti bear, otter, twink, wolf, hunk, jock. Voglio tronisti effeminati e tronisti masc4masc #uominiedonne #tronogay." Twitter, March 30, 2016. http://www.twitter.com/SaintPoppy.

Barretta, Nicolò, and Santon, Maria Elisabetta. *La signora della tv. Fenomenologia di Maria De Filippi*. Milano: Unicolpi, 2013.

Bastioni, Simona. "Mia mamma, che ha sempre voluto un maschio, adesso vorrebbe un gay. Grazie Maria! #uominiedonne #mammina #tronogay." Twitter, November 2, 2016. http://www.twitter.com/SimonaBastioni.

Be.Mon. "L'annuncio della figlia del marò Latorre: 'Pronta a partecipare al trono gay della De Filippi'." *Corriere.it,* May 5, 2016. http://www.corriere.it/cronache/16_maggio_05/annuncio-figlia-maro-latorre-pronta-partecipare-trono-gay-de-filippi-ecc131a8-128c-11e6-918d-cff62dc61260.shtml.

Bernini, Lorenzo. "La 'teoria del gender', i 'negazionisti' e la 'fine della differenza sessuale'." *AboutGender* 5, no. 10 (2016): 367–381.

Bianca, Christian. "Ipocrisia Sovrana . . . #uominedonne #uominieuomini #tronogay #tronoclassico #censura #bacio #primobaciogay #nonvale #peccato." Twitter, December 13, 2016. http://www.twitter.com/XiaNb82.

Bitchyf. "Trono gay: pioggia di commenti omofobi contro il bacio di Claudio e Mario." *bitchyf.it,* December 13, 2016. http://www.bitchyf.it/trono-gay-pioggia-commenti-omofobi-bacio-claudio-mario/.

Bitchyf. "Emma Marrone lesbica e fidanzata con Maria De Filippi? Parla la cantante su Grazia." *bitchyf.it,* Jannuary, 25 2018. https://www.bitchyf.it/emma-marrone-lesbica-fidanzata-con-maria-de-filippi.

Bourdieu, Pierre. *Distinction: A Social Critique of the Judgement of Taste.* London: Routledge, 1984.

Brokeback Mountain. Directed by Ang Lee. 2005.

Buckingham, David, and Bragg, Sara. *Young People, Sex and the Media: The Facts of Life?* Basingstoke: Palgrave Macmillan, 2004.

Capatti, Irene. *Le donne in televisione. Analisi degli stereotipi sul corpo e sui ruoli attraverso il programma Uomini e donne.* PhD diss., Università di Bologna, 2015.

Carini, Stefania. "Uomini e donne." In *Televisione convergente. La tv oltre il piccolo schermo*, edited by Aldo Grasso and Massimiliano, Scaglioni, 147–156. Milan: RTI, 2010.

C'è posta per te. Created by Maria De Filippi. Italy: Canale 5, 2000–present.

CENSIS. *I media tra élite e popolo, 13° Rapporto Censis-Ucsi sulla comunicazione.* September 28, 2016. http://www.censis.it/7?shadow_comunicato_stampa=121073.

Chambers, Samuel A. *The Queer Politics of Television.* London; New York: I. B. Tauris, 2009.

Cicchini, Alessio. "La parte per il tutto: ecco perché il trono gay di Uomini e Donne non può (e non deve) rappresentare tutta la comunità LGBT." *Gay.it*, October 1, 2016. http://www.gay.it/televisione/news/uomini-e-donne-trono-gay-stereotipi-lgbt.

Cirinnà, Monica. "Da oggi il #tronogay entra con normalità a #uominiedonne. Grazie a #MariaDeFilippi per il coraggio contro #omofobia." Twitter, September 14, 2016. http://www.twitter.com/ MonicaCirinna.

Clariofanfiction 2016. *Love is Love.* Accessed May 30, 2018. https://www.wattpad.com/story/91862078-loveislove/parts.

Coco, Rosario. "Trono gay: Maria De Filippi riempie il vuoto Rai." September 15, 2016. http://www.anddos.org/trono-gay-maria-de-filippi-riempie-il-vuoto-rai/.

Colli, Alberto. "Ma lo chiamate #tronogay perché c'è un puntello al centro della seduta?" Twitter, March 30, 2016. http://www.twitter.com/MrTurtelen.

Cominetti, Andrea. "Il trono gay fa bene all'Italia." *Letteradonna.it*, September 30, 2016. http://letteradonna.it/263475/trono-gay-uomini-e-donne-pareri-politici-persoonagg.

COTINO 5. "Santa Maria mater gay #tronogay." Twitter, March 30, 2016. http://www.twitter.com/cotiedp.

Dall'Orto, Giovanni. "I turbamenti del giovane Gender." *H-ermes: Journal of Communication*, no. 7 (2016): 33–60.

D'Amato, Marina. "Le donne dello schermo. Uno studio di caso." *Storia delle donne*, no. 3 (2007): 61–76. Firenze: University Press.

Davis, Glyn, and Needham, Gary. *Queer TV: Theories, Histories, Politics*. London: Routledge, 2009.

De Filippi, Maria. *Amici di sera. Gli adolescenti e la famiglia*. Milano: Oscar Mondadori, 1998.

de Lauretis, Teresa. "Queer Theory: Lesbian and Gay Sexualities. An Introduction." *differences* 3, no. 2 (1991): iii–xviii.

Dell'Acqua, Francesco. "Da Maria De Filippi a Nonno Libero: la nuova stagione arcobaleno della televisione italiana." *Il sole 24 ore.com*, November 7, 2016. http://www.alleyoop.ilsole24ore.com/2016/11/07/da-maria-de-filippi-a-nonno-libero-la-nuova-stagione-arcobaleno-della-televisione-italiana/.

Diamanti, Barbara. "#tronogay sono molto più virili dei concorrenti etero. Fa piacere che siano persone molto lontane dallo stereotipo della checca. Ci piace." Twitter, September 14, 2016. http://www.twitter.com/barbaradiamanti.

Di Girolamo, Giulia. "Per un mondo migliore: #unionicivili in Italia e #tronogay a #uominiedonne al posto del Trono Classico #svegliatitalia." Twitter, January 25, 2016. http://www.twitter.com/ giugidigir.

Dines, Martin, and Rigoletto, Sergio. "Country Cousins: Europeanness, Sexuality and Locality in Contemporary Italian Television." *Modern Italy* 12, no. 4 (2012): 479–491.

Dollimore, Jonathan. *Sexual Dissidence: Augustine to Wilde, Freud to Foucault*. Oxford: University Press, 1991.

Duggan, Lisa. "The New Homonormativity: The Sexual Politics of Neoliberalism." In *Materializing Democracy: Toward a Revitalized Cultural Politics*, edited by Russ Castronovo and Dana D. Nelson, 175–194. Durham, NC: Duke University Press, 2002.

Durante, Ruben, Pinotti, Paolo, and Tesei, Andrea. "The Political Legacy of Entertainment TV." *American Economic Review* 109, no. 7 (July 2019): 2497–2530.

Elevctraheart. "Va bene il #tronogay, ma le #unionicivili se ne sono andate a fanculandia?" Twitter, March 30, 2016. http://www.twitter.com/elevctraheart.

Emanuele_DottorGay. "Se Maria ha deciso che deve esserci il #tronogay vuol dire che è tempo di matrimonio egualitario. E i bigotti muti." Twitter, March 30, 2016. http://www.twitter.com/ dottor_gay.

Enrico. "#tronogay immagino quanti diventeranno gay x le telecamere, nulla contro i gay se nn ci fosse la scienza avremmo scoperto cm ci estingueremo." Twitter, March 30, 2016. http://www.twitter.com/enrico_v.

Erbaggio, Pierluigi. "#*GomorraLaSerie*: Convergin Audience and Enhanced Authorship on Twenty-First-Century Italian Screens." *Modern Italy* 20, no. 4 (2015): 335–349.

Eurotrash. Created by Peter Stuart. UK: Channel 4, 1993–2004.

Fabb, Luca. "Grazie per questa orrenda ed ulteriore spettacolarizzazione del sesso. Ci mancava. #tronogay #uominieuomini." Twitter, March 30, 2016. http://www.twitter.com/luca_fabb.

FiglieDellaServa. "Col #tronogay si realizza la vera parificazione, i gay diventano parte integrante del #trash." Twitter, March 30, 2016. http://www.twitter.com/FigliedelaServa.

Fraciraffo. "Farà molto di più #MariaDeFilippi per #gay che legge #Cirinà #unionicivili #tronogay." Twitter, March 30, 2016. http://www.twitter.com/fraciraffo.

Francesco. "Si dice che il nome del programma cambierà in: Uomini e Donne mancate. #tronogay." Twitter, March 30, 2016. http://www.twitter.com/macheansia.

Franci. "Vladimir Luxuria dice la sua sull'eventualità di un trono gay a Uomini e Donne: 'Finalmente si parlerebbe d'amore a prescindere dal sesso!'." *isaechia.it*, April 2, 2016. http://www.isaechia.it/2016/04/02/vladimir-luxuria-dice-la-sua-su lleventualita-di-un-trono-gay-a-uomini-e-donne-finalmente-si-parlerebbe-dam ore-a-prescindere-dal-sesso/.

Fumarola, Silvia. "Basta esclusioni Uomini e donne adesso si apre al tronista gay." *Repubblica.it*, September 2, 2016. http://ricerca.repubblica.it/repubblica/archivio/r epubblica/2016/09/02/basta-esclusioni-uomini-e-donne-adesso-si-apre-al-tronista-gay41.html.

Gamson, Joshua. *Freaks Talk Back: Tabloid Talk Shows and Sexual Noncomformity*. Chicago: University of Chicago Press, 1998.

Gandini, Erik. *Videocrazy*. DVD. Directed by Erik Gandini. New York: Lorber Kino, 2009.

Garbagnoli, Sara, and Prearo, Massimo. *La crociata "anti-gender." Dal Vaticano alle manif pour tous*. Torino: Kaplan, 2018.

Gay.it. "Un'estate all'insegna dell'omofobia." *Gay.it*, September 2, 2009. http://www.gay.it/attualita/news/un-estate-all-insegna-dell-omofobia.

Gay.it. "'Che schifo', 'malati', 'gente aberrante': la scelta di Claudio Sona al Trono Gay presa di mira dagli omofobi." *Gay.it*, December 17, 2016. http://www.gay.it/televisione/gallery/commenti-omofobi-claudio-sona.

Gentili, Beatrice. "Uomini e Donne, trono gay: sui social commenti omofobi contro il casting." *Lineadiretta24.it*, June 1, 2016. http://www.lineadiretta24.it/tv-costume/arriva-ufficialmente-il-trono-gay.html.

Grasso, Aldo, and Scaglioni, Massimiliano. *Televisione convergente. La tv oltre il piccolo schermo*. Milan: RTI, 2010.

Grazioli, Tina. "È una vergogna che nessuno abbia ancora aperto un processo di beatificazione per Maria #tronogay." Twitter, March 30, 2016. http://www.twitter.com/TinaGrazioli.

Gretaebasta. "Queen Mary che ascolta le nostre preghiere e finalmente farà il #tronogay!! Era ora!!!" Twitter, March 30, 2016. http://www.twitter.com/greta_pittana.

Grindstaff, Laura. *The Money Shot: Trash, Class and the Making of TV Talk Shows*. Chicago: University of Chicago Press, 2002.

Hipkins, Danielle. "'Whore-ocracy': Show Girls, the Beauty Trade-Off, and Mainstream Oppositional Discourse in Contemporary Italy." *Italian Studies* 66, no. 3 (2011): 413–430.

Hipkins, Danielle. "Who Wants to be a TV Showgirl?: Auditions, Talent and Taste in Contemporary Popular Italian Cinema." *The Italianist*, no. 32 (2012): 154–190.

How to Get Away with Murder. Created by Peter Nowalk. USA: ABC, 2014–present.

I Diari del Disagio. "Rendersi conto che per la comunità gay, in materia di uguaglianza, #mariadefilippi fa più dell'intero Parlamento. #uominiedonne #tronogay." Twitter, March 30, 2016. http://www.twitter.com/diarideldisagio.

Ilenia. "#MariaDeFilippi SANTA SUBITO #uominiedonne waiting for #tronogay." Twitter, March 30, 2016. http://www.twitter.com/Ilenia_aca.

il Maschilista. "L Italia quel paese dove il progresso è promosso da una conduttrice tv #tronogay." Twitter, March 30, 2016. http://www.twitter.com/MaschilistaITA.

Imberti, Michele. "'Cosa dico ai miei figli?!' Cazzi tuoi. Mica sono i miei. #uominiedonne #tronogay." Twitter, August 27, 2016. http://www.twitter.com/MicheleImberti.

Jenkins, Henry. *Convergence Culture.* New York: New York University Press, 2006.

Kellakiara. "Maria De Filippi che move il sole e l'altre stelle." Twitter, March 30, 2016. http://www.twitter.com/Kellakiara.

Kellakiara. "Noi scherziamo ma quando la casalinga di Gela scoprirà che STI FROCI ALLA FINE SO' BRAVI, sarà davvero una rivoluzione culturale #tronogay." Twitter, March 30, 2016. http://www.twitter.com/kellakiara.

Krashaar, Emanuele. *Iconoclasti. Maria De Filippi.* Padova: Alet edizioni, 2011.

Kristeva, Julia. *Powers of Horror: An Essay on Abjection.* New York: Columbia University Press, 1982.

Labranca, Tommaso. *Andy Warhol era un coatto. Vivere e capire il trash.* Rome: Castelvecchi, 2004.

Lalli, Chiara. *Tutti pazzi per il gender.* Roma: Fandango, 2016.

La Stampa. "Tronista e Subprime entrano nello Zingarelli 2009." *La Stampa.it,* October 7, 2008. http://www.lastampa.it/2008/10/07/societa/tronista-e-subprime-entrano-nello-zingarelli-RB66uO6whsxVGtzY8cH3QN/pagina.html.

La Torre, Cathy. "#DeFilippi lancia #tronogay. Io invece vorrei sapere che fine hanno fatto #unionicivili. O dobbiamo andare a C'è posta per te per scoprirlo?" Twitter, March 30, 2016. http://www.twitter.com/catlatorre.

Legrottaglie, Pasqua. *Una telespettatrice particolare: una counselor alla corte di Maria.* PhD diss., Accademia per la Riprogrammazione, 2013.

Lezpop.it. "Uomini e Donne trono gay: arriva l'annuncio ufficiale e i commenti omofobi!" *Lezpop.it,* May 31, 2016. http://www.lezpop.it/uomini-donne-trono-gay-arriva-lannuncio-ufficiale-commenti-omofobi/.

Lo sfigatto. "Però so carini maschio e maschio che ballano (cit. mi nonna) #uominiedonne #tronogay." Twitter, October 25, 2016. http://www.twitter.com/TheSfigatto.

Luxuria, Vladimir. "#uominiedonne Maria please dopo il #tronogay dammi il #tronotrans: cerco marito vivo e paziente! magari il miracolo lo fai tu . . . :))))" Twitter, September 14, 2016. http://www.twitter.com/vladiluxuria.

Maietta, Marco. "Sono contento del #tronogay Così ci rendiamo conto che la sessualità prescinde sempre da tutte le cose, anche quando si parla di idiozia." Twitter, March 30, 2016. http://www.twitter.com/MaiettaMarco.

Maggio, Davide. "Auditel: Ascolti TV del giorno," 2016. Accessed May 30, 2018. www.davidemaggio.it/archives.

Malici, Luca. "Queer in Italy: Italian Televisibility and the 'Queerable' Audience." In *Queer in Europe: Contemporary Case Studies,* edited by Lisa Downing and Robert Gillett, 113–128. London: Ashgate, 2011.

Malici, Luca. "Italian S-queer Eyes: Surveying and Voicing Television Representations." In *Queer Crossings: Theories, Bodies, Texts,* edited by Silvia Antosa, 105–122. Milan: Mimesis, 2012.

Malici, Luca. "Queer TV Moments and Family Viewing in Italy." *Journal of GLBT Family Studies* 10, nos. 1–2 (2014): 188–210.

Malici, Luca. *Watching Queer Television: A Case Study of the Representation, Circulation and Reception of Sexual Dissidence on Italian Mainstream TV from 1990 to 2012*. PhD diss., University of Birmingham, 2015.

Manga, Julie. *Talking Trash: The Cultural Politics of Daytime TV Talk Shows*. New York: New York University Press, 2003.

Marzano, Michela. *Papà, mamma e gender*. Novara: UTET, 2015.

Mavih. "Il trash non discrimina #tronogay." Twitter, March 30, 2016. http://www.twitter.com/mavih.

McCoy, Charles, and Scarborough, Roscoe. "The Guilty Pleasure of Watching Trashy TV." *The Conversation*, May 20, 2015. https://theconversation.com/the-guilty-pleasure-of-watching-trashy-tv-40214.

Michele. "Si auto-censurano il bacio #uominedonne #tronogay." Twitter, December 13, 2016. http://www.twitter.com/xMikele87.

Mister, G. "Solo perchè ci son le telecamere tutti contenti . . . se fossero stati soli sarebbe volato qualche insulto purtroppo #uominiedonne #tronogay." Twitter, December 16, 2016. http://www.twitter.com/MisterG1991.

Mujeres, Hombres y Viceversa. Created by Maria De Filippi. Spain: Telecinco, 2008–present.

Murthy, Dhiraj. "The Ontology of Tweets: Mixed-Method Approaches to the Study of Twitter." In *The Sage Handbook of Social Media Research Methods*, edited by Sloan Luke and Anabel Quan-Haase, 559–572. London: Sage, 2017.

Napolitano, Paolo. "Quindi si chiamerà Uomini, Gay & Donne? #tronogay." Twitter, March 30, 2016. http://www.twitter.com/NapolitanoPaul.

Naso, Domenico. "Rai Due censura il sesso in 'Le regole del delitto perfetto' Ma solo quello gay." *Il fatto quotidiano.it*, July 9, 2016a. http://www.ilfattoquotidiano.it/2016/07/09/rai-due-censura-il-sesso-le-regole-del-delitto-perfetto-ma-solo-quello-gay/2893053/.

Naso, Domenico. "Uomini e Donne, da settembre arriva il 'trono gay'. E così Maria De Filippi sdogana le coppie omosessuali in tv." *Il fatto quotidiano.it*, March 31, 2016b. http://www.ilfattoquotidiano.it/2016/03/31/uomini-e-donne-da-settembre-arriva-il-trono-gay-e-cosi-maria-de-filippi-sdogana-le-coppie-omosessuali-in-tv/2595468/.

O'Leary, Alan. "The Phenomenology of the Cinepanettone." *Italian Studies* 66, no. 3 (2011): 431–443.

O'Leary, Alan. *Fenomenologia del cinepanettone*. Soveria Mannelli: Rubbettino, 2013.

Panarari, Massimiliano. "Dal costume al coattume nazionale: Maria De Filippi 'arbitra' *elegantiarum* della neo-Italia." In *L'egemonia sottoculturale: L'Italia da Gramsci al gossip*, 73–88. Turin: Einaudi, 2010.

Panarari, Massimiliano. "Maria De Filippi, critica della ragion televisiva." *La stampa.it*, March 3, 2012. http://www.lastampa.it/2012/03/10/cultura/maria-de-filippi-critica-della-ragion-televisiva-RMWc1oRltXwv74lVwCj0eJ/pagina.html.

Patriarca, Salvatore. *Il mistero di Maria. La filosofia, la De Filippi e la televisione*. Milano-Udine: Mimesis Edizioni, 2012.

Pennisi, Martina. "Uomini e Donne, Maria De Filippi ha deciso: da settembre il trono gay." *corriere.it*, March 30, 2016. http://www.corriere.it/spettacoli/16_marzo_30/uomini-donne-trono-gay-ufficiale-maria-de-filippi-921fe566-f656-11e5-b728-3bdfea23c73f.shtml.

Peruzzo, Manuel. "Uomini e Donne gay, così Maria De Filippi non fa altro che seguire il suo pubblico." *Il foglio.it*, March 31, 2016. http://www.ilfoglio.it/cultura/2016/03/31/news/uomini-e-donne-gay-cosi-maria-de-filippi-non-fa-altro-che-seguire-il-suo-pubblico-94414/.

P.L. "A Settembre trono gay a Uomini e Donne. Ed è subito 'Uomini e Gonne'." Twitter, March 30, 2016. http://www.twitter.com/PieroLatino.

P. Luca. "Nella vita reale avrebbero limonato dopo 24 ore E a #uominiedonne fanno le esterne filosofiche #tronogay #uominiedonne." Twitter, October 21, 2016. http://www.twitter.com/tznlucas.

Proia, Roberto. "'Le regole del delitto perfetto', Raidue si scusa e manda in onda la versione integrale." *Il fatto quotidiano.it*, July 10, 2016. https://www.ilfattoquotidiano.it/2016/07/10/le-regole-del-delitto-perfetto-raidue-si-scusa-e-manda-in-onda-la-versione-integrale/2894951/.

Radio_zek. "Sono partiti i casting per il #tronogay di #uominiedonne. -Trono gay? Al pomeriggio? E come lo spiego a mio figlio?" Twitter, May 31, 2016. http://www.twitter.com/MrTurtelen.

Romano, Luca. "Teoria gender e ascolti flop, la Bignardi si dimetta." *Il gionrale.it*, December 27, 2016. http://www.ilgiornale.it/news/spettacoli/teoria-gender-e-ascolti-flop-bignardi-si-dimetta-1346249.html.

Sad fluffy grinch. "Quindi poi avremo anche il trono black, asiatico, transessuale, pansessuale, asessuale, bisessuale. Giusto per non fare differenze #tronogay." Twitter, March 30, 2016. http://www.twitter.com/hemmoschannel.

Sloan, Luke. "Social Science 'Lite'? Deriving Demographic Proxies from Twitter." In *the Sage Handbook of Social Media Research Methods*, edited by Sloan Luke and Anabel Quan-Haase, 90–104. London: Sage, 2017.

Stanoeva, Milena. *Hate Watching Trash TV: Intersections of Class and Anti-Fandom*. PhD diss., York University, Toronto, Ontario, 2016.

Stato Civile: l'amore è uguale per tutti. Directed by Giampaolo Marconato. Italy: RAI 3, December 2016–September 2017.

The Bachelor. Created by Mike Fleiss. USA: ABC, 2002–present.

Titta. "Maria De Filippi a 'Tv Talk' parla del Trono gay di Uomini e Donne: 'È stato giusto e pacato. Baci censurati? No, uno deve ancora andare in onda!'." *isaechia.it*, December 4, 2016. http://www.isaechia.it/2016/12/04/maria-de-filippi-a-tv-talk-parla-del-trono-gay-di-uomini-e-donne-e-stato-giusto-e-pacato-baci-censurati-no-uno-deve-ancora-andare-in-onda/.

Townsend, Leanne, and Wallace, Claire. *Social Media Research: A Guide to Ethics*. The University of Aberdeen, 2017. Accessed May 30, 2018. https://www.gla.ac.uk/media/media_487729_en.pdf.

Uomini e donne. Created by Maria De Filippi. Italy: Canale 5, 1996–present.

Uomini e donne. "Il quartetto." Created by Maria De Filippi. Italy: Canale 5, September 14, 2016. http://www.wittytv.it/uomini-e-donne/mercoledi-14-settembre-il-quartetto/.

Uomini e donne. "Il bacio non visto." Created by Maria De Filippi. Italy: Canale 5, November 22, 2016. http://www.wittytv.it/uomini-e-donne/martedi-22-novembre-il-bacio-non-visto/.

Uomini e donne. "Il bacio e il bivio." Created by Maria De Filippi. Italy: Canale 5, Decembre 13, 2016. http://www.wittytv.it/uomini-e-donne/martedi-13-dicembre-il-bacio-e-il-bivio/.

Uomini e donne. "Un giorno speciale." Created by Maria De Filippi. Italy: Canale 5, Decembre 16, 2016. http://www.wittytv.it/uomini-e-donne/venerdi-16-dicembre-un-giorno-speciale/.

Van Dam, Andrew. "How Trashy TV Made Children Dumber and Enabled a Wave of Populist Leaders." *The Washington Post*, July 20, 2019. https://www.washingtonpost.com/business/2019/07/20/how-trashy-tv-made-children-dumber-enabled-wave-populist-leaders/?utm_term=.a34ab8a1933f.

Vieneskifo. "Qualcuno avvisa #adinolfi di cosa trasmettono ora a #uominiedonne ? Esterna a Napoli con bagno di folla pro #tronogay #clario." Twitter, December 16, 2016. http://www.twitter.com/stoabestemmia.

West, Andy. "The Rise of Campophobia. Why Does there Seem to be Such an Increase in Rejecting Campness?" *The Independent*, December 18, 2012. http://www.independent.co.uk/voices/comment/the-rise-of-campophobia-8422628.html.

Whitaker, Brian. "The Value of Trash TV." *The Guardian*, May 22, 2007. https://www.theguardian.com/commentisfree/2007/may/22/thevalueoftrashtv.

Wood, Helen, and Skeggs, Beverly. *Reality Television and Class*. New York: Palgrave Macmillan, 2011.

Zeni, Simone. "Trono gay, perché quella di Maria De Filippi è una rivoluzione culturale." *Wired.it*, September 14, 2016. https://www.wired.it/play/televisione/2016/09/14/trono-gay-uomini-donne-omosessuali/.

Zia enri. "Spero solo non lo riempiano di 'steriotipi' tipo solo tizi effeminati o donne macho #tronogay." Twitter, March 30, 2016. http://www.twitter.com/louisstrawberry.

Chapter 6

Queer Italian Communities and Alternative Televisual Re/Mediations

Julia Heim

SPECTATORS, MEDIA, AND NATIONHOOD

Italian television is a particularly fruitful place to start when understanding the social position of lesbian, gay, bisexual, transgender, queer, intersex, and asexual (LGBTQIA)[1] people for three main reasons. First, Italian national identity and language unification were developed alongside the development of Italian television in a way that challenges essentialist notions of identity formation. In light of this relationship between media and nationhood, identity can be immediately understood as a construct. Secondly, Italy has been openly ambivalent about conceding rights to these marginalized peoples, making their depictions on television particularly telling of their position in Italian society. Lastly, Italian television's reliance on foreign content and formats complicates the *national* aspects of this national television, expands the kinds of representations Italians have access to, and contributes to the creation of various communities that engage with these programs in different ways at different times. All of this factors in not only to discussions of LGBTQIA people's social standing, but also to the ways that televisions and audiences shape and are shaped by one another.

The current sociopolitical climate of negotiation with regard to LGBTQIA identities in Italy and on Italian television does not give us the full story when exploring representations of these minority populations, queer televisual identifications, and the relationship between theories of queerness and Italian television consumption and production. Because while television is, as Amy Villarejo notes, "one of the most [. . .] gendered and sexualized repetition apparatuses of modern technoscience," we must explore the temporalities (as Villarejo herself has done), technologies, and modes of consumption of the texts themselves to broaden our understanding of the sociocultural-political relationships between nation, television, and queerness.[2] In doing so, this chapter seeks to create a queer lens with which we may view the rise of Italian media producer-consumers (pro-sumers), the bodies of work they create, and the shifting technological landscape with which they engage. In exploring the relationship between queer representation and consumer viewing practices, we may come to find that the dynamic exposes a queer practice and engagement that, while embodied and performative, lies outside the frame of identity politics. The methodology at the base of this analysis is speculative and operates exclusively theoretically; it does not, therefore, seek to make specific claims about Italian audience reception and lived spectator experience.

FRAGMENTED COMMUNITIES IN THE AGE OF MEDIA CONVERGENCE

The beginning of contemporary media convergence—understood as the mixing, overlapping, and combining of all means of communication—was due in part to or, as some scholars argue, completely caused by, the digitalization of television.[3] This convergence is often discussed in terms of a rise in spectator participation as television shifts, as Pulcini says, from a "mass" medium to "my" medium.[4] Participation in television content is one of the primary ways that television continues to redefine itself. The proliferation of the internet, along with other technological advancements, creates a foundation for an ultimate convergence between televisions and computers; these technological changes have helped to redefine the relationship between producers and consumers of televisual content. In this way, to only talk about the global and national forces creating and disseminating content within the television industry suggests a one-sidedness in television's relationship to the spectators consuming its content. Spectators not only help to shape the industry's content, they often actively create their own. Thus, audience reception studies of mainstream content might falsely suggest a unity within the various spectator communities and within the identities of the individuals who form them.

Furthermore, in this current state of televisual convergence we have a blurring of the boundaries of both technology and content. In terms of the televisual text, extensions (or paratexts) created by the networks and those created by consumers across technological platforms all work to form a kind of "megatext." In other words, official Twitter feeds, websites, interviews, spin-off series, books, fan fiction, and fan art all extend the narrative universe of a program. Technology, in turn, creates the means by which these extensions are possible. It is important to keep in mind that participation and enjoyment of each extension of the megatext are not necessarily determined by the extension's creator. Tertiary extensions—extensions created from the "bottom-up," namely by the public actively participating in the text's narrative, are often sparked by the necessity to fill voids not being met by the institutions that created or imported the brand.[5] In terms of viewer creation and consumption, spectator participation in content production is one of the elements that facilitate the coming together of a community around a character, an episode, a season, a series, a moment, or a narrative line of a text. The kinds of communities that are created by televisual convergence depend largely on desired engagement with a brand, but also on the chosen mode of consumption—"chosen," of course, is a loose word that is not meant to dismiss any economic limitations that might actively force consumers into a category with which they might not otherwise identify. In light of the multitude of individuals and communities contributing to the creation, as well as the consumption, of the various parts of the televisual megatext, we may begin to reframe our understanding of the content, the communities, the temporalities, and the technological modes of content production and experience as fractured mediatic moments of engagement.

In *In a Queer Time and Place*, Jack Halberstam introduces the term "technotopic" when discussing representations of the transgender body in art, in order to "refer to the spatial dimensions of this aesthetic, its preoccupation with the body as a site created through technological and aesthetic innovation. Technotopic inventions of the body resist idealizations of body integrity, on the one hand, and rationalizations of disintegration on the other."[6] The composition of the technotopic transgendered body of which he speaks contains a multiplicity of both body parts and their representations, but the end result has no unifying sense. Using the idea of technotopic bodies to look into the relationship between queerness and contemporary television we may identify at least four such bodies at play: the individual consumer/producer as body; the community as body; the consumed televisual text as body; and the produced televisual text as body (see figure 6.1).

While I have identified them as four, they should not be viewed as necessarily separate from one another or whole in themselves. Let us consider these bodies as materializations; they are matter-in-performance, and as such lack fixity both in their relationships to one another, and in their mercurial and fractured individualities. The indeterminacy of this speaks directly to Jasbir Puar's elaborations of assemblage. Assemblage can be understood as "a series of dispersed but mutually implicated and messy networks" which "allow us to attune to movements, intensities, emotions, energies, affectivities, and textures as they inhabit events, spatialities, and corporealities."[7] The televisual bodies we are exploring may thus be seen as technotopic assemblages whose multiplicities run both inward (in the case of the individual body, the bodies of community in which the individual partakes, and the

The Four Televisual Bodies

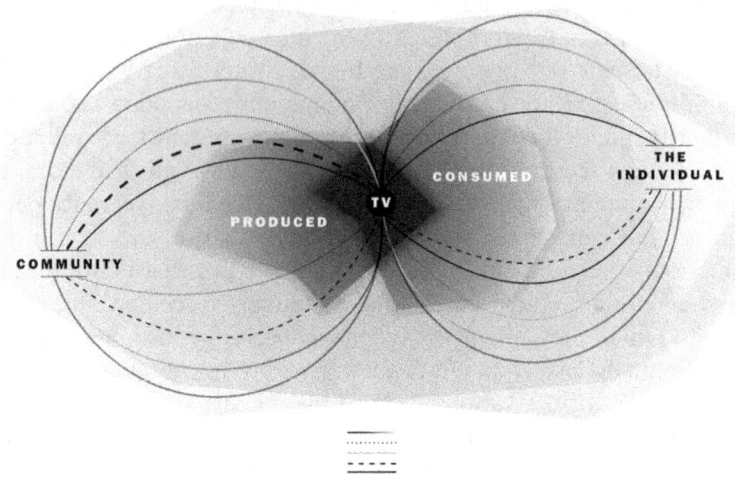

DENOTES ENGAGEMENT VARIANCE

Figure 6.1 *The Four Televisual Bodies. Source:* Created by Kate Dautrich and J. Heim.

televisual body's reception and conceptualization) and outward (as for the body of the televisual product, and the bodies' affective response to reception). Analyzing Italian webseries, remediations, and fan fiction depicting LGB subjects using these bodies as our frame will reveal a queerness in *how* these bodies mean something more so than in *what* these bodies mean, create, and consume.

WEBSERIES

In the last several years there has been a rise in television content available on the web that focus on LGBT narratives and characters. The programs under investigation in this section, *G&T*, *Tris*, *Bowtieboy*, *LSB*, and *Re(l)azioni a catena* are all Italian webseries with LGB content created between 2012 and 2015.[8] The first three shows center on gay men and the latter three on women who fall somewhere along the lesbian continuum. Many of the shows (*Re(la)zioni a catena*, *Bowtieboy*, and *G&T*, for example) are fictionalized video adaptations of real life events and situations, and most of the shows' creators are explicit about the fact that their work stems from a desire to fill a gap in mainstream LGBT representations (*Tris* and *LSB*).

To avoid the classic stereotypes that have plagued LGBT representation in television's past, many contemporary Italian mainstream fictional serials erase all signs of difference (read gayness) in their tokenized characters.[9]

While reality TV may still often cater to representations of gays as stereotypically flamboyant, for example, fictional series and serials have recently begun depicting LGBT people who embody normative societal expectations. Looking at the Diversity Media Awards for best Italian series in recent years reveals a celebration of normative sameness portrayed through characters who desire procreative futurity and monogamy, and exhibit gender binarism. Broadening our lens to include foreign fictional programming, and performing a generalized survey of programming with LGBT characters on public and private networks and streaming platforms reveals the same.[10] Both LGBT and straight characters in these webseries, instead, seem to celebrate their diversity and weirdness; traits that are presented as separate from and unrelated to their orientations or identifications.

From a representational perspective these shows offer viewers more variety, not necessarily by covering more of the acronym—indeed we are still shown only the L, G, and B, and no T, Q, A, or I—or any racial diversity, but more range of gender presentation and types of identities within each sexual orientation category. In the first season of *LSB* (a show about the lives of a group of lesbian and bisexual friends), for example, viewers are exposed to a gamut of aesthetics and modes of lesbian living. Couple Giulia (lesbian identified and masculine-of-center presenting) and Martina (bisexual and femme-presenting) are in a monogamous, albeit troubled relationship; Filomena, the hard-femme bisexual who lives with Martina, is single and always looking to fall in love; Nic is fairly androgynous and very promiscuous; and Benedetta is questioning her sexuality and, after a makeover from Nic, reveals herself to be more femme and sexually attractive to the other characters than anyone expected. In terms of gay male representation, from twink identified Alex in *Tris*, to bear identified Alex in *Bowtieboy*, and all the drag queens, otters, and unreadable characters in between, spectators are given a huge visual variety of what gayness can look like.

In these webseries the assumed desires for and expectations of the normativity that is present on mainstream broadcast television seem to disappear. Some of the characters do desire monogamous relationships, as is the case with Giulio and Tommy (*G&T*), Alex (*Tris*), and Martina and Giulia (*LSB*) to name a few. Others like Daniele and Giulio on *Tris*, Benedetta, Filomena, and Nic on *LSB*, and Alex on *Bowtieboy* are single, looking to date, and engage in various levels of promiscuity, but their desires for monogamy are never made clear. In fact, even straight characters are vocal about rejecting domestic and procreative familial expectation. Sara, Giulio's straight roommate and best friend on *G&T* for example, is the one to intentionally seek out an alternative to normativity. After getting impregnated by her "friend with benefits" Gianluca, Sara asks Giulio to be the father instead of seeking domestic stability with the biological father of her child.

It is only when the future or social expectations are brought up in these shows that we are introduced to normativity or the possibility of societal difficulty. In *LSB* for example, Martina is in a relationship with Giulia but during a period of romantic strife she begins to voice her concerns about the future. She notes that one day she would like to have a family of her own but her family and society would judge her if she chose to do that with a woman.[11] Likewise, in *Re(l)azioni a catena*—a series about scientist Silvia who suddenly finds herself both in love and taking care of her two estranged adolescent cousins—Silvia's mother attempts to set her brother up with a woman that she believes is wife-material. Silvia scolds her mother for her constant meddling, and in response she replies, "of course I am, he's the only one in the family that I can set up, seeing how you are."[12] The results are depictions that problematize not the characters for their sexual orientation or choice of partners, but the societies that turn these attributes into issues.

The diversities present in these programs push against any clear idea of normalcy, and reject any essentialism that would reaffirm the straight/gay and man/woman binaries. Ultimately weirdness becomes a cause for celebration or appreciation more than anything. In *Bowtieboy*, for example, gay main character Alex's love of everything "kawaii" or cute and Asian, is matched by his friend Victory's obsession with the color pink, her Hello Kitty car, and her anthropomorphizing of cakes and cupcakes. Similarly, on *Re(l)azioni a catena*, when Chiara, aka "Skemmy," Silvia's cousin, finds out that Silvia is a lesbian, the two engage in a pivotal discussion that challenges the meaning and foundations of normalcy:

Chiara: I thought you were normal.
Silvia: Am I not normal because I don't have a husband, kids, and a color TV? Am I not normal because I like women? Look, you're not so normal yourself: you steal, you spend more time lying down than on your feet, and you have secret boyfriends.
Chiara: But I'm seventeen years old, I have a right not to be normal.
Silvia: Well, I'd also like this right, is that asking too much?
Chiara: Okay, you win; you have the right not to be normal.[13]

Determinants of normalcy are proven to encompass many more behavioral tendencies than those that foretell sexual orientation. Not only does Chiara realize that she too lives her life outside the boundaries of expectation and acceptability, but abnormality ultimately becomes something to desire and be celebrated. These shows, thus, tend to afford all characters the ability to seek ways of living that lie outside restrictive normative boundaries; boundaries that are so naturalized that questioning them would jeopardize the very foundations at the heart of the televisual narratives that create and perpetuate them.

In addition to what seems to be a celebration of difference in these webseries, spectators are privy to representations of same-sex sexual intimacy that is not visually equated with or substituted by images of heterosexual sex, is not complicated by psychological angst or regret, is not problematized for not having procreative ends, and is as varied as the desires and investments of the parties participating in these acts. We must not overlook the fact that webseries are not constrained by networks and do not face scrutiny and threats of censorship in the same way that programs being aired on RAI or Mediaset might.[14] This plays a very large role in what may or may not be depicted. That being said, after the show *Tris* aired a gay kiss on YouTube the number of complaints received led the site to block the episode. After an influx of grievances about this censorship were aired, however, YouTube agreed to publish the episode once again.[15] It is also important to keep in mind that viewers must seek out these webseries, which, in turn, rely heavily on festival circuits and word of mouth for publicity. The comparatively limited reach of these shows and the niche market that must intentionally look for such programs allow the creators to make certain assumptions about what their audiences want or are willing to watch. The benefit for viewers when seeking out and consuming these webseries is that they are given a broader range of representations that may provide more points of identification. Furthermore, from a queering perspective, the lack of necessary correlation between the straight and LGB characters means that binary understandings of gender and sexuality are not foundational for viewer comprehension or pleasure.

Discussions of the potential for increased and more varied visibilities in these webseries must be placed in relation to an acknowledgment of the silences and invisibilities within these television shows. Invisibilities in televisual representations help us understand the boundaries of the legible and socially acceptable. In this respect, we may say that the major commonalities linking these programs are the ultimate source of their invisibilities. Made by Italians who are not necessarily in the TV or film industries, produced with low or next to no budgets, born from a desire to see more gays on TV, these shows are produced by relatively young LGBTQ people looking to represent themselves and their communities in ways that reflect their actual lives. Because of this the age range of the characters is extremely limited (most of them are in their twenties and early thirties). The plus side of this is that the characters are presented as unfettered by normative social expectation since they are not necessarily ready to settle down and are largely at ease with their sexuality. The inevitable downside is that these shows lack diversity in age, race, and gender variance—invisibilities which should not be taken lightly or cast aside.

Unlike these representational voids, the linguistic silences that spectators may notice in these webseries seem intentionally positioned to highlight the inevitable problems with invisibility or presumed heterosexuality. As we saw in *Re(l)azioni a catena,* for example, Silvia's mother tries to set her brother Stefano up with Alessia, assuming that the woman she has chosen for her son is straight. Presuming heterosexuality ends up creating moments of confusion and drama as Alessia has feelings for Silvia and not for her brother Stefano.

Misunderstanding is created within these narratives time and again when expectation is paired with silence. We have a similar situation in *G&T* when Tommy hears that his ex-friend Giulio is roommates with another old friend Sara. Tommy assumes that the two are a couple which causes a lot of anger and confusion later when Tommy catches Giulio making out with a man on the roof of a bar. Likewise, in *Tris*, when Alex assumes that he and his boyfriend are monogamous but the couple never has a conversation about it, this lack of clarity creates the drama that ultimately leads to their breakup. Language not only provides a certain level of social legibility and interpellation, it also helps expand or destroy expectations based on compulsory heterosexuality and normativity. Taken to the extreme this silence often results in violence against LGBTQ people, as is the case in *Tris* when Alex gets gay bashed while walking alone at night. The assumptions the aggressors make about Alex and their tacit understanding that they are both ready and willing to perform this act of violence show the power of silence surrounding normative expectation and the potential dangers it signifies for those who lack semiotic representation. It becomes, therefore, linguistically significant that Daniele in *Tris* mispronounces "gay" as "ghee" until he is finally ready to come out of the closet. Often in these webseries, and very much in contrast with mainstream Italian television serials, these silences and invisibilities are used as devices to highlight the damages they create for LGBT characters.

On the other side of this semiotic coin, these shows use verbal and visual language to depict actions and expressions that are culturally coded within LGBTQIA communities. Perpetuating these semiotic signs serves to broaden their reach and deepen the understanding of nonnormative signification within dominant linguistic discourses. In terms of languages used within gay communities, when Alex in *Bowtieboy* joins online dating and hookup apps, we learn along with him that acronym AOP (which in English would be TOB—"top or bottom") stands for active or passive and is used by gay men to communicate sexual preference.[16] Similarly in *Tris* when Daniele says that he doesn't know where to meet men, Alex immediately lends him his dog and tells him to go to the park, giving spectators access to the LGBTQ connotative codes for this everyday space. Semiotic signification becomes multilayered or complicated by the verbalization and visualization of subcultural codes. At times this even leads to moments of intersection between LGBTQIA and heterosexual cultures, especially, for example, in *Bowtieboy*, when Alex asks Victory if she is menstruating because she is acting strange.

Victory's response, "you are just a typical gay misogynist, a miso-gay-nist," points out a known grievance in the LGBTQIA community, namely that gay men are often presented and present themselves as hating women.[17] Two things happen in Victory's comment: first, gay men are acknowledged for their gender and as such have the ability to be as misogynist as any straight man, and second, the common societal phenomenon of seeing gay men as either a third sex or more in tuned with women because they are more feminized is dismantled.

By problematizing assumption by making silence the catalyst for drama, these shows point to a need for semiotic representation. And it is through their visual and linguistic representations of LGBT characters that the cultural codes of these groups may ultimately merge into the semiotics of the larger society, the result of which just might be a level of interpellation for LGBTQ people that allows for greater diversity and greater legibility.

BEYOND THE NARRATIVES

Looking beyond the narratives of these shows, we spectators may find a queerness within these programs' temporal structure that facilitates a queerness of engagement and pleasure. Indeed the brevity of these programs—generally ranging from seven to twenty-five minutes—means that viewers do not need a very substantial time commitment to enjoy these shows. They themselves, just like the content they depict, are fleeting queer moments of engagement for spectators. Furthermore, their existence online and not on traditional broadcasting platforms means that viewers have more power to control both the content's flow (just like DVR or watching a program on DVD) and the time and place of consumption.

Existing outside the television industry, and relying on very limited budgets, the aesthetics of these shows run in direct contrast to the stylized and sutured framings of big budget small screen productions. BADhOLE, the cultural association that created and produced *Re(l)azioni a catena*, and more recently *10percento*—a lesbian film for Instagram made up of one hundred ten-second clips—is comprised of only five women (see figure 6.2). These women-activists made these works from a sense of indignation in the face of societal ills like discrimination, and not from a desire to become rich or be discovered.[18] The aesthetic result, as with *LSB*, is a stylistic rawness of sound, editing, attire, and location. *Bowtieboy*, which began as a blog, is written and produced by Simone Botte who also plays Alex, the main character in the program. The do-it-yourself attitude of these small-scale productions gets reflected in the amateurish aesthetics of the programs.[19] This is not a negative judgment of the shows, to the contrary, *Bowtieboy*'s use of clips

Figure 6.2 *10percento*, **BADhOLE Video.** *Source*: Screenshot.

from movies and television, and the often fragmented frames that seem to intentionally refuse to show viewers a character's face or whole body, give the show a postmodern "mash-up" feel. The cut-and-paste quality recreates the fragmentation that we find in queer identity construction, and that, I have argued, is fundamental to the bodies at play in contemporary televisual creation and consumption. As Robert J. Hill notes, "Queer shares with postmodern perspectives the refusal to be positioned as solitary and intact. Queer is a category that no one can ever fully own or possess because it requires a shifting identity to practice."[20] Through these aesthetics audiences are visually reminded that these programs are constructions. While for Kaja Silverman the cinematic suture that erased the technology behind a representation allowed for easier identification between the viewer and the viewed, it is the lack of suture, the evidence of the technology, which makes identification with the *process* of constructing the characters a queer identification.[21] The technology used to make these shows is shown to be the same technology on which we are watching them. Thus, the textual body of these webseries can be understood as an unstable technotopic assemblage that actively invites the audience to break the traditional mediatic fourth wall.

Webseries are not the only method for creating other representations of LGBTQIA populations or responding to those produced by the television industry. In addition to the production of new material and narrative worlds, spectators looking to queer their televisual content often engage in acts of remediation or fan fiction to create the things they would like to see in the content that is already available to them.

REMEDIATIONS

"Remediation" is a word used to define a repurposing of content, or as Jay David Bolter and Richard Grusin explain, it is "the representation of one medium in another."[22] While Bolter and Grusin do make the claim that remediation within one medium is also possible, for this investigation a cross-media perspective on repurposing is fitting.

The gay, lesbian, and trans storylines within mainstream programs become, in this digital age of convergence and participatory media, fodder for remediation, especially on online platforms such as YouTube and Dailymotion. Users with names such as Yukimax79, Edos90, and Alterego have remediated mainstream programs by stripping them of the heterosexual narratives and pasting together only the storylines of the gay or lesbian characters. Alterego, who previously posted on YouTube but, out of frustration for all of the erasing of her videos, has turned to other online platforms such as altervista.org and Google+ (on which she is now known as alterego198x), is a perfect exemplar of user renegotiation and remediation.

Both on Google+ and her altervista website alterego1983.altervista.org, Alterego has created various playlists of remediated lesbian film and television content from Italy, Germany, France, and Anglophone nations—giving audiences access to exclusively lesbian transnational media content. In *Ethereal Queer*, Amy Villarejo discusses the potential for queerness in the spatio-temporal dynamics of remediated television. When discussing the made-for-TV movie *Losing Chase* she refers to a fan who has, like Alterego, cut up the film and pieced together the lesbian love scenes. Villarejo remarks, "Where *Losing Chase* requires quite a bit of effort to bring Chase Philips (Mirren) and Elizabeth Cole (Sedgwick) together [. . .] [this YouTube user] cuts, as it were, right to the chase of lesbian desire [. . .] We get all the good stuff [. . .] and almost none of the bad stuff."[23] Alterego, like the user Villarejo discusses, reduces these shows to their lesbian narratives and in so doing eliminates some of the inequalities between them and the heterosexual love stories. The show, obviously, does not change and, as such, nor do the problems of the representation of the characters, but without the presence of the straight narratives there is no juxtaposition. Viewers need not come face to face with the show's choice to exclude intimacy only for the same-sex couple, as such a large part of the representational imbalance is removed.[24] That being said, whether we watch scenes with problematic LGB representations on mainstream television networks or through Alterego's sites we are still faced with the very same depictions. The shows are shortened, and those watching explicitly for lesbian narratives can enjoy them without wading through a predominantly straight program for glimpses of homosexuality, but the presentation of the lesbian content comes with all the problems of its representation regardless of the platform on which it gets viewed. bell hooks has attested that for black women watching mainstream Hollywood movies "to experience fully the pleasure of that cinema they had to close down critique, analysis; they had to forget racism."[25] Similarly, though these are abbreviated and explicitly LGB narratives, the act of remediation through abridgment reaffirms many of the issues of representation, and those watching may be forced to "forget homophobia" to find pleasure much like the women of which hooks speaks.

We might argue that it is precisely the problems within mainstream representations that make the kinds of remediations performed by Alterego, Yukimax79, and Edos90 possible. The lack of any LGBTQIA community present in these shows and the normative monogamy of the plotlines streamline the content. Without a complex web of relations, these LGB people can be literally plucked out of their original narratives and repositioned as isolated stories. What these online users do, however, is create a different (read, a queer technotopic assemblaged) kind of community for these characters. Alterego's placement of Italian programs alongside the lesbian narratives of other countries—providing Italian, English, and German subtitles for her audiences—creates a new kind of community of lovers of lesbian stories that transcends national borders. Providing a locus for multinational LGBT representation is an act of what Henry Jenkins has called "pop cosmopolitanism," by which he means, "the ways that the transcultural flows of popular culture inspire new forms of global consciousness and cultural competency."[26] Jenkins emphasizes the importance of grassroots intermediaries such as Alterego in facilitating the cultural exchange of products and media. Acknowledging that perceptions of these media products cannot necessarily be controlled, and are often left to the mercy of these bottom-up culture sharers, he is optimistic about its potential: "What cosmopolitanism at its best offers us is an escape from parochialism and isolationism, the beginnings of a global perspective, and the awareness of alternative vantage points."[27] Viewers now have access to a larger textual body of LGBT stories, creating a new content context and broader transnational technological consumption community, both of which speak to the technotopic assemblaged nature of the televisual bodies of which we spoke earlier.

Through the remediation of mainstream LGB narratives, these Italian media pro-sumers create a kind of queerness that the stories they cut up and stream do not. Much like the webseries discussed above, these narratives come in abbreviated clip form. Often the "episodes" of remediated content are just a few minutes long, giving viewers fleeting moments of gay narrative.

In addition, the ability to watch a storyline that traditionally spanned an entire season in just a few short clips strips the story of its future-oriented trajectory and forward movement. Viewers can experience all the futurity in the now, no anticipation or extended viewer fidelity required. The elasticity and fragmentation indicative of the queer temporalities created by these users and sites is mirrored in the way they play with both physical and textual space.

On the one hand Grusin and Bolter speak of a certain "seamlessness" of digital technology, which disguises mediation and renders the depicted images as "realistic" as possible. The streaming and automatic flow of one "episode" to the next facilitate a sutured aesthetic that, together with the high definition images, work to perpetuate normative time and the notion of unity and wholeness.[28] On the other hand, I argue that these LGB remediations call into question the very boundaries needed to establish wholeness in the first place. By cutting up the original programs, viewers are presented with a fractured part of what was a "whole" story and this new text is put into conversation with all the surrounding textual fragments, producing a mosaic body of narratives that span across both shows and nations. Furthermore, these cut-ups still bear the trace of their shows of origin. Grusin and Bolter have noted that "the digital medium can be more aggressive in its remediation. It can try to refashion the older medium or media entirely while still marking the presence of the older media and therefore maintaining a sense of multiplicity or hypermediacy."[29] The multiplicity of this remediation is increased even further by the addition of subtitles and other text written on the older media products. Thus, these remediations contract and expand the body of the text as they layer and refashion media and put them in conversation with other similar textual bodies. Far from being sutured to appear seamless, it is precisely this piecing together, and the highlighting of these remediations as constructions, that make them queer and allow them to expand the textual landscape of the original work. Here the stability of boundaries, or the limits of the political geographies used to produces ideas of nationhood and of media are called into question and rendered futile. The multiplicities of time, space, and technology that help produce these mediations would therefore seem queerer than the images and narratives of which they are comprised.

SLASH FICTION

Fan fiction, generally speaking, is a work of fiction written by a fan of a particular book, film, television show, comic or other narrative medium. Usually fan fiction creates an extension of some area of the original text. These works range from the extremely short (known as "drabble") to the long form multiple chapter works. Those who engage in fan fiction largely take part in active online or real-life communities and exchange, comment on, and enjoy each other's stories.

Slash fiction, a subcategory of fan fiction, puts two heterosexual male characters in situations of homoerotic intimacy. Femslash, its less common counterpart, does the same with straight female characters. Many scholars, like Henry Jenkins, have theorized as to the roots and possible effects of slash fiction in these communities and in society more generally. Jenkins argues two key points: First that "slash is not so much a genre about sex as it is a genre about the limitations of traditional masculinity."[30] And second, that "slash allows for a more thorough exploration of issues of intimacy, power, commitment, partnership, competition and attraction."[31] Slash as a genre, regardless of content, exists, therefore, because of a need not being met by traditional depictions of desire in mainstream media products.

The content of these slash works, while depicting acts of same-sex sexual intimacy, are constrained by the narratives and characters within the works they paratextually extend. Slash writers seek to maintain the voices of the characters and generally the types of situations in which they find themselves, thus "slash, like most of fan culture, represents a negotiation rather than a radical break with the ideological construction of mass culture; slash like other forms of fan writing, strives for a balance between reworking the series material and remaining true to the original characterizations."[32] In this way these slash works are very much like the remediations discussed in the previous section: both are limited by the mainstream narratives and character constructions of the works from which they derive.

Those who read and write slash fiction may not necessarily produce queer content but we may understand their work as containing, producing, and facilitating queerness from the perspectives of both community formation and technology. Furthermore, we may view slash fiction sharing sites as a locus of queer potentiality in that they are spaces where alternatives to hegemonic representations of gender and sexuality get created and disseminated.

Italian-speaking slashers (writers of slash fiction) can find their largest outlet on efpfanfic.net, which was created in 2001 by webmaster Erika.[33] The texts these Italian-speaking communities engage with vary enormously in terms of nation of origin and genre, and slashers may choose to remain specific to a genre or program or move between them.

Reflecting for a moment on the content produced by these Italian slashers, what stand out are the myriad programs being slashed that already contain LGBT narratives or moments. Of particular relevance within the scope of this chapter is the slashing of the American sitcom *Modern Family*—which won the Diversity Media Award for best foreign series in 2017. Used by the Italian media to position—and laud—the show *È arrivata la felicità*, *Modern Family* is celebrated for its depiction of gay couple Mitchell and Cameron. Italian slashers, however, consider it a text wanting for actual sexual intimacy between the gay characters. A text entitled "Problemi in paradiso" ["Trouble in Paradise"] written by slasher Whity on Efpfanfic.net, takes Cameron and Mitchell's relationship to the next level. In her story, after a day of turmoil caused largely by Cam's body insecurities, Mitchell orchestrates a night of romance for the two, which ends up in the consummation of their relationship. The reviews of Whity's story are flush with compliments regarding the "authenticity" of the characters, and her ability to make the couple seem introspective while maintaining the comic nature of the genre. Most telling for our purposes, however, is a remark made by user Memi91, who writes, "finally we know who gives it to whom."[34] Here slash fiction is used to fill a void, to give audiences what is lacking in the narratives of origin, namely a clear sexual dynamic.

The same can be said for the Italian slash fiction about the teen drama *Gossip Girl*. In 2011 Mediaset aired the third season of the show as part of their summer programming, and decided to censure a gay kiss between main character Chuck Bass and secondary character Josh Elliot.[35] Many Italian online blogs and magazines responded by criticizing the censure and providing links to the cut content. But while mainstream media was questioning the motives for eliminating a tongue-less kiss between two men, Italian slash fiction was busy inserting much more than kisses into the narrative. Slashers are providing audiences with the sexual expressions lacking or removed from mainstream depictions, and in this case Chuck Bass becomes a point of convergence for gay and straight audience desire.

In these slash works a direct connection gets created between those spectator/authors who desire depictions of gay sex, because they more fully represent LGBTQI populations and those spectator/authors who find the depictions of the female characters to be unsubstantive and therefore create same-sex intimacy between straight-male characters in an effort to better represent the complexity of heterosexual relationships. Given that the majority of slash fiction writers are straight women, scholars have theorized several possible reasons for their desire to produce homoerotic narratives. Alexis Lothian et al., reiterating many dominant understandings for this authorship, note that:

> Few female role models are available in media texts [. . .] if they are, their overdetermination for female viewers complicates or even prohibits identifications [. . .] feminist readings offer same-sex relationships as models for a more equal relationship; psychoanalytic analyses address the fact that women can be and desire both subjects within a given pairing, thus offering a wider variety of identificatory options.[36]

Representations of women lack the depth of the men in these programs and women respond by looking elsewhere. In this way slash fiction affords them multiple possibilities for identification and pleasure. The very same or similar reasons draw those who seek better representations of LGBTQAI people to slash fiction. The result is that "slash fandom has become a place where a young urban dyke shares erotic space with a straight married mom in the American heartland, and where women whose identity markers suggest they would find few points of agreement have forged erotic, emotional, and political alliances."[37] This diverse community comes together because of the limitations of representation in these mainstream programs. In rejecting normative standards of gender and sexuality, these slashers produce bodies of work that challenge the strict categorizations enforced by imposed sociocultural binaries. The result is threefold.

These slashers challenge the foundations of identity politics by producing and performing works and acts that often run counter to the socially accepted understanding of their identity which is based on their chosen sexual partners. In other words, writing gay and acting straight questions the validity of identity categories that cannot reconcile these differences. In this way, Westernized social constructions centering on identity may be replaced with alternative understandings of the flexibility of positionality based on performativity.

Secondly, just as their actions seem to reject "the automatic primacy and singularity of the disciplinary subject and its identitarian interpellation," so too do the communities they form reject the identity politics too often at the heart of feminist discourses of intersectionality.[38] I am arguing here that the queerness of these slash fiction communities lies in the "affective tendencies" that bring them together as an assemblage.[39] We may look at these communities as queer performing bodies made up of the multiple bodies which in and of themselves are also "unstable assemblages that cannot be seamlessly disaggregated into identity formations."[40]

Lastly, though from a textual perspective not all the works produced can be considered queer—especially in light of their desire to conform stylistically to their works of origin—their existence as paratextual extensions calls into question the boundaries of the televisual text as a fixed entity. Just as knowledge about actors seeps into spectator perception of a program and alters it, so too do these texts extend and obfuscate the definition of the text. We might say that slashers put homosexual intimacy within these texts, but, more importantly, we may argue that by extending the texts slashers queer the produced televisual body through the dismantling of its textual boundaries.

QUEER TELEVISION ASSEMBLAGES

The content of the bodies of work in this chapter varies greatly both from the webseries, to the remediations, to the slash fiction discussed, and from one work to the next within each category. Webseries are limited largely by resource availability due to financial constraints, and potentially by the time limits imposed by the online platforms on which they have chosen to stream, while remediations and slash fictions are constrained in content or genre and style by their works of origin.

LGB webseries, like slash fiction, afford characters a level of sexual expression not limited by acceptable representations of identity. In presenting more than one or two token LGB characters they have the space to express diversity within each sexual orientation and gender identity, and use culturally connoted codes that are more specific to the represented populations. These shows also make use of queer aesthetics that highlight the technological aspects most mainstream programs are quick to suture. Though these Italian webseries tend to lack variety in the age and ethnicity of their characters, they speak to the potential for more and other kinds of representations on grassroots programs. The limits of what they depict are matched by their limit of accessibility. In fact, many of these webseries are prohibited from being streamed outside of Italy.

For remediated material, problems of LGB representation are for the most part inherited from the shows they cut up. Homonormative characters remain such even when the stories of the straight characters are removed from the narrative. Furthermore, the choice to re-air these normativities and make them available on more online platforms essentially spreads these problematic depictions by making them available to broader audiences. Despite these issues, the reshaping of this content still creates new bodies of work whose stories are focused entirely on LGB characters, taking them from their secondary roles and positioning them front and center. We might also say that the sites created by these remediators are assemblaged LGBQ spaces; each remediation—which is an assemblage onto itself—is placed next to other LGBQ remediated assemblages that, when grouped on these user generated content sites, enter into new conversation with one another.

The works of slash fiction, as I have mentioned, largely attempt to stick to the genre and tone of their work of origin, and seek to capture the voices of their characters. The same-sex erotic acts that slashers create are essentially inserted into the narrative worlds they are slashing. Thus, where remediators take content out of the show and reposition it, slashers put content in while repositioning the content in the frame of fan community sites. Both the action of remediating and that of slashing change and extend the bodies of the televisual texts with which they play. This repositioning consequently puts the texts in contact with new texts, creating a space that changes both the experience of consumption and the works themselves. In their extensions of these narrative worlds, the slashers also dismantle the misconception of a single televisual author; the work is now collectively created by all those who add to or rewrite it. No longer are these programs industry texts, they become texts created both from the top down and the bottom-up, often crossing nations and languages along the way.

We have seen how these Italian grassroots media makers and sharers embrace changing technology as a tool and an aesthetic, and dismantle the linearity of time and the politics of space in so doing. Likewise, they create communities that break linguistic and class barriers to collaborate in creating and sharing modes of understanding and representation that challenge the hegemonic structures on which local and global television industry depend. Perhaps, then, it isn't the content we should be looking at when considering queerness' relationship to television, not yet at least. Perhaps looking past the censorship, the normativity, the marginalizations and erasures, we might see Italian television serials—with their assemblaged structures, technological mutability, temporal play, and grassroots engagement—as a locus for queer potentiality. Television's queer potentiality is created by and through moments of interaction between bodies made possible by technology and the dissolution of prescriptive definitions of what television is, and is reliant on, as Puar states, "the capacity to *regenerate*" and we might add, remediate.[41]

There are, indeed, consequences to what I am saying. If collective and individual transitory unstable identities are being created by and through television in this age of media convergence—during which temporalities and the technologies multiply the languages that form the way we talk to ourselves about ourselves—these are queer identities. What this means is that the queering of television content and our queer engagements with it are merely a moment we are experiencing. Television has gone through other developmental moments that have helped shape society's understandings of identity, and soon this moment will also pass, and the changes of television will produce different identities that we as a society will use to create meaning. But, like the programs and representations that make up the history of our televisual experience, the texts being produced now, the texts that are queering us and our televisions will not disappear. In the true spirit of the television archive that gets consumed and re-consumed, mediated and remediated, this queer moment will live on in the multiplicity that is the perpetual temporal present of the medium.

NOTES

1. In this chapter the acronym LBGTQIA will often be shortened according to the populations being referred to in each specific context. The term "queer," unless otherwise stated, will be used when referring to a particular theoretical framework.

2. Amy Villarejo, *Ethereal Queer* (Durham: Duke University Press, 2014), 7.

3. Aldo Grasso and Massimo Scaglioni, *Televisione convergente: La TV oltre il piccolo schermo* (Cologno Monzese: Link-RTI, 2010), 11; Henry Jenkins, *Convergence Culture: Where Old and New Media Collide* (New York: New York University Press, 2006), 11. Jenkins has argued for a direct causal link between digitalization and media convergence while others like Grasso and Scaglioni propose a more moderate relation.

4. Enrico Pulcini, *Click TV* (Milan: Angeli, 2006), 114. In his work Pulcini maps out shifts from broadcast television culture, to a move toward narrowcasting due to a rise in number of channels available, to a shift toward increase niche-market programming, and finally to a *me-casting* designed for and determined by the audiences themselves.

5. Luca Barra, Cecilia Penati, and Massimo Scaglioni, "Estensione Accesso, Brand: Le Tre Dimensioni Della Televisione Convergente," in *La TV oltre il piccolo schermo*, eds. Aldo Grasso and Massimo Scaglioni (Cologno Monzese: Link-RTI, 2010), 26.

6. Judith Halberstam, *In A Queer Time and Place* (New York: New York University Press, 2005), 124. Note that Jack Halberstam published under the name Judith at the time but has since changed his name to Jack, as such all references to him in this text will use his name.

7. Jasbir Puar, *Terrorist Assemblages* (Durham: Duke University Press, 2007), 212–215.

8. Francesco D'Alessio and Matteo Rocchi, *G&T* (2012), Web; Antonio Back, *Tris* (2012), Web; Simone Botte, *Bowtieboy* (2015), Web; Floriana Buonomo and Geraldine Ottier, dirs. *LSB* (2013), Web; Badholevideo, *Re(l)azioni a catena* (2013), Web. These shows were chosen because they are the most publicized, most available Italian webseries with LGB content release during the three-year period that marks the very start of Italian webseries production with LGBTQIA+ narratives. Since then other webseries have been released, notably *L-ever*, a lesbian webseries from Turin that very much resembles *LSB* in content and structure, and *Ice the Webseries*, created by the Roman musical group Calypso Chaos as a marketing tool to promote their music.

9. For more on this, see Andrea Jelardi et Al., *Queer TV: Omosessualità e trasgressione nella television italiana* (Rome: F. Croce, 2006).

10. See, for example, *Tutti pazzi per amore, È arrivata la felicità, Tutti insieme all'improvviso, Una grande famiglia*, and *Tutti i padri di maria, I bastardi di Pizzofalcone*, and foreign shows such as *Grace and Frankie*, and *Modern Family*, which were both nominated for DMAs.

11. *LSB*, "1x06," directed by Floriana Buonomo and Geraldine Ottier, 2013, YouTube, Youtube.com.

12. *Re(l)azioni a catena*, Season 1, episode 3, "Innocua apparenza," created by Badhole, 2013, YouTube, Youtube.com.

13. *Re(l)azioni a catena*, Season 1 episode 7, "Zero assoluto." Translation mine.

14. In 2017, for example, Mediaset censured a gay kiss on Maria De Filippi's show *Uomini e donne*, as did RAI for the American imported show *How to Get Away with Murder* in 2016.

15. Marta Premoli, "Tris, Tre Tipi Travolgenti," *Citizen Post*, August 7, 2013, https://www.citizenpost.it/2013/08/07/tris-tre-tipi-travolgenti/. Note that in addition to showcasing the freedom nonbroadcast programming is afforded, this particular back and forth is a clear example of the participatory power of contemporary television audiences.

16. *Bowtieboy*, Episode 1, "Un nuovo inizio," created by Simone Botte, 2015, YouTube, Youtube.com.

17. *Bowtieboy*, Episode 6, "Rompiamo le uova."

18. Badhole, "Chi siamo," accessed July 3, 2018, http://www.badholevideo.com/chi-siamo/.

19. "Bowtieboy, la webserie nata da un blog," *Gayburg Blogspot*, last modified July 28, 2015, https://gayburg.blogspot.com/2015/07/bowtieboy-la-webserie-nata-da-un-blog.html.

20. Robert J. Hill, "Activism as Practice," *New Directions for Adult and Continuing Education* no. 102 (2004): 87, accessed December 6, 2016, https://doi.org/10.1002/ace.141.

21. See Kaja Silverman, *The Subject of Semiotics* (New York: Oxford University Press, 1983).

22. David Jay Bolter and Richard Grusin, *Remediation: Understanding New Media* (Massachusetts: MIT Press, 2000), 45.

23. Villarejo, *Ethereal Queer*, 156.

24. As is the case for *Tutti pazzi per amore*, and *Tutti insieme all'improvviso*, for example, both of which are remediated by Alterego.

25. bell hooks, "The Oppositional Gaze," in *Film and Theory: An Anthology*, eds. Robert Stam and Toby Miller (Massachusetts: Blackwell Publishing, 2000), 514. The use of lowercase in hooks' name is a reflection of the author's preferred self-representation.

26. Henry Jenkins, "Pop Cosmopolitanism," in *Fans, Bloggers, and Gamers* (New York: New York University Press, 2006), 156.

27. Ibid., 166.

28. Bolter and Grusin, *Remediation: Understanding New Media*, 24.

29. Ibid., 46.

30. Henry Jenkins, *Textual Poachers* (New York: Routledge, 1992), 191.

31. Ibid., 202.

32. Ibid., 119.

33. Slasher may also interact with Italian fan fiction communities on sites such as fanfic-italia.livejournal.com or post and comment on slash fiction and art on Facebook.com/slashandfemslash, for example.

34. Memi91, "Recensioni per problem in paradise di Whity," last modified October 13, 2015, https://efpfanfic.net/reviews.php?sid=2032563&a=1, translation mine.

35. "Mediaset censura il bacio gay di Gossip Girl," last modified June 21, 2011, https://gayburg.blogspot.com/2011/06/mediaset-censura-il-bacio-gay-di-gossip.html.

36. Alexis Lothian, Robin Anne Reid, and Kristina Busse, "Yearning Void and Infinite Potential," *English Language Notes* 45, no. 2 (2007): 106, http://queergeektheory.org/docs/Lothian_QFS.pdf.

37. Ibid., 104.

38. Puar, *Terrorist Assemblages*, 206.
39. Puar, "I Would Rather Be a Cyborg than a Goddess," *Meritum* 8, no. 2 (2013): 387, https://muse.jhu.edu/article/486621.
40. Ibid., 378–379.
41. Puar, *Terrorist Assemblages*, 211.

BIBLIOGRAPHY

Badholevideo. "Chi siamo." Accessed February 15, 2017. Badholevideo.com/chi-siamo/.

Barra, Luca, Cecilia Penati, and Massimo Scaglioni. "Estensione, Accesso, Brand: Le Tre Dimensioni Della Televisione Convergente." In *Televisione Convergente: La TV Oltre Il Piccolo Schermo*, edited by Aldo Grasso and Massimo Scaglioni, 21–31. Cologno Monzese: Link-RTI, 2010.

Bolter, Jay David, and Richard Grusin. *Remediation: Understanding New Media*. Massachusetts: MIT Press, 2000.

Bowtieboy, episode 1, "un nuovo inizio." Created by Simone Botte, aired September 7, 2015, on YouTube, https://www.youtube.com/watch?v=2Y82n38kAZk&list=PLcQmceuB42aF6oiJ1pCTBZESk4DjOP_3v&index=1.

———, episode 6, "Rompiamo le uova." Created by Simone Botte, aired October 16, 2015, on YouTube, https://www.youtube.com/watch?v=E12cUa2nNcI&list=PLcQmceuB42aF6oiJ1pCTBZESk4DjOP_3v&index=6.

"Bowtieboy, la webserie nata da un blog." Last modified July 28, 2015. Gayburg.blogspot.com.

G&T. Directed by Francesco D'Alessio and Matteo Rocchi, launched December 14, 2012, on YouTube, https://www.youtube.com/GETwebserie.

Grasso, Aldo, and Massimo Scaglioni. *Televisione Convergente: La TV Oltre Il Piccolo Schermo*. Cologno Monzese: Link-RTI, 2010.

Halberstam, Judith. *In A Queer Time and Place: Transgender Bodies, Subcultural Lives*. New York: New York University Press, 2005.

Hill, Robert J. "Activism as Practice: Some Queer Considerations." *New Directions for Adult and Continuing Education* 102 (2004): 85–94. https://doi: 10.1002/ace.141.

hooks, bell. "The Oppositional Gaze: Black Female Spectators." In *Film and Theory: An Anthology,* edited by Robert Stam and Toby Miller, 510–523. Massachusetts: Blackwell Publishing, 2000.

Jenkins, Henry. *Convergence Culture: Where Old and New Media Collide*. New York: New York University Press, 2006.

———. "Pop Cosmopolitanism: Mapping Cultural Flows in an Age of Media Convergence." In *Fans, Bloggers, and Gamers,* 152–172. New York: New York University Press, 2006.

———. *Textual Poachers*. New York: Routledge, 1992.

Lothian, Alexis, Kristina Busse, and Robin Anne Reid. "'Yearning Void and Infinite Potential': Online Slash Fandom as Queer Female Space." *English Language Notes* 45, no. 2 (2007): 103–111. www.queergeektheory.org/docs/Lothian_QFS.pdf.

LSB, episode 2. Directed by Floriana Buonomo and Geraldine Ottier, aired May 7, 2013, on YouTube, https://www.youtube.com/watch?v=abkdv1iaVBg&list=PL5vyHtukUK0OdthvgF23ypCoeI_WiAPQR&index=2.

———, episode 6. Directed by Floriana Buonomo and Geraldine Ottier, aired May 21, 2013, on YouTube, https://www.youtube.com/watch?v=XdkT7ymAWZk&list=PL5vyHtukUK0OdthvgF23ypCoeI_WiAPQR&index=6.

"Mediaset censura il bacio gay di Gossip Girl." Last modified June 21, 2011. https://gayburg.blogspot.com/2011/06/mediaset-censura-il-bacio-gay-di-gossip.html.

Memi91. "Recensioni per Problemi in paradiso di Whity." Last modified October 13, 2015. https://efpfanfic.net/reviews.php?sid=2032563&a=1.

Premoli, Marta. "Tris, Tre Tipi Travolgenti." *Citizen Post*, August 7, 2013. https://www.citizenpost.it/2013/08/07/tris-tre-tipi-travolgenti/.

Puar, Jasbir. "'I Would Rather be a Cyborg than a Goddess': Intersectionality, Assemblage, and Affective Politics." *Meritum* 8, no. 2 (2013): 371–390. http://www.fumec.br/revistas/meritum/article/viewFile/2172/1332.

———. *Terrorist Assemblages: homonationalism in Queer Times*. Durham: Duke University Press, 2007.

Pulcini, Enrico. *Click TV: Come Internet E Il Digitale Cambieranno La Televisione*. Milano: Angeli, 2006.

Re(l)azioni a catena, Season 1 episode 3, "Innocua apparenza." *Re(l)azioni a catena.* Directed and written by Badholevideo, aired May 9, 2013, on YouTube, https://www.youtube.com/watch?v=LKuVJSkjTvo.

———, Season 1 episode 7, "Zero assoluto." Directed and written by Badholevideo, aired January 24, 2014, on YouTube, https://www.youtube.com/watch?v=pkeILH0rpq8.

Tris. Created by Antonio Back, launched April 2012, on YouTube, https://www.youtube.com/watch?v=HIDiliMwktA&index=2&list=PL79CBE336A657E260.

Villarejo, Amy. *Ethereal Queer*. Durham: Duke University Press, 2014.

Index

Note: Page numbers in italics indicate illustrative material.

10percento (webseries), 141, *142*

ABC (magazine), 21
abnormal behavior, 15–20, 21–22
abortion, 39–40, 51nn22–23
Accolla, Dario, 111
Adinolfi, Mario, 107
aesthetic citation, 63
affective tendencies, 148
Ahmed, Sara, 5
Alliva, Simone, 102–3
altervista.org, 143
anti-homosexuality, 3–4, 11n9, 15–21, 77–79, 83–85, 108–9
Antosa, Silvia, 43–44
Archivio Queer, 6
Ardizzoni, Michela, 2
asexuality, 36
assemblages, 17, *18*, 135–36, 142, 148

backwardness, 83–85
BADhOLE, 141, *142*
Baeri, Emma, 37
Baldisseri, Marco, 14–15, 16
Balletti Verdi (green ballets) scandal, 15
Benedetti, Andrea, 14, 17
Benedetti, Pablo, 60

Benedict XVI, Pope, 39, 51n23
BGILQT acronym, 113n4
binaries, 61, 66, 85, 137, 138, 139, 148
birth control, 39–40
bisexuals, 49n2, 85, 111
Bolter, Jay David, 143, 145
Il Borghese (newspaper), 17, 20
Borghi, Liana, 40
Borri, Giovanni, 15
Botte, Simone, 141
Bowtieboy (webseries), 136, 137, 138, 140, 141–42
Braidotti, Rosi, 48, 58
Brokeback Mountain (film), 97
Butler, Judith, 5

Cado dalle nubi (film), 77, 77–78, 83, 84, 87, *89*, 93n36
camp, 72n23, 77–78, 87, 88, 100–101
Campbell, Timothy, 67
Carini, Stefania, 99
Cavarero, Adriana, 49–50n14
censorship, 97–98, 108, 109, 114n9, 147, 151n14
Centro Interuniversitario di Ricerca Queer (Interuniversity Center for Queer Research), 6

C'è posta per te (TV program), 120n78
children, and pedophilia, 15, 16–17, 20
Cicchini, Alessio, 102
cinema. *See* film
cinematic suture, 141–42
Cirinnà, Monica, 106, 110
Cirinnà Law, 97, 106, 113n3
citizenship, 21, 22
civil unions, 97, 104, 106, 113n3
class, 81–82, 100
Come non detto (film), 84
Comizi d'amore (documentary), 49n7
communist press, 16, 19–20
connotative codes, 140
conservative thought, 3–4, 11n9, 16, 17, 20, 46
consumption communities, 144
contraception, 39–40
convergence: culture, 1–2; media, 1–2, 99, 134–35
Corazones de mujer (film): and migrant film genre, 60; nomadism in, 58–59, 60–61, 64–65, 69; overview, 57; queering of Leone's films in, 62–64, 67; queering of *Thelma & Louise* in, 65–69
Corriere della Sera (newspaper), 15, 16
Costanzo, Maurizio, 115n12
Cronaca (magazine), 21, 24
cross-dressing, 17, *18*, 59, 60
cultural coding, 140–41
CUNTemporary, Deep Trash Italia, 100, 117n34

Dailymotion, 143
De Filippi, Maria, 98, 102, 103, 105, 106, 109, 111, 115n12, 120n78
De Lauretis, Teresa, 3, 34, 37, 45
Deleuze, Giles, 5
Dell'Acqua, Francesco, 103
Della Latta, Rodolfo, 14–15
Demau, 50n14
DICO law, 46
Diotima, 50n14
disease paradigm, 19, 21

Diversity Media Awards (DMA), 3, 97, 137, 146, 151n10
divorce law, 49n10
Dollimore, Jonathan, 114n7
Dominijanni, Ida, 44, 45
Doty, Alexander, 86
drag, 59, 60
Duncan, Derek, 70n2
Dyer, Richard, 86

Epoca (magazine), 16
L'Espresso (magazine), 16

Facebook, 101–2, 108
fan fictions, 110, 145–48, 149–50
far-right activists, 14–15
femicide, 53–54n52
femininity, 17, *18*, 59, 141
feminists and feminism: abandonment of 'women,' 46–48; and reproductive rights, 39–41; separatism ideology, 36–37, 44–45; sexual difference ideology, 41, 42–43, 49–50n14. *See also* lesbian feminists
femslash fictions, 146
Ferrara, Giuliano, 39
film: homophobia critiques in, 77–79, 83–85; migrant film genre, 60; parodies of cultural anxieties, 80–82; queer potential of, 85–90; role in shaping female sexuality, 33–34. *See also specific films*
A Fistful of Dollars (film), 67
For a Few Dollars More (film), 67
Foucault, Michel, 5
Francis, Pope, 4
Frasca, Giampiero, 66
freedom, national models, 61
frocia, as term, 4–5, 11n13
FUORI!, 37–38
Fuori! Donna (journal), 38, 41
futurity, 57, 65, 68, 69, 138

Gabbana, Stefano, 118n51
Galt, Rosalind, 58, 84–86, 90

gender: binaries, 66, 85, 137, 138, 139, 148; and homonormativity, 86, 97, 98–99, 112–13, 149; neutrality, 46–48; nomadism, 58–59, 60–61, 64–65, 69; nonconformity, 17, 18; stereotypes, 87, 136–37; theory education, 3; violence based on, 48, 53–54n52, 67–68
GendErotica, 6
Gente (magazine), 16, 17
GIFTS: Genere Intersex Femministi Trans Sessualità (Gender Intersex Feminist Trans Sexuality), 6
Gitelman, Lisa, 7
The Good, the Bad, the Ugly (film), 63, 64, 67
Google+, 143
Gossip Girl (TV program), 147
Gramolini, Cristina, 45
Grasso, Aldo, 151n3
Griggers, Cathy, 68
Grindstaff, Laura, 100
Grusin, Richard, 143, 145
G&T (webseries), 136, 137, 140

Halberstam, Jack, 135, 151n6
Haraway, Donna, 42
heterosexuality and heteronormativity: assumptions of, 140; compulsory, 35–36; defined, 49nn2–3; indoctrination in media, 33–36; parodied in film, 80–81; patriarchy and misogyny, 34–38, 53–54n52, 65, 67–68, 141; queer "savior" symbol, 79; and reproductive rights, 39–41; right-wing preservation of, 3–4, 11n9, 46; and separatism, 36–38
Hill, Robert J., 142
Hipkins, Danielle, 81
homoerotic narratives, 146–48
homonormativity, 86, 97, 98–99, 112–13, 149
homophobia, 3–4, 11n9, 15–21, 77–79, 83–85, 108–9

homosexuals and homosexuality: anti-homosexuality press campaign, 15–21; counterreaction to negative press representation, 21–24; criminalization of, 15–17, 19–20; lesbian feminists in collectives, 37–38; underworld, 14, 19
hooks, bell, 144
How to Get Away with Murder (TV program), 97–98, 114n9
hustlers and hustling, 14, 17
hypermediacy, 145

identity politics, 37, 148
ILGA (International Lesbian Gay Bisexual Trans and Intersex Association), 4
Instagram, 108, 141
intersectionality, 37, 59, 88, 140, 148
Io che amo solo te (film), 83, 84, 88
Io e lei (film), 76
Irigaray, Luce, 48, 50n14
Italian Association of Homosexuals' Parents and Relatives (AGEDO), 97
Italian Center for Sexology (Centro Italiano Sessuologia, CIS), 38
Italy: ethnic identity, 60–61, 81–82; freedom discourse, 61; Italianness, 1–3; laws, 19, 20, 39, 49n10, 51n22, 97, 106, 113n3; national identity, 1–3, 70n2, 133; political borders, 57–58; and transnationalism/culturalism, 6, 60–61, 71n11

Jenkins, Henry, 7, 144, 146, 151n3

Khouri, Callie, 57
Kinsey, Alfred, 20, 26n36

Labranca, Tommaso, 100–101
La Torre, Giulia, 118n51
Lavorini, Ermanno, murder case: anti-homosexuality campaign following, 15–21; homosexual counterattack

following, 21–24; investigation and resolution, 13, 14–15
laws, 19, 20, 39, 49n10, 51n22, 97, 106, 113n3
Lee, Ang, 97
Leone, Sergio, 57, 62–64, 67, 70n2
lesbian feminists: and reproductive rights issues, 40–41; and separatism ideology, 37–38, 41, 44–45; and sexual difference ideology, 41, 52n28
lesbians and lesbianism: and compulsory heterosexuality, 35–36; as term, 31, 43–44, 52n38; in *We Want Roses Too*, overview, 31–33
LGBTQIA+ acronyms, 11n11, 113n4, 137
Libreria delle donne di Milano, 50n14
Lonzi, Carla, 36–37, 40, 42, 50n14
Lothian, Alexis, 147
Love, Heather, 86
LSB (webseries), 136, 137, 138, 141
LSD (magazine), 24
Luxuria, Valdimir, 111, 112

Manga, Julie, 100
Manzoli, Giacomo, 77
Marazzi, Alina, 31. *See also We Want Roses Too*
Marcasciano, Porpora, 4–5
Maschi contro femmine (film), 81, 85
masculinity, 17, 48, 59, 69, 80–81, 83, 111
Mazzara, Federica, 58, 60, 61
Mazzocchi, Pierluigi, 14
McCoy, Charles, 101
Meciani, Adolfo, 14, 15
media, as term, 6–7
media convergence, 1–2, 99, 134–35
media representations. *See* film; press; television
Mediaset, 98, 115n12, 139, 147, 151n14
Men (magazine), 24
Mieli, Mario, 5
MigraBO, 6

migration: migrant and post-migrant films, 60; and nomadism, 58–59, 60–61, 64–65, 69. *See also Corazones de mujer*
Milletti, Nerina, 38, 44
Mine vaganti (film), 83
misogyny and patriarchy, 34–38, 53–54n52, 65, 67–68, 141
Mittell, Jason, 4
Modern Family (TV program), 146–47
Monarchist Front, 14
Mora, Lele, 118n51
Morley, David, 2
Moroccan identity, 61
movies. *See* film
Movimento Identità Trans (Trans Identity Movement), 6
Movimento Pro-Family (Pro-Family Movement), 46
Movimento Sociale Italiano, 14
Muñoz, José, 58, 69
Muraro, Luisa, 50n14

Nathan, Vetri, 60
national identity and nationhood: and borders, 57–58; in film, 70n2; and freedom, 61; shaped by media, overview, 1–3; in television, 133; and transnationalism/culturalism, 6, 60–61, 71n11
La Nazione Sera (newspaper), 15, 16, 20–23
neo-Fascism, 14, 15
Nessuno mi può giudicare (film), 82, 83
nomadism, 58–59, 60–61, 64–65, 69
Non Una Di Meno, 46–48, 53n49
normalization, of queer identity, 76, 85, 86, 105, 106–7, 137–38
normal *vs.* abnormal behavior, 21–22

Oggi (magazine), 17, 18–19, 20, 21
O'Healy, Áine, 1
O'Leary, Alan, 80, 99
Once Upon a Time in the West (film), 64

Ortoleva, Peppino, 1
Ozpetek, Ferzan, 76, 83

Il padre delle spose (film), 84
Pananari, Michele, 99, 102
paratexts, 134, 146, 148
Pasolini, Pier Paolo, 49n7
Patriarca, Salvatore, 102
patriarchy and misogyny, 34–38, 53–54n52, 65, 67–68, 141
pedophilia, 15, 16–17, 20
pensiero femminista, 41
Perfetti sconosciuti (film), 78, 78–79, 88–89
Peruzzo, Manuel, 103
PoliTeSse, 6
Pomeranzi, Bianca, 35–36
pop cosmopolitanism, 144
post-migrant films, 60
Prearo, Massimo, 5
press: anti-homosexuality campaign, 15–21; homosexual counterreaction to negative representation by, 21–24
private *vs.* political action, 41, 44, 53n44
prostitution, 15
Pro-Vita (Pro-Life), 46
psychoanalysis, 19, 34–35, 37
Puar, Jasbir, 59, 135, 150
Puglia, 83–84
Pulcini, Enrico, 134, 151n4
Puoi baciare lo sposo (film), 84

queer: aesthetics, 141–42, 145, 149; engagement, 141, 150; excess, 62–63; experiential *vs.* theoretical, 5; futurity, 57, 65, 68, 69, 138; genealogy, 65; kinships, 61–62; pleasure, 141, 147–48; potentiality, 85–90, 143–44, 146; as term, 4–6, 44, 112
Queer Italia Network (QuIR), vii, 113
queer representations. *See* film; press; television

Quo vado? (film), 75

race, 60, 81–82, 144
radical lesbian separatists, 41
ragazzi di pineta (pine forest boys), 14, 16–17
RAI (Radiotelevisione Italiana), 97–98, 139, 151n14
regional prejudice, 83–85
Re(l)azioni acatena (webseries), 136, 138, 140
remediations, 143–45, 149
reproductive rights, 39–41, 51nn22–23
Rich, Adrienne, 35, 48
right-wing thought, 3–4, 11n9, 16, 17, 20, 46
Rivolta Femminile, 36, 50n14
Robé, Christopher, 62
Ross, Charlotte, 43–44
Russo, Vito, 86

Salvini, Matteo, 3
Scaglioni, Massimo, 151n3
Scarborough, Roscoe, 101
sceneggiati, 2
Schiavo, Maria, 38, 41
Schoonover, Karl, 58, 84–86, 90
Scott, Ridley, 57
Scusate se esisto (film), 88
Sedgwick, Eve, 5, 11n8
semiotics, 140–41
separatism, 36–38, 41, 44–45
sexuality: asexuality, 36; bisexuals, 49n2, 85, 111; inversion, 17, 18; liberation, 36, 39–40; sexual difference ideology, 41, 42–43, 49–50n14, 52n28; transvestites and transvestitism, 14, 88. *See also* heterosexuality and heteronormativity; homosexuals and homosexuality; lesbians and lesbianism; transgenderism
shame, 34–35
Silverman, Kaja, 142
slash fictions, 145–48, 149–50

social media: Facebook, 101–2, 108; Instagram, 108, 141; Twitter, 104–12, 116n26
Sona, Claudio, 112
Sordella, Davide, 60
South, Italian, 83–84
space-off, 3
Spaghetti Westerns, 57, 62–64, 67
Lo Specchio (magazine), 16
Sperti, Gianni, 107
Spinelli, Simonetta, 44
Stanoeva, Milena, 101
Stato Civile: l'amore è uguale per tutti (TV program), 97
stereotypes, 87, 136–37
subcultural coding, 140–41
Svegliatitalia!, 102

Tasker, Yvonne, 72n29
technotopic assemblages, 135–36, 142
Il Telegrafo (newspaper), 15, 16, 20
television: and media convergence, 134–35; remediations, 143–45, 149; sexual dissidence representation, overview, 97–98, 115n14; slash fictions, 145–48, 149–50; televisual bodies, 135–36, *136*; trash TV genre, 100–101, 116n24, 117n40; webseries, 136–42, 149, 151n8. *See also specific programs*
terrorism, 14, 15
Thelma & Louise (film), 57, 62, 65–69, 70n2, 72n29
Third Person Perception, 107
third sex, 16, 19, 20
Tognazzi, Maria Sole, 76
transgenderism: and gender neutrality, 46–48; and nomadism, 59, 61; and technotopic bodies, 135
transnationalism and transculturalism, 6, 60–61, 71n11
transvestites and transvestitism, 14, 88
trash TV, 100–101, 116n24, 117n40. *See also Uomini e Donne*

Tris (webseries), 136, 137, 139, 140
trono gay. *See Uomini e Donne*
Tutta colpa di Freud (film), 80, *80*, 84, 88
Twitter, 104–12, 116n26

Una piccola impresa meridionale (film), 82–84, 88
Uomini e Donne (TV program): audience, 103–4, *104*; overview, 98–99, 101–3; reactions to trono gay airing, 109–12; reactions to trono gay announcement, 104–9, *105*
user-generated content: fan fictions, 110, 145–48, 149–50; femslash fictions, 146; remediations, 143–45, 149; slash fictions, 145–48, 149–50

Valeria Mercandino, 44
Vangioni, Pietro, 14–15
Vendola, Nichi, 84
Vie Nuove (newspaper), 19–20
Villarejo, Amy, 133, 143
violence: and control, 67, 68–69; against women, 48, 53–54n52, 67–68. *See also* Lavorini, Ermanno, murder case
virgin/whore paradigm, 34
Vozza, Andrea, 15

webseries, 136–42, 149, 151n8
Westerns, Spaghetti, 57, 62–64, 67
We Want Roses Too (film): feminist collectives in, 42–43; heterosexual agenda in, 33–36; overview, 31–33; sexual liberation in, 39–40
Wittig, Monique, 40–41
World Congress of Families (WCF), 3, 46, 53n48

YouTube, 139, 143

Zacconi, Giuseppe, 14, 15
Zalone, Checco, 75, *77*, 77–78
Zeni, Simone, 103

About the Editors

Sole Anatrone holds a PhD in Italian Studies and a Designated Emphasis in Women, Gender and Sexuality Studies from the University of California, Berkeley. Her publications include "'Almeno non hai un nome da negra': Race, Gender and National Belonging in Laila Wadia's *Amiche per la pelle*," *Gender/Sexuality/Italy Journal*; "Disciplining Narratives and Damaged Identities in Rossana Campo's *Lezioni di arabo*," *California Italian Studies*; and the forthcoming "Why LGBTQIA+ Inclusivity Matters for Italian Studies," chapter in *Diversity in Italian Studies*, ed. A. Tamburri (New York: John D. Calandra Italian American Institute). She is an assistant professor of Italian Studies at Vassar College, a member of the advisory board to the Queer Studies Caucus of the American Association of Italian Studies, and a cofounder of Asterisk, an LGBTQIA+ Inclusivity taskforce.

Julia Heim holds a PhD in Comparative Literature with a specialization in Italian from City University of New York, and a master's in Italian Language, Literature and Culture from Middlebury College. Heim's publications include "Queer Italian Studies: Critical Reflections from the Field," *Italian Studies*; "Race, a Floating Signifier, or, Rudy Guede in the Italian Press," in *Transmedia Crime Stories: The Trial of Amanda Knox and Raffaele Sollecito in the Globalised Media Sphere* (Palgrave Macmillan, 2016); and the forthcoming "Why LGBTQIA+ Inclusivity Matters for Italian Studies," chapter in *Diversity in Italian Studies*, ed. A. Tamburri (New York: John D. Calandra Italian American Institute). She is also a prolific translator with titles including G. Burgio's "Boundless Desires: Migrant Sexuality and Cultural Borders," *Queen Mob's Treehouse* (*Queenmobs.com*); L. Bernini's *Queer Apocalypses.* Translation of *Apocalissi Queer* (Palgrave Macmillan, 2017). In addition to her research, Dr. Heim is the cofounder and advisory board member of the Queer Studies Caucus of the American Association of Italian Studies, and a cofounder of Asterisk, an LGBTQIA+ Inclusivity taskforce. She is currently a Lecturer of Italian Studies at the University of Pennsylvania.

About the Contributors

Dom Holdaway is a research fellow at the University of Milan. His research focuses on Italian and international film and TV studies, with an emphasis on cinema, politics, and representation. He has published both in the area of cultural studies (concentrating on politics in Italian film and contemporary US TV series) and production studies (working on public film funding in Italy and global circulation patterns of European cinema). He completed his PhD in Italian at the University of Warwick, and then moved to Italy to work as a research fellow and lecturer in film and media at the Universities of Bologna and Milan.

Luca Malici, PhD, is Italian assistant coordinator at the University of Sheffield. His principal research interests lie in the fields of Sexuality, Film and Media Studies with a particular focus on Television, Reception and Audience studies. He has published "Queer TV Moments and Family Viewing in Italy," in *the Journal of GLBT Family Studies* 10, nos. 1–2 (2014): 188–210; "Italian S-queer Eyes: Surveying and Voicing Television Representations," in *Queer Crossings: Theories, Bodies, Texts*, edited by Silvia Antosa (Milan: Mimesis, 2012), 105–122; and the chapter "Queer in Italy: Italian Televisibility and the 'Queerable' Audience," in *Queer in Europe: Contemporary Case Studies*, edited by Lisa Downing and Robert Gillett (London: Ashgate, 2011), 113–128. Luca Malici is currently working on a monograph on the representation, circulation, and reception of sexual dissidence on Italian mainstream TV before Italy's passage to digital terrestrial television in 2012.

Alessia Palanti received her PhD from Columbia University's Department of Italian and a certification from the Institute for Research on Women's Gender and Sexuality. She teaches writing in the department of English and

Comparative Literature at Columbia University where she leads a theme in the performing arts, and designed writing curricula for incarcerated and formerly incarcerated student populations. Her dissertation, "Stranded, Isolated, Cloistered, and Confined: Women Queering Space in Twenty-first Century Italian Cinema," investigates the uses of restricted spatial configurations in an emerging wave of Italian films. Alessia has published her work in the *Journal for Modern Italian Studies* and in the *Pirandello Society of America* journal. Outside of academia, she's been a consultant for the United Nation Women's HeForShe Initiative, for a project that investigates gender bias in cinema. She co-programmed an American independent film showcase *American Fringe* for Paris's 2016 Festival D'Automne; and in 2015 she was on the selection committee of the Rome Film Festival. Alessia is also a contemporary dancer, choreographer, and cofounder of *Gravity*, a queer and feminist dance and acrobatics company in New York City.

Alessio Ponzio received his PhD in history and politics from the Università Roma Tre and his PhD in women's studies and history from the University of Michigan, Ann Arbor. Ponzio is author of several articles and two books. His last monograph, *Shaping the New Man. Youth Training Regimes in Fascist Italy and Nazi Germany*, was published by the University of Wisconsin Press in 2015. He is an assistant professor in European History of Gender and Sexualities in the Department of History at the University of Saskatchewan.

www.ingramcontent.com/pod-product-compliance
Lightning Source LLC
Chambersburg PA
CBHW070831300426
44111CB00014B/2522